Solutions Manual

for use with

Corporate Finance

Sixth Edition

Stephen A. Ross
Massachusetts Institute of Technology

Randolph W. Westerfield
University of Southern California

Jeffrey Jaffe
University of Pennsylvania

Prepared by
John A. Helmuth
University of Michigan

McGraw-Hill
Irwin

Boston   Burr Ridge, IL   Dubuque, IA   Madison, WI   New York   San Francisco   St. Louis
Bangkok   Bogotá   Caracas   Kuala Lumpur   Lisbon   London   Madrid   Mexico City
Milan   Montreal   New Delhi   Santiago   Seoul   Singapore   Sydney   Taipei   Toronto

McGraw-Hill Higher Education

A Division of The McGraw-Hill Companies

Solutions Manual for use with
CORPORATE FINANCE
Stephen A. Ross, Randolph W. Westerfield and Jeffrey Jaffe

234567890 CUS/CUS 0987654321

ISBN 0-07-233884-9

www.mhhe.com

Contents

CONCEPT QUESTIONS - CHAPTER 1

1.1 • **What are the three basic questions of corporate finance?**
   a. Investment decision (capital budgeting): What long-term investment strategy should a firm adopt?
   b. Financing decision (capital structure): How much cash must be raised for the required investments?
   c. Short-term finance decision (working capital): How much short-term cash flow does company need to pay its bills.

• **Describe capital structure.**
   Capital structure is the mix of different securities used to finance a firm's investments.

• **List three reasons why value creation is difficult.**
   Value creation is difficult because it is not easy to observe cash flows directly. The reasons are:
   a. Cash flows are sometimes difficult to identify.
   b. The timing of cash flows is difficult to determine.
   c. Cash flows are uncertain and therefore risky.

1.2 • **What is a contingent claim?**
   A contingent claim is a claim whose payoffs are dependent on the value of the firm at the end of the year. In more general terms, contingent claims depend on the value of an underlying asset.

• **Describe equity and debt as contingent claims.**
   Both debt and equity depend on the value of the firm. If the value of the firm is greater than the amount owed to debt holders, they will get what the firm owes them, while stockholders will get the difference. But if the value of the firm is less than equity, bondholders will get the value of the firm and equity holders nothing.

1.3 • **Define a proprietorship, a partnership and a corporation.**
   A proprietorship is a business owned by a single individual with unlimited liability. A partnership is a business owned by two or more individuals with unlimited liability. A corporation is a business which is a "legal person" with many limited liability owners.

• **What are the advantages of the corporate form of business organization?**
   Limited liability, east of ownership transfer and perpetual succession.

1.4 • **What are the two types of agency costs?**
   Monitoring costs of the shareholders and the incentive fees paid to the managers.

• **How are managers bonded to shareholders?**

a. Shareholders determine the membership to the board of directors, which selects management.
b. Management contracts and incentives are build into compensation arrangements.
c. If a firm is taken over because the firm's price dropped, managers could lose their jobs.
d. Competition in the managerial labor market makes managers perform in the best interest of stockholders.

- **Can you recall some managerial goals?**
  Maximization of corporate wealth, growth and company size.

- **What is the set-of-contracts perspective?**
  The view of the corporation as a set of contracting relationships among individuals who have conflicting objectives.

1.5 • **Distinguish between money markets and capital markets.**
  Money markets are markets for debt securities that pay off in less than one year, while capital markets are markets for long-term debt and equity shares.

- **What is listing?**
  Listing refers to the procedures by which a company applies and qualifies so that its stock can be traded on the New York Stock Exchange.

- **What is the difference between a primary market and a secondary market?**
  The primary market is the market where issuers of securities sell them for the first time to investors, while a secondary market is a market for securities previously issued.

CONCEPT QUESTIONS - CHAPTER 2

2.1 • **What is the balance-sheet equation?**
  Assets = Liabilities + Stockholders' equity

- **What three things should be kept in mind when looking at a balance sheet?**
  Accounting liquidity, debt vs. equity, and value vs. cost.

2.2 • **What is the income statement equation?**
  Revenue - expenses = Income

- **What are the three things to keep in mind when looking at an income statement?**
  Generally Accepted Accounting Principles (GAAP), noncash items, and time and costs.

- **What are noncash expenses?**
  Noncash expenses are items included as expenses but which do not directly affect cash flow. The most important one is depreciation.

2.3 • **What is net working capital?**
  It is the difference between current assets and current liabilities.

  • **What is the change in net working capital?**
  To determine changes in net working capital you subtract uses of net working capital from sources of net working capital.

2.4 • **How is cash flow different from changes in net working capital?**
  The difference between cash flow and changes in new working capital is that some transactions affect cash flow and not net working capital. The acquisition of inventories with cash is a good example of a change in working capital requirements.

  • **What is the difference between operating cash flow and total cash flow of the firm?**
  The main difference between the two is capital spending and additions to working capital, that is, investment in fixed assets and "investment" in working capital.

CONCEPT QUESTIONS - CHAPTER 3

3.1 • **What is an interest rate?**
  It is the payment required by the lender of money for the use of it during a determined period of time. It is expressed in percentage.
  • What are institutions that match borrowers and lenders called?
  They are called financial institutions.

  • **What do we mean when we say a market clears? What is an equilibrium rate of interest?**
  A market clears if the amount of money borrowers want to borrow is equal to the amount lenders wish to lend. An equilibrium rate of interest is the interest rate at which markets clear.

3.2 • **How does an individual change his consumption across periods through borrowing and lending.**
  By borrowing and lending different amounts the person can achieve any of all consumption possibilities available.

  • **How do interest rate changes affect one's degree of impatience?**
  A person's level of patience depends upon the interest rate he or she faces in the market. A person eager to borrow money at a low interest rate will become less

eager if that interest rate is raised and may prefer to *lend* money to take advantage of higher interest rates.

3.3 • **What is the most important feature of a competitive financial market?**
No investor, individual or corporation can have a significant effect on total lending or on interest rates. Therefore, investors are price takers.

• **What conditions are likely to lead to this?**
a. Trading is costless.
b. Information about borrowing and lending opportunities is available
c. There are many traders.

3.4 • **Describe the basic financial principle of investment decision-making?**
An investment project is worth undertaking only if it is mores desirable than what is available in the financial markets.

3.5 • **Describe how the financial markets can be used to evaluate investment alternatives?**
The financial markets can be used as a benchmark. If the proposed investment provides a better alternative than the financial markets, it should be undertaken.

• **What is the separation theorem? Why is it important?**
The separation theorem says that the decision as to whether to undertake a project (compared to the financial markets) is independent of the consumption preferences of the individual. It is important because we can make investment decisions based on objective data, disregarding personal preferences.

3.6 • **Give the definitions of net present value, future value and present value?**
New present value is the difference in present value terms between cash inflows and cash outflows. Given the financial market, the future value is an amount equivalent to the amount currently held, and present value is the amount equivalent now to an amount to be received or given in the future.

• **What information does a person need to compute an investment's net present value?**
Cash inflows, cash outflows and an interest or discount rate.

3.7 • **In terms of the net-present-value rule, what is the essential difference between the individual and the corporation.**
The main difference is that firms have no consumption endowment.

CONCEPT QUESTIONS - CHAPTER 4

4.1 • **Define future value and present value.**

Future value is the value of a sum after investing over one or more periods. Present value is the value today of cash flows to be received in the future.

- **How does one use net present value when making an investment decision?**
  One determines the present value of future cash flows and then subtracts the cost of the investment. If this value is positive, the investment should be undertaken. If the NPV is negative, then the investment should be rejected.

4.2 - **What is the difference between simple interest and compound interest?**
  With simple interest, the interest on the original investment is not reinvested. With compound interest, each interest payment is reinvested and one earns interest on interest.

- **What is the formula for the net present value of a project?**
$$NPV = -C_0 + \sum_{t=1}^{T} C_t /(1+I)^t$$

4.3 - **What is a stated annual interest rate?**
  The stated annual interest rate is the annual interest rate without consideration of compounding.

- **What is an effective annual interest rate?**
  An effective annual interest rate is a rate that takes compounding into account.

- **What is the relationship between the stated annual interest rate and the effective annual interest rate?**
  Effective annual interest rate $= (1 + (r/m))^m - 1$.

- **Define continuous compounding.**
  Continuous compounding compounds investments every instant.

4.4 - **What are the formulas for perpetuity, growing-perpetuity, annuity, and growing annuity?**
  Perpetuity: $PV = C/r$
  Growing Perpetuity: $PV = C/(r-g)$
  Annuity: $PV = (C/r) [1-1/(1+r)^T]$
  Growing Annuity: $PV = [C/(r-g)] [1-((1+g)/(1+r))^T]$

- **What are three important points concerning the growing perpetuity formula?**
  1. The numerator.
  2. The interest rate and the growth rate.
  3. The timing assumption.

- **What are four tricks concerning annuities?**

1. A delayed annuity.
2. An annuity in advance
3. An infrequent annuity
4. The equating of present values of two annuities.

CONCEPT QUESTIONS - CHAPTER 5

5.2 • Define pure discount bonds, level-coupon bonds, and consols.
A pure discount bond is one that makes no intervening interest payments. One receives a single lump sum payment at maturity. A level-coupon bond is a combination of an annuity and a lump sum at maturity. A consol is a bond that makes interest payments forever.

• Contrast the state interest rate and the effective annual interest rate for bonds paying semi-annual interest.
Effective annual interest rate on a bond takes into account two periods of compounding per year received on the coupon payments. The state rate does not take this into account.

5.3 • What is the relationship between interest rates and bond prices?
There is an inverse relationship. When one goes up, the other goes down.

• How does one calculate the yield to maturity on a bond?
One finds the discount rate that equates the promised future cash flows with the price of the bond.

5.8 • What are the three factors determining a firm's P/E ratio?
1. Today's expectations of future growth opportunities.
2. The discount rte.
3. The accounting method.

5.9 • What is the closing price of General Data?
The closing price of General Data is 6 3/16.

• What is the PE of General House?
The PE of General House is 29.

• What is the annual dividend of General Host?
The annual dividend of General Host is zero.

CONCEPT QUESTIONS - Appendix to Chapter 5

• What is the difference between a spot interest rate and the yield to maturity?

The yield to maturity is the geometric average of the spot rates during the life of the bond.

- **Define the forward rate.**
  Given a one-year bond and a two-year bond, one knows the spot rates for both. The forward rate is the rate of return implicit on a one-year bond purchased in the second year that would equate the terminal wealth of purchasing the one-year bond today and another in one year with that of the two-year bond.

- **What is the relationship between the one-year spot rate, the two-year spot rate and the forward rate over the second year?**
  The forward rate $f_2 = [(1+r_2)^2 / (1+r_1)] - 1$

- **What is the expectation hypothesis?**
  Investors set interest rates such that the forward rate over a given period equals the spot rate for that period.

- **What is the liquidity-preference hypothesis?**
  This hypothesis maintains that investors require a risk premium for holding longer-term bonds (i.e. they prefer to be liquid or short-term investors). This implies that the market sets the forward rate for a given period above the expected spot rate for that period.

CONCEPT QUESTIONS - CHAPTER 6

6.2 • **List the problems of the payback period rule.**
  1. It does not take into account the time value of money.
  2. It ignores payments after the payback period.
  3. The cutoff period is arbitrary.

- **What are some advantages?**
  1. It is simple to implement.
  2. It may help in controlling and evaluating managers.

6.4 • **What are the three steps in calculating AAR?**
  1. Determine average net income.
  2. Determine average investment
  3. Divide average net income by average investment.

- **What are some flaws with the AAR approach?**
  1. It uses accounting figures.
  2. It takes no account of timing.
  3. The cutoff period is arbitrary.

6.5 • **How does one calculate the IRR of a project?**

Using either trial-and-error or a financial calculator, one finds the discount rate that produces an NPV of zero.

6.6 • **What is the difference between independent projects and mutually exclusive projects?**
An independent project is one whose acceptance does not affect the acceptance of another. A mutually exclusive project, on the other hand is one whose acceptance precludes the acceptance of another.

• **What are two problems with the IRR approach that apply to both independent and mutually exclusive projects?**
1. The decision rule depends on whether one is investing of financing.
2. Multiple rates of return are possible.

• **What are two additional problems applying only to mutually exclusive projects?**
1. The IRR approach ignores issues of scale.
2. The IRR approach does not accommodate the timing of the cash flows properly.

6.7 • **How does one calculate a project's profitability index?**
Divide the present value of the cash flows subsequent to the initial investment by the initial investment.

• **How is the profitability index applied to independent projects, mutually exclusive projects, and situations of capital rationing?**
1. With independent projects, accept the project if the PI is greater than 1.0 and reject if less than 1.0.
2. With mutually exclusive projects, use incremental analysis, subtracting the cash flows of project 2 from project 1. Find the PI. If the PI is greater than 1.0, accept project 1. If less than 1.0, accept project 2.
3. In capital rationing, the firm should simply rank the projects according to their respective PIs and accept the projects with the highest PIs, subject to the budget constrain.

CONCEPT QUESTIONS - CHAPTER 7

7.1 • **What are the three difficulties in determining incremental cash flows?**
1. Sunk costs.
2. Opportunity costs
3. Side effects.

• **Define sunk costs, opportunity costs, and side effects.**
1. Sunk costs are costs that have already been incurred and that will not be affected by the decision whether to undertake the investment.

2. Opportunity costs are costs incurred by the firm because, if it decides to undertake a project, it will forego other opportunities for using the assets.
3. Side effects appear when a project negatively affects cash flows from other parts of the firm.

7.2 • **What are the items leading to cash flow in any year?**
Cash flow from operations (revenue-operating costs-taxes) plus cash flow of investment (cost of new machines + changes in net working capital + opportunity costs).

• **Why did we determine income when NPV Analysis discounts cash flows, not income?**
Because we need to determine how much is paid out in taxes.

• **Why is working capital viewed as a cash outflow?**
Because increases in working capital must be funded by cash generated elsewhere in the firm.

7.3 • **What is the difference between the nominal and the real interest rate?**
The nominal interest rate is the real interest rate with a premium for inflation.

• **What is the difference between nominal and real cash flows?**
Real cash flows are nominal cash flows adjusted for inflation.

7.4 • **What is the equivalent annual cost method of capital budgeting?**
The decision as to which of various mutually exclusive machines to buy is based on the equivalent annual cost. The EAC is determined by dividing the net present value of costs by an annuity factor that has the same life as the machines. The machine with the lowest EAC should be acquired.

• **Can you list the assumptions that we must to use EAC?**
1. All machines do the same job.
2. They have different operating costs and lives
3. The machine will be indefinitely replaced.

CONCEPT QUESTIONS - CHAPTER 8

8.1 • **What are the ways a firm can create positive NPV.**
1. Be first to introduce a new product.
2. Further develop a core competency to product goods or services at lower costs than competitors.
3. Create a barrier that makes it difficult for the other firms to compete effectively.
4. Introduce variation on existing products to take advantage of unsatisfied demand

5. Create product differentiation by aggressive advertising and marketing networks.
6. Use innovation in organizational processes to do all of the above.

- **How can managers use the market to help them screen out negative NPV projects?**

8.2 • What is a decision tree?
It is a method to help capital budgeting decision-makers evaluating projects involving sequential decisions. At every point in the tree, there are different alternatives that should be analyzed.

- **What are potential problems in using a decision tree?**
Potential problems 1) that a different discount rate should be used for different branches in the tree and 2) it is difficult for decision trees to capture managerial options.

8.3 • What is a sensitivity analysis?
It is a technique used to determine how the result of a decision changes when some of the parameters or assumptions change.

- **Why is it important to perform a sensitivity analysis?**
Because it provides an analysis of the consequences of possible prediction or assumption errors.

- **What is a break-even analysis?**
It is a technique used to determine the volume of production necessary to break even, that is, to cover not only variable costs but fixed costs as well.

- **Describe how sensitivity analysis interacts with break-even analysis.**
Sensitivity analysis can determine how the financial break-even point changes when some factors (such as fixed costs, variable costs, or revenue) change.

CONCEPT QUESTIONS - CHAPTER 9

9.1 • What are the two parts of total return?
Dividend income and capital gain (or loss)

- **Why are unrealized capital gains or losses included in the calculation of returns?**
Because it is as much a part of returns as dividends, even if the investor decides to hold onto the stock and not to realize the capital gain.

- **What is the difference between a dollar return and a percentage return?**

A dollar return is the amount of money the original investment provided, while percentage return is the percentage of the original investment represented by the total return.

9.2 • **What is the largest one-period return in the 63-year history of common stocks we have displayed, and when did it occur? What is the smallest return, and when did it occur?**
Largest common stock return: 53.99% in 1933. Smallest common stock return: -43.34% in 1931.

• **In how many years did the common stock return exceed 30 percent, and in how many years was it below 20 percent?**
It exceeded 30% in 16 years. It was below 20% in 39 years.

• **For common stocks, what is the longest period of time without a single losing year? What is the longest streak of losing years?**
There are 6 consecutive years of positive returns. The longest losing streak was 4 years.

• **What is the longest period of time such that if you have invested at the beginning of the period, you would still not have had a positive return on your common-stock investment by the end?**
The longest period of time was 14 years (from 1929 to 1942).

9.4 • **What is the major observation about capital markets that we will seek to explain?**
That the return on risky assets has been higher on average than the return on risk-free assets.

• **What does the observation tell us about investors for the period from 1926 through 1994.**
An investor in this period was rewarded for investment in the stock market with an extra or excess return over what would have achieved by simply investing in T-bills.

9.5 • **What is the definition of sample estimates of variance and standard deviation?**
Variance is given by Var $(R) = (1 / (T-1)) \Sigma_t (R_t - R)^2$ where T is the number of periods, R_t is the period return and R is the sample mean. Standard deviation is given by $SD = Var^{1/2}$. For large T, (T-1) may be approximated by T.

• **How does the normal distribution help us interpret standard deviation?**
For a normal distribution, the probability of having a return that is above or below the men by a certain amount only depends on the standard deviation.

9.6 • **How can financial managers use the history of capital markets to estimate**

the required rate of return on nonfinancial investments with the same risk as
the average common stock?

They can determine the historical risk premium and add this amount to the current
risk-free rate to determine the required return on investments of that risk.

CONCEPT QUESTIONS - CHAPTER 10

10.3 • **What are the formulas for the expected return, variance, and standard deviation of a portfolio of two assets?**

$$E\{R_p\} = X_i\,R_i + X_j\,R_j$$

$$\text{Var}_p = (X_i^2\,(R_i - R_i)^2 + X_j^2\,(R_j - R_j)^2 + 2X_i\,X_j(R_i - R_i)\,(R_j - R_j)$$

$$\text{SD}_p = \text{Var}_p{}^{1/2}$$

• **What is the diversification effect?**

As long as the correlation coefficient between two securities is less than one, the
standard deviation of a portfolio of two securities is less than the weighted
average of the standard deviations of the individual securities.

• **What are the highest and lowest possible values for the correlation coefficient?**

+1 and -1.

10.4 • **What is the relationship between the shape of the efficient set for two assets and the correlation between the two assets?**

The less correlation there is between two assets the more the efficient set bends in
toward the y-axis.

10.5 • **What is the formula for the variance of a portfolio for many assets?**

$$\text{Var}_p = \sum_{I=1}^{N}\sum_{j=1}^{N}[X_iX_j(R_i - R_i)(R_j - R_j)]$$

• **How can the formula be expressed in terms of a box or matrix?**

The terms on the diagonal of the matrix represent the variances of each term and
the off-diagonal elements represent the covariances.

10.6 • **What are the two components of the total risk of a security?**

Portfolio risk and diversifiable risk.

• **Why doesn't diversification eliminate all risk?**

Because the variances of the portfolio asymptotically approaches the portfolio
risk. This risk is the covariance of each pair of securities, which always remains.

10.7 • **What is the formula for the standard deviation of a portfolio composed of one riskless and one risky asset?**

$SD_P = (X_A^2 Var_A)^{1/2} = X_A SD_A$ where A is the risky asset

• **How does one determine the optimal portfolio among the efficient set of risky assets?**
This portfolio lies at the point at which a line drawn from the risk-free rate is tangent to the efficient set.

10.8 • **If all investors have homogeneous expectations, what portfolio of risky assets do they hold?**
The market portfolio.

• **What is the formula for beta?**
$B_i = COV(R_i R_m)/Var(R_m)$

• **Why is the beta the appropriate measure of risk for a single security in a large portfolio?**
Because beta measures the contribution of that single security to the variance of the portfolio.

10.9 • **Why is the SML a straight line?**
Because investors could form homemade portfolios that dominate portfolios that don't lie on a straight line. Buying and selling of these portfolios would then drive any outliers back to the line.

• **What is the Capital-Asset-Pricing model?**
The CAPM is a linear model that relates the expected return on an asset to its systematic risk (beta).

• **What are the differences between the capital market line and the security market line?**
The SML relates expected return to beta, while the CML relates expected return to the standard deviation. The SML holds both for all individual securities and for all possible portfolios, whereas the CML holds only for efficient portfolios.

CONCEPT QUESTIONS - CHAPTER 11

11.1• **What are the two basic parts of a return?**
1. The expected part
2. The surprise part

• **Under what conditions will some news have no effect on common stock prices?**

If there is no surprise in the news, there will not be any effect on prices. That is, the news was fully expected.

11.2• **Describe the difference between systematic risk and unsystematic risk.**
A systematic risk is any risk that affects a large number of assets, each to a greater or lesser degree. An unsystematic risk is a risk that specifically affects a single asset or a small group of assets.

• **Why is unsystematic risk sometimes referred to as idiosyncratic risk?**
Because information such as the announcement of a labor strike, may affect only some companies.

11.3 • **What is an inflation beta? A GNP beta? An interest-rate beta?**
An inflation beta is a measure of the sensitivity of a stock's return to changes in the expected inflation rate. A GNP beta measures the sensitivity of a stock's return to changes in the expected GNP. An interest rate beta reflects the sensitivity of a stock's return to changes in the market interest rate.

• **What is the difference between a k-factor model and the market model?**
The main difference is that the market model assumes that only one factor, usually a stock market aggregate, is enough to explain stock returns, while a k-factor model relies on k factors to explain returns.

• **Define the beta coefficient.**
The beta coefficient is a measure of the sensitivity of stock's return to unexpected changes in one factor.

11.4• **How can the return on a portfolio be expressed in terms of a factor model?**
It is the weighted average of expected returns plus the weighted average of each security's beta times a factor F plus the weighted average of the unsystematic risks of the individual securities.

• **What risk is diversified away in a large portfolio?**
The unsystematic risk.

11.5• **What is the relationship between the one-factor model and CAPM?**
Assuming the market portfolio is properly scaled, it can be shown that the one-factor model is identical to the CAPM.

11.7 • **Empirical models are sometimes called factor models. What is the difference between a factor as we have used it previously in this chapter and an attribute as we use it in this section?**
A factor is generally a market wide or industry wide factor proxying the systematic risk. An attribute is related with the returns of the stocks.

- **What is data mining and why might it overstate the relation between some stock attribute and returns?**
  Choosing parameters because they have been shown to be related to returns is data mining. The relation found between some attribute and returns can be accidental, thus overstated.

- **What is wrong with measuring the performance of a U.S. growth stock manager against a benchmark composed of English stocks?**
  Using a benchmark composed of English stocks is wrong because the stocks included are not of the same style as those in a U.S. growth stock fund.

CONCEPT QUESTIONS - CHAPTER 12

12.1• **What is the disadvantage of using too few observations when estimating beta?**
Small samples can lead to inaccurate estimations.

- **What is the disadvantage of using too many observations when estimating beta?**
  Firms may change their industries over time making observations from the distant past out-of-date.

- **What is the disadvantage of using the industry beta as the estimate of the beta of an individual firm?**
  The operations of a particular firm may not be similar to the industry average.

12.2• **What are the determinants of equity betas?**
  1. The responsiveness of a firm's revenues to economy wide movements.
  2. The degree of a firm's operating leverage.
  3. The degree of a firm's financial leverage.

- **What is the difference between an asset beta and an equity beta?**
  Financial leverage.

12.6 • **What is liquidity?**
  Liquidity in this context means the cost of buying and selling stocks. Those stocks that are expensive to trade are considered less liquid.

- **What is the relation between liquidity and expected return?**
  There is a high expected return for illiquid stocks with high trading costs.

* ☐**What is adverse selection?**

  Adverse selection occurs when individuals have ignorance about traits, trends, or other information hidden in a population. For instance, a trader may suffer from adverse selection if certain market knowledge is hidden from him but is available to some investors.

* ☐**What can a corporation do to lower its cost of capital?**

  A corporation can be proactive in taking actions that will lower trading costs, thereby lowering its cost of capital.

CONCEPT QUESTIONS - CHAPTER 13

13.1● List the three ways financing decisions can create value.
1. Fool investors
2. Reduce costs or increase subsidies
3. Create a new security

13.2 ● Can you define an efficient market?
It is a market where current prices reflect all available information.

13.3 ● Can you describe the three forms of the efficient-market hypotheses?
1. Weak-from EMH postulates that prices reflect all information contained in the past history of prices.
2. Semistrong form EMH says that prices not only reflect the history of prices but all publicly available information.
3. Strong form EMH contends that prices reflect all available information, public and private (or "inside").

* **What kinds of things could make markets inefficient?**
1. Large costs of acquiring and skillfully utilizing information
2. The existence of private information
3. Large transactions costs

* **Does market efficiency mean you can throw darts at a Wall Street Journal listing of New York Stock Exchange stocks to pick a portfolio.**
No. All it says is that, on average, a portfolio manager will not be able to achieve excess returns on a risk-adjusted basis.

* **What does it mean to say the price you pay for a stock is fair?**
It means that the stock has been priced taking into account all publicly available information.

13.5 • What are three implications of the efficient-market hypothesis for corporate finance?
1. The prices of stocks and bonds cannot be affected by the company's choice of accounting method.
2. Financial managers cannot time issues of stocks and bonds.
3. A firm can sell as many stocks and bonds as it wants without depressing prices.

CONCEPT QUESTIONS - CHAPTER 14

14.1• What is a company's book value?
It is the sum of the par value, capital surplus and accumulated retained earnings.

• What rights do stockholders have?
1. Voting rights for board members
2. Proxy rights
3. Asset Participation in case of liquidation
4. Voting rights for mergers and acquisitions
5. Preemptive rights to new shares issued.

• What is a proxy?
It is the grant of authority by a shareholder to someone else to vote his or her shares.

14.2• What is corporate debt? Describe its general features.
Corporate debt is a security issued by corporations as a result of borrowing money and represents something that must be repaid. Its main features are:
1. It does not represent ownership interest in the firm.
2. Payment of interest on debt is tax deductible because it is considered a cost of doing business.
3. Unpaid debt is a liability of the firm.

• Why is it sometimes difficult to tell whether a particular security is debt or equity?
Because it has characteristics that are particular to both. Companies are very adept at creating hybrid securities that are considered debt by the IRS but have equity features.

14.3• What is a preferred stock?
It is a security that has preference over common stock in the payment of dividends and in the distribution of assets in the case of liquidation.

- **Do you think it is more like debt or equity?**
  Preferred stock is similar to both debt and common equity. Preferred shareholders receive a stated dividend only, and if the corporation is liquidated, preferred receive a stated dividend only, and if the corporation is liquidated, preferred stockholders get a stated value. However, unpaid preferred dividends are not debts of a company and preferred dividends not a tax deductible business expense.

- **What are three reasons why preferred stock is issued?**
  1. Because of the way utility rates are determined in regulatory environments, regulated public utilities can pass the tax disadvantage of issuing preferred stock on to their customers.
  2. Companies reporting losses to the IRS may issue preferred stock.
  3. Firms issuing preferred stock can avoid the threat of bankruptcy that exists that debt financing.

14.4 • **What is the difference between internal financing and external financing?**
Internal financing comes from internally generated cash flows and does not require the issuing securities.

- **What are the major sources of corporate financing?**
  1. Internal financing
  2. External financing (new long-term borrowing, equity)

- **What factors influence a firm's choices of external versus internal equity financing?**
  1. The general economic environment, specifically, business cycles.
  2. The level of stock prices
  3. The availability of positive NPV projects.

- **What pecking order can be observed in the historical patterns of long-term financing?**
  The first form of financing is internally generated funds, then external financing; debt is used before equity.

CONCEPT QUESTIONS - CHAPTER 15

15.1 • **What is the pie model of capital structure?**
It is a model in which the value of the firm is pictured as a pie cut into debt and equity slices.

15.2 • **Why should financial managers choose the capital structure that maximizes the value of the firm.**
Because this capital structure also maximizes the value of equity.

15.3 • **Describe financial leverage**.
It is the extent to which a company relies on debt in its capital structure.

- **What is levered equity?**
The equity of a firm that has debt in its capital structure.

- **How can a shareholder of Trans Am undo the company's financial leverage?**
By selling shares of Trans Am and buying bonds or investing the proceeds in another company's debt.

15.4 • **Why does the expected return on equity risk with firm leverage?**
Because increasing leverage raises the risk of equity.

- **What is the exact relationship between the expected return on equity and firm leverage?**
$R_s = r_0 + (r_0 - r_b) (B/S)$

- **How are market-value balance sheets set up?**
They are set up the same way as accounting balance sheets with assets on the left side and liabilities on the right side. However, instead of valuing assets in terms of historical values, market values are used.

15.5 • **What is the quirk in the tax code making a levered firm more valuable than an otherwise-identical unlevered firm?**
Interest payments are tax deductible and dividend payments are not.

- **What is MM Proposition under corporate taxes?**
$V_L = V_U + T_C B$

- **What MM Proposition II under corporate taxes?**
$r_s = p + (B/S)(1 - T_c)(p - r_B)$

CONCEPT QUESTIONS - CHAPTER 16

16.1 • **What does risk-neutrality mean?**
Investors are indifferent to the presence of risk.

- **Can one have bankruptcy risk without bankruptcy costs?**
Yes. When a firm takes on debt the risk of bankruptcy is always present but bankruptcy cost may not be.

- **Why do we say that stockholders bear bankruptcy costs?**
Because in the presence of bankruptcy costs, bondholders would pay less for any debt issued. This then will reduce the value of potential future dividends.

16.2• What is the main direct cost of financial distress?
Legal and administrative costs of liquidation or reorganization.

• What are the indirect costs of financial distress?
Those that arise because of an impaired ability to conduct business.

• Who pays the costs of selfish strategies?
Ultimately, the stockholders.

16.4 • List all the claims to the firm's assets.
Payments to stockholders and bondholders, payments to the government, payments to lawyers, and payments to any al all other claimants to the cash flows of the firm.

• Describe marketed claims and nonmarketed claims.
Marketed claims are claims that can be sold or bought in capital markets. Nonmarketed claims are claims that cannot be sold in capital markets.

• How can a firm maximize the value of its marketed claims?
By minimizing the value of nonmarketed claims such as taxes.

16.5 • What are agency costs?
Costs that arise from conflicts of interest between managers bondholders and stockholders.

• Why are shirking and perquisites considered an agency cost of equity?
Because managers will act in their own best interests rather than those of shareholders.

• How do agency costs of equity affect the firm's debt-equity ratio?
The optimal debt-equity ratio is higher in a world with agency costs than in a world without such costs.

• What is the Free Cash Flow Hypothesis?
We might expect to see more wasteful activity in a firm capable of generating large cash flows.

16.6 • What is the pecking-order theory?
This theory states that when a firm seeks new capital it faces 'timing' issues of new stock.

• What are the problems of issuing equity according to this theory?
The theory implies that only overvalued firms have an incentive to issue equity and given market reactions to a stock issue, virtually no firm will issue equity. The model results in firms being financed virtually entirely by debt. Moderating the pure theory and we would predict that debt should be issued before equity.

Answers to Concept Questions

- **What is financial slack?**
  If a firm expects to fund a profitable project in the future it will start to accumulate a cash reservoir today, thus avoiding the need to go to the capital markets.

16.7 • **How do growth opportunities decrease the advantage of debt financing?**
  Growth implies significant equity financing, even in a world with low bankruptcy costs. To eliminate the potential increasing tax liability resulting from growing EBIT, the firm would want to issue enough debt so that interest equals EBIT. Any further increase in debt would, however, lower the value of the firm in a world with bankruptcy costs.

16.9• **List the empirical regularities we observe for corporate capital structure?**
  1. Most corporations have low debt ratios.
  2. Changes in financial leverage affect firm value.
  3. There are differences in the capital structure of different industries.

- **What are the factors to consider in establishing a debt-equity ratio?**
  1. Taxes
  2. Financial distress costs
  3. Pecking order and financial slack.

CONCEPT QUESTIONS - CHAPTER 17

17.1• **How is the APV method applied?**
  APV is equal to the NPV of the project (i.e. the value of the project for an unlevered firm) plus the NPV of financing side effects.

- **What additional information beyond NPV does one need to calculate A|PV?**
  NPV of financing side effects (NPVF)>

17.2 • **How is the FTE Method applied?**
  FTE calls for the discounting of the cash flows of a project to the equity holder at the cost of equity capital.

- What information is needed to calculate FTE?
  Levered cash flow and the cost of equity capital.

17.3• **How is the WACC method applied?**
  WACC calls for the discounting of unlevered cash flows of a project (UCF) at the weighted average cost of capital, WACC.

17.4• **What is the main difference between AAPV and WACC?**
  WACC is based upon a target debt rate and APV is based upon the level of debt.

- **What is the main difference between the FTE approach and the two other approaches?**
  FTE uses levered cash flow and other methods use unlevered cash flow.

- **When should the APV method be used?**
  When the level of debt is known in each future period.

- **When should the FTE and WACC approaches be used?**
  When the target debt ratio is known.

CONCEPT QUESTIONS - CHAPTER 18

18.2 • **Describe the procedure of a dividend payment.**
  1. Dividends are declared: The board of directors passes a resolution to pay dividends.
  2. Date of record: Preparation of the list of shareholders entitled to dividends.
  3. Ex-Dividend date: A date before the date of record when the brokerage firm entitles stockholders to receive the dividend if they buy before this date.
  4. Date of payment: Dividend checks are sent to stockholders.

- **Why should the price of a stock change when it goes ex-dividend?**
  Because in essence the firm is reducing its value by the amount paid out in cash for the dividend.

18.3 • **How can an investor make homemade dividends?**
  By selling shares of the stock.

- **Are dividends irrelevant?**
  If we consider a perfect capital market, dividend policy, and therefore the timing of dividend payout, should be irrelevant.

- **What assumptions are needed to show that dividend policy is irrelevant?**
  1. Perfect markets exist.
  2. Investors have homogeneous expectations
  3. This investment policy of the firm is fixed.

18.5 • **Why does a stock repurchase make more sense than paying dividends?**
  When the capital gain tax rate is lower than the ordinary income (on dividends), stockholders should prefer a repurchase to a dividend. In addition, stock repurchase is associated with a lower effective tax since one can defer the tax until the gains are realized but taxes are due when dividends are paid.

- **Why don't all firms use stock repurchases?**
  When there is no tax disadvantage of dividend, or there is signaling value in dividend distribution, firms would like to pay out dividends rather than repurchase their own stocks.

18.6 • **What is the relationship between expected returns and dividend yields?**
  Theory implies a direct relationship between expected returns and dividend yields. Empirical results are not consistent regarding this relationship.

18.7 • **What are the real-world factors favoring a high-dividend policy?**
  1. Desire for current income
  2. Resolution of uncertainty
  3. Brokerage and other transactions costs
  4. Fear of consumption out of principal

18.8 • **Do dividends have information content?**
  Often. An increase in dividend payouts may signal that future earnings are expected to rise enough so that dividends will not likely be reduced later on.

- **What are tax clienteles?**
  Different types of shareholders that prefer one kind of dividend policy due to difference in tax brackets.

CONCEPT QUESTIONS - Appendix to Chapter 18

- **What is a stock dividend? A stock split?**
  Stock dividend is a dividend in the form of stocks. In a stock split, each shareholder receives additional shares of stock for each one held originally.

- **What is the value of a stock dividend and a stock split?**
  It can be positive, zero or negative. The possible benefits are lowered commission in stock trades within the proper trading range. The costs are related to the financial procedures.

CONCEPT QUESTIONS - CHAPTER 19

19.1 • **Describe the basic procedures in a new issue.**
  1. Obtain approval of the Board of Directors.
  2. File registration statement with the SEC
  3. Distribute prospectus
  4. Determine offer price
  5. Place tombstone advertisements.

- **What is a registration statement?**
  A document filed with the SEC containing information relevant to the offering.

19.3 • **Describe a firm commitment underwriting and a best-efforts underwriting.**
  In a firm commitment underwriting, the underwriter buys the entire issue and then resells it. In a best efforts underwriting, the underwriter is only legally bound to use "best efforts" to sell the securities at the agreed upon offering price.

- **Suppose that a stockholder calls you up out of the blue and offers to sell you some shares of a new issue. Do you think the issue will do better or worse than average?**
  It will probably do worse because otherwise it would have been oversold and there would be no need for the broker to try to sell it to you.

19.4 • **What are some reasons that the price of stock drops on the announcement of a new equity issue?**
  1. Managers are disinclined to issue stock when the share price is below their estimate of intrinsic value. Equity offerings signal that management considers the share price high.
  2. Equity offerings are more likely when the firm is over-levered.

19.5 • **Describe the costs of a new issue of common stock.**
  1. Spread: The difference between the offering price and what the underwriter pays the issuing company.
  2. Other direct expenses: Filing fees, legal fees and taxes.
  3. Indirect expenses: Management time spent analyzing the issuance.
  4. Abnormal returns: The drop in the current stock price by 1% to 2% in a seasoned new issue of stock.
  5. Underpricing: Setting the offering price below the correct value in an initial new issue of stock.
  6. Green shoe option: The underwriter's right to buy additional shares at the offer price to cover overallotments.

- **What conclusions emerge from an analysis of Table 19.5?**
  1. There are substantial financial economies of scale.
  2. Direct costs are somewhat greater than indirect ones.
  3. Higher costs for best efforts offers.
  4. More underpricing for firm commitment than for best efforts offers.
  5. Both direct and indirect costs are higher for initial offerings than for seasoned ones.

19.6 • **Describe the details of a rights offering.**
  In a rights offering, each shareholder is issued an option to buy a specified number of shares from the firm at a specified price within a certain time frame. These rights are often traded on securities exchanges or over the counter.

Answers to Concept Questions

- **What are the questions that financial management must answer in a rights offerings?**

    1. What price should existing shareholders pay for a share of new stock?
    2. How many rights will be required to purchase one share of stock?
    3. What effect will the rights offering have on the price of the existing stock?

- **How is the value of a right determined?**
  Value of one right
  = Rights-on stock price - ex-rights stock price
  = (Ex-rights price - Subscription price) / (rights/share)
  = (Rights-on price - Subscription price) / (rights/share+1)

19.7 • **What are the several kinds of dilution?**
    1. Dilution of ownership
    2. Dilution of market value
    3. Dilution of book value

- **Is dilution important?**
  True dilution, of ownership or market value, is very important because it is an economic loss to current shareholders. Book value dilution, on the other hand, is irrelevant.

- **Why might a firm prefer a general cash offering to a rights offering?**
    1. Underwriters provide insurance regarding the amount raised by the firm regardless of true stock value.
    2. Proceeds are available sooner.
    3. Underwriters will provide wider distribution of ownership
    4. Underwriters provide consulting advice.

19.8 • **Describe shelf registration.**
  It is registration allowed by Rule 415 of the SEC whereby a corporation registers stock that will be sold within two years of registration.

- **What are the arguments against shelf registration?**
    1. The costs of new issues might go up because underwriters may be unable to provide as much information to potential investors as would be true otherwise.
    2. It may cause "market overhand" which will depress market prices.

19.9 • **What are the different sources of venture-capital financing?**
  Private partnerships and corporations, large industrial or financial corporation, and wealthy families and individuals.

- **What are the different stages for companies seeking venture capital financing?**
  Seed money, start-up, and then first through fourth round financing as the company gets off the ground.

- **What is the private equity market?**
  The private equity market involves the issuance of securities to a small number of private investors or certain qualified institutional investors.

- **What is Rule 144A?**
  Rule 144A establishes a legal framework for the issuance of private securities to qualified institutional investors.

CONCEPT QUESTIONS - CHAPTER 20

20.2 • **Do bearer bonds have any advantage? Why might Mr. "I Like to Keep My Affairs Private" prefer to hold bearer bonds?**
They have the advantage of secrecy.

- **What advantages and what disadvantages do bondholders derive from provisions of sinking funds?**
  They provide additional security as an early warning system if sinking fund payments are not made. But if interest rates are high, the company will buy the bonds from the market, and if rates are low, it will use the lottery, exercising an option that makes sinking fund bonds less attractive to bondholders.

- **What is a call provision? What is the difference between the call price and the stated price?**
  It is an option that allows the company after a certain number of years to repurchase the bonds at the call price. This option will only be exercised if interest rates drop. The difference between the call price and the stated price is the call premium.

20.3 • **What the advantages to a firm of having a call provision?**
If interest rates go down and the market bond prices are higher than the call price, the firm can exercise its call option and buy the bonds at less than the market price.

- **What are the disadvantages to bondholders of having a call provision?**
  If the firm decides to exercise its option, bondholders will have to sell their bonds to the firm at less than the market price.

20.4 • **List and describe the different bond rating classes.**
  1. Investment grade |AAA/Aaa to BBB/Baa: extremely strong to adequate capacity to pay interest and principal.
  2. Speculative BB/Ba to CC/Ca: slightly to extremely speculative capacity to pay interest and principle.
  3. C: Debt not currently paying interest
  4. D: Debt in default.

• **Why don't bond prices change when bond ratings change?**
  The bond ratings are based on publicly available information and therefore may not provide information that the market did not have before the change.

• **Are the costs of bond issues related to their ratings?**
  Investment –grade issues have much lower direct costs than non-investment grade issues.

20.5 • **Create an idea of an unusual bond and analyze its features.**
  The text provides an example of an unusual bond; income bonds are a hybrid between debt and equity. For the firm interest is tax deductible, but the payment depends on income rather than being fixed. This feature makes it riskier than normal bonds, and although the tax deductibility may make them appear cheaper, the market prices them according to risk as well.

20.6 • **What are the differences between private and public bond issues?**
  1. Direct private placement of long-term debt does not require SEC registration.
  2. Direct placement is more likely to have more restrictive covenants.
  3. Distribution costs are lower for private bonds.
  4. It is easier to renegotiate a private placement because there are fewer investors.

• **A private placement is more likely to have restrictive covenants than is a public issue. Why?**
  It is arranged between a firm and a few financial institutions, such as banks or insurance companies, that are very much interested in avoiding the transfer of wealth from them to stockholders. It is easier for a few financial institutions to renegotiate restrictive covenants if circumstances change.

CONCEPT QUESTIONS – CHAPTER 21

21.1 • **What are some reasons that assets like automobiles would be leased with operating leases, whereas machines or real estate would be leased with financial leases?**
  1. Operating leases have a cancellation option that protects the lessee from technological obsolescence in the case of equipment.

2. The service provided by the lessor in an operating lease eliminates the problem of retraining employees to service the new equipment or the problem of repairs in the case of a person leasing a car.

- **What are the differences between an operating lease and a financial lease?**
  1. Operating leases are not fully amortized.
  2. In an operating lease the lessor maintains and insures the leased asset. With financial leases the lessee must do both himself.
  3. Operating leases have a cancellation option.

21.2 • Define capital lease.
Capital leases meet at least one of the following:
  1. Transfer of ownership by the end of the lease term.
  2. Bargain purchase price option.
  3. Lease term at least 75 percent of asset's economic life.
  4. PV (lease payments) at least 90 percent of asset's fair value.

- **Define operating lease.**
  "Operating lease" is a general term applied to leases which are typically not fully amortized, are maintained by the lessor, and have a cancellation option.

21.3• What are the IRS guidelines for treating a lease contract as a lease for tax purposes?
Very generally, the guidelines are set up to identify lease contracts which are purely a tax dodge.

21.5 • How should one discount a riskless cash flow?
At the after-tax riskless interest rate.

21.9 • Summarize the good and bad arguments for leasing.
Good Arguments:
  a. Leasing reduces taxes because firms are in different tax bracket.
  b. Leasing reduces uncertainty by eliminating the residual value risk.
  c. Leasing lowers transactions costs by reducing the changes of ownership of an asset over its useful life.
Bad Arguments:
  a. Leasing improves accounting income and the balance sheet if leases are kept off the books.
  b. Leasing provides 100% financing, but secured equipment loans require an initial down payment.
  c. There are special reasons like government appropriations for acquisitions and circumventing bureaucratic firms.

CONCEPT QUESTIONS - CHAPTER 22

22.2 • What is a call option?
A call option is a contract that gives the owner the right to buy an asset at a fixed price within a certain time period.

• How is a call option's price related to the underlying stock price at the expiration date?
If the stock is "in the money" (above the striking price), stock price and option price are linearly related. If it's "out of the money", the call option is worthless.

22.3 • What is a put option?
A put option is a contract that gives the owner the right to sell an asset at a fixed price within a certain time period.

• How is a put option related to the underlying stock price at expiration date?
If the stock is "in the money" (below the striking price), stock price and option price are linearly related. If it's "out of the money", the put option is worthless.

22.6 • What is a put-call parity?
The theorem says that because a call's payoff is the same as payoffs from a combination of buying a put, buying the underlying stock and borrowing at the risk-free rate, the call and the combination should be equally priced.

22.7 • List the factors that determine the value of options?
1. Exercise price
2. Maturity
3. Price of the underlying asset
4. Variability of the underlying asset
5. Interest rate

• Why does a stock's variability affect the value of options written on it?
The more variable the stock the higher the possibility that it will go over the exercise price in the case of a call or under the exercise price in the case of a put. The variability increases the changes of the stocks price extremes.

22.8 • How does the two-state option model work?
It uses the fact that buying call can be made equivalent to buying the stock and borrowing to determine option value.

• What is the formula for the Black-Scholes option-pricing model?
$$C = S_o N(d_1) - E e^{-r_f t} d N(d_2)$$

Where $d_1 = [\ln(S/E) + d(r_f + (1/2)\sigma^2)^t] / (\sigma^2 t)^{1/2}$

$d_2 = d_1 - (\sigma^2 t)^{1/2}$

22.9 • **How can the firm be expressed in terms of call options?**
Bondholders own the firm and have written a call to stockholders with an exercise price equal to the promised interest payment.

• **How can the firm be expressed in terms of put options?**
Stockholders own the firm and have purchased a put option from the bondholders with an exercise price equal to the promised interest payment.

• **How does put-call parity relate these two expressions?**
A call option's payoff is the same as the payoff from a combination of buying a put, buying the underlying stock and borrowing at the risk-free rate. Consequently, puts and calls can always be stated in terms of the other.

22.12 •Why are the hidden options in projects valuable?
Even the best laid plans of men and mice often go astray. The option to adapt plans to new circumstances is a valuable asset.

CONCEPT QUESTIONS - CHAPTER 23

23.1 • **Why do companies issue options to executives of they cost the company more than they are worth to the executive? Why not just give cash and split the difference? Wouldn't that make both the company and executive better off?**
One of the purposes to give stock options to CEOs (instead of cash) is to bond the performance of the firm's stock with the compensation of the CEO. In this way, the CEO has an incentive to increase shareholder value.

23.2 • **What are the two options that many businesses have?**
Most businesses have the option to abandon under bad conditions and the option to expand under good conditions.

• **Why does a strict NPV calculation typically understate the value of a firm or a project?**
Virtually all projects have embedded options, which are ignored in NPV calculations and likely leads to undervaluation.

CONCEPT QUESTIONS - CHAPTER 24

24.2 • **What is the key difference between a warrant and a traded call options?**
When a warrant is exercised, the number of shares increases. Also, the Warrant is an option sold by the firm.

- **Why does dilution occur when warrants are exercised?**
  Because additional shares of stock are sold to warrant holders at a below market price.

- **How can the firm hurt warrant holders?**
  The firm can hurt warrant holders by taking any action that reduces the value of the stock. A typical example would be the payment of abnormally high dividends.

24.4 • **What are the conversion ratio, the conversion price, and the conversion premium?**
  The conversion ratio is the number of shares received for each debenture. The conversion price is equivalent to the price which the holders of convertible bonds pay for each share of common stock they receive. The conversion premium is the excess of the conversion price over the common stock price.

24.5 • **What three elements make up the value of a convertible bond.**
  Convertible bond value = Greater of (straight bond value and conversion value) plus option value.

- **Describe the payoff structure of convertible bonds?**
  It is the value of the firm if the value of the firm is less than total face value. It is the face value if the total face value is less that the value of the firm but greater than its conversion value. It is the conversion value if the value of the firm and the conversion value are greater than total face value.

24.6 • **What is wrong with the simple view that it is cheaper to issue a bond with a warrant or a convertible feature because the required coupon is lower?**
  In an efficient capital market the difference between the market value of a convertible bond and the value of straight bond is the fair price investors pay for the call option that the convertible or the warrant provides.

- **What is wrong with the Free Lunch story?**
  This story compares convertible financing to straight debt when the price falls and to common stock when price rises.

24.7 • **Why do firms issue convertible bonds?**
  1. To match cash flows, that is, they issue securities whose cash flows match those of the firm.
  2. To bypass assessing the risk of the company (risk synergy). The risk of company start-ups is hard to evaluate.
  3. To reduce agency costs associated with raising money by providing a package that reduces bondholder-stockholder conflicts.

24.8 • **Why will convertible bonds not be voluntarily converted to stock before expiration?**

Because the holder of the convertible has the option to wait and perhaps do better than what is implied by current stock prices.

• **When should firms force conversion of convertibles? Why?**

Theoretically conversion should be forced as soon as the conversion value reaches the call price because other conversion policies will reduce shareholder value. If conversion is forced when conversion values are above the call price, bondholders will be allowed to exchange less valuable bonds for more valuable common stock. In the opposite situation, shareholders are giving bondholders the excess value.

CONCEPT QUESTIONS – CHAPTER 25

25.1 • **What is a forward contract?**

An agreement to trade at a set price in the future.

• **Give examples of forward contracts in your life.**

A forward contract is formed when you contract an artisan to construct a banjo and agree to pay him $1,200 on delivery.

25.2 • **What is a futures contract?**

Futures contracts are like forward contracts except that:
1. They are traded on organized exchanges.
2. They let the seller choose when to make delivery on any day during the delivery month.
3. They are marked to market daily.

• **How is a futures contract related to a forward contract?**

In both contracts, it is the obligation of both the buyer and seller to settle the contract at the future date.

• **Why do exchanges require futures contracts to be marked to the market?**

Because there is no accumulation of loss, the mark to the market convention reduces the risk of default.

25.3 • **Define short and long hedges.**

A short futures hedge involves selling a futures contract. A long futures hedge involves buying a futures contract.

• **Under what circumstances is each of the two hedges used?**

Short hedges are used when you will be making delivery at a future date and wish to minimize the risk of a drop in price. Long hedges are used when you must purchase at a future date and wish to minimize the risk of a rise in price.

- **What is a rolling stock strategy?**
  A rolling stock strategy involves buying a short-term futures contract and simultaneously selling a long-term futures contract. After the short-term elapses, the rolling stock involves buying another short-term futures contract. The strategy is implemented over a series of short-term contracts.

25.4 • **How are forward contracts on bonds priced?**
  The same as any other cash flow stream – as the sum of discounted cash flows:
$$P_{\text{FORW.CONT}} = (1 + r_1)[\textstyle\sum_{t=1} (I_t/(1+r_t)^t + PAR/(1 + r_T)^T]$$

- **What are the differences between forward contracts on bonds and futures contracts on bonds?**
  Futures contracts on bonds have the following characteristics:
  1. They are traded on organized exchanges.
  2. The seller can make delivery on any day during the month.
  3. They are marked to market daily.

- **Give examples of hedging with futures contracts on bonds.**
  Your partnership has just leased commercial space in a downtown hotel to a department store chain. The lessee has agreed to pay $1 million per year for 8 years. You can hedge the risk of a rise in inflation (and hence a fall in the value of the lease contract) over this period by forming a short hedge in the T-bond futures market.

25.5 • **What is duration?**
  The weighted average maturity of a cash flow stream in present value terms.

- **How is the concept of duration used to reduce interest rate risk?**
  By matching the duration of financial assets and liabilities, a change in interest rates has the same impact on them value of the assets and liabilities.

25.6 • **Show that a currency swap is equivalent to a series of forward contracts.**
  Assume the swap is for five year at a fixed term of 100 million DM for $50 million each year. This is equivalent to a series of forward contracts. In year one, for example, it is equivalent to a one-year forward contract of 100 million DM at 2 DM/$.

CONCEPT QUESTIONS – CHAPTER 26

26.1 • **What are the two dimensions of the financial-planning process?**
  The time frame and the level of aggregation.

- **Why should firms draw up financial plans?**
  It accomplishes various goals:
  1. It improves interactions between investment proposals for the different operating activities of the firm.
  2. It provides opportunities for the firm to work through various investment and financial alternatives.
  3. It provides greater flexibility.
  4. It avoids surprises.

- **When might the goals of growth and value maximization be in conflict and when would they be aligned?**
  They might be in conflict if management is willing to accept negative NPV projects just for the sake of growth. They would be aligned if growth is an indeterminate goal that leads to higher value.

- **What are the determinants of growth?**
  1. Profit margin
  2. Asset utilization
  3. Payout ratio
  4. Debt ratio

CONCEPT QUESTIONS – CHAPTER 27

27.2 • What is the difference between net working capital and cash?
  Net working capital includes not only cash, but also other current assets minus current liabilities.

- **Will net working capital always increase when cash increases?**
  No. There are transactions such as collection of accounts receivable that increase cash but leave net working capital unchanged. Any transaction that will increase cash but produce a corresponding decrease in another current asset account or an increase in a current liability will have the same effect.

- **List the potential uses of cash.**
  1. Acquisition of capital
  2. Acquisition of marketable securities
  3. Acquisition of working capital
  4. Payment of dividends
  5. Retirement of debt
  6. Payment for labor, management and services rendered

- **List the potential sources of cash.**
  1. Sale of services or merchandise
  2. Collection of accounts receivable
  3. Issuance of debt or stock
  4. Sale of marketable securities
  5. Sale of fixed assets
  6. Short-term bank loans
  7. Increased accrued expenses, wages, or taxes.

27.3• What does it mean to say that a firm has an inventory-turnover ratio of four?

It means that on average the inventory is kept on hand for (365 days per year/4 times per year) = 91.25 days.

- **Describe operating cycle and cash cycle. What are the differences between them?**

  The operating cycle is the period of time from the acquisition of raw material until the collection of cash from sales. It includes conversion of raw materials into finished goods, inventories, sales and collection of accounts receivable. The cash cycle is the period of time from the cash payment for raw materials to the collection of cash. The difference between the two is the accounts payable stage, the time between the acquisition of raw materials and the cash payment for them.

27.4• What keeps the real world from being an ideal on where net working capital could always be zero?

A long-term rise is sales level will result in permanent investment in current assets. In addition, any day-to-day and month-to-month fluctuation in the level of sales will produce a nonzero NWC.

- **What considerations determine the optimal compromise between flexible and restrictive net-working-capital policies?**
  1. Cash reserves: How much cash does management want?
  2. Matching of asset and liability maturity (maturity hedging)
  3. Term structure: The difference between short-term and long-term interest rates

27.5 • How would you conduct a sensitivity analysis for Fun Toys' net cash balance?

By determining the net cash balance under different scenario assumptions – changing factors that will affects net cash balance and figuring out the result.

- **What could you learn from such an analysis?**

  It will give you an idea of what the range of net cash balances will be under the different scenarios and how sensitive the net cash balance is to each of the factors that affect it.

27.6 • What are the two basic forms of short-term financing?
Unsecured bank borrowing and secured bank borrowing.

• **Describe two types of secured loans.**
1. Accounts receivable financing. In this type of borrowing, accounts receivable are either assigned or factored. In the latter case receivables are actually sold at a discount.
2. Trust receipt. This is one of the three types of inventory loans in which the borrower holds the inventory in "trust" for the lender.

CONCEPT QUESTIONS – CHAPTER 28

28.1 • What is the transactions motive, and how does it lead firms to hold cash?
It is the necessity to hold cash for disbursements to pay wages, trade debts, taxes and dividends. A firm that does not have cash for these transactions will not be able to meet its obligations. Because cash inflows and outflows are seldom synchronized, firms need cash balances to serve as a buffer.

• **What is a compensating balance?**
It is the amount of cash banks require firms to keep permanently in their accounts to compensate the bank for services rendered.

28.2 • What is a target cash balance?
It is a firm's desired level of cash holdings to satisfy the transactions and compensating balance needs.

• **What are the strengths and weaknesses of the Baumol model and the Miller-Orr model?**
The Baumol model is a very simple and straightforward model with sensible conclusions, but it assumes a constant disbursement rate, lack of cash receipts during the projected period, and makes no allowance for "safety stock." It also assumes discrete, certain cash flows. The Miller-Orr model improves the understanding of the problem by determining the relationships among the different variables, but it neglects other factors that affect the target cash balance.

28.3 • Describe collection and disbursement float.
Collection float is the time that elapses from the moment the customer mails the payment until cash is received. Disbursement float is the time that elapses from the moment a company mails a check and the time cash is withdrawn from the company's bank account.

- **What are lockboxes? Concentration banks? Wire transfers?**
  Lockboxes are postal boxes strategically located in such a way that the mailing time from customers to the box is minimized. The firm's bank has direct access to the boxes, and thus in-house handling is eliminated and collection float is reduced. Concentration banks are regional banks in which the company has accounts and to which it sends excess cash at the end of the day. In this fashion checks obtained from nearby customers can be collected daily. Wire transfers are electronic transfers of surplus funds from local deposit banks to concentration banks.

- **Suppose an overzealous financial manager writes checks on uncollected funds. Aside from legal issues, who is the financial loser in this situation?**
  The bank where the firm has its accounts.

- **Why do firms find themselves with idle cash?**
  To finance seasonal or cyclical activities (transactions motive), to finance planned expenditures (investment motive), and to provide for unanticipated contingencies (precautionary motive).

- **What are the types of money market securities?**
  1. U.S. Treasury bills and notes
  2. Federal agency securities
  3. Municipal securities
  4. Commercial paper
  5. Certificates of deposit
  6. Repurchase agreements
  7. Eurodollar certificates of deposit
  8. Bankers' acceptances

CONCEPT QUESTIONS - CHAPTER 29

29.1 • What considerations enter into the determination of the terms of sale?
  1. Probability of non-payment
  2. Size of the account
  3. Perishability of goods
  4. Industry standards and competition
  5. Standard speed of collection
  6. Price of the goods

29.2 • List the factors that influence the decision to grant credit.
  1. The delayed revenues from granting credit
  2. The immediate cost of granting credit
  3. The probability of non-payment
  4. The appropriate required rate of return for delayed cash flows.

29.4 • What is credit analysis?

It is the process of trying to determine the probability that a customer will default. It involves:
a. gathering relevant information, and
b. determining creditworthiness

• What are the five Cs of credit?

Character, capacity, capital, collateral, conditions.

29.5 • What tools can a manager use to analyze a collection policy?

Average collection period, the aging schedule, and the payments pattern.

CONCEPT QUESTIONS - CHAPTER 30

30.1 • What is a merger? How does a merger differ from other forms of acquisition?

A merger is the absorption of one firm by another, where the acquiring firm retains its identity and the acquired firm ceases to exist. It differs from other forms of acquisition in that no new firm is created, and there is no need of buying the individual assets of the acquired firm or its stock.

• What is a takeover?

It is the transference of control of a firm from one group of shareholders to another by means of a majority vote of the board of directors.

30.3 • What is the difference between purchase accounting and pooling-of-interest accounting.

The most important difference is the creation of goodwill for a purchase.

30.8 • Why can a merger create the appearance of earnings growth?

If a high price-earnings ratio company acquires a low price-earnings company, the market might assume that the price-earnings ratio does not change.

30.9 • In an efficient market with no tax effects, should an acquiring firm use cash or stock?

It would not matter because the NPV of the acquisition will be zero, and so the acquired firm's shareholders obtain nothing but the value of the stock. If they use cash, the value of the acquired firm's stockholders is the same as the value of the original firm.

30.10 •What can a firm do to make a takeover less likely?
1. It can change the corporate charter by requiring a higher percentage of share approval for a merger or staggering the election of board members.
2. It can engage in standstill agreements (greenmail).
3. It can make an exclusionary self-tender

y about the benefits of mergers and acquisitions?
efit the shareholders of the acquired firm but do not holders of the acquiring firm. In terms of the new n be created.

iu?
usually affiliated around a large bank, industrial firm,

iu?
ial distress.

CONCEPT QUESTIONS - CHAPTER 31

31.1 • Can you describe financial distress?
It is a situation where operating cash flows at a firm are not sufficient to satisfy current obligations and the firm is forced to take corrective action.

• What are stock based insolvency and flow based insolvency?
Stock based insolvency occurs when a firm has negative net worth. Flow based insolvency occurs when a firm has a short fall in cash flow.

31.2 • Why doesn't financial distress always cause firms to die?
Financial restructuring may make a firm worth more"alive than dead".

• What is a benefit of financial distress?
It can serve as an early warning system or "wake up call.

31.3 • What is bankruptcy?
Legal bankruptcy occurs when a firm files for bankruptcy under chapter 7 (liquidations) or chapter 11 (reorganization). 1 the Bankruptcy Reform Act, 1978.

• What is the difference between liquidation and reorganization?
Liquidation occurs when the assets of a firm are sold and payments are made to creditors (usually based upon the APR). Reorganization is the restricting of the firm's finances.

31.4 • **What are two ways a firm can restructure its finances?**
Private workouts may be more expensive because of complex capital structure or conflicts of interest.

• **Why do firms use formal bankruptcy?**
Equity holdouts
Private workouts may be more expensive because of complex capital structure or conflicts of interest.

31.5 • **What is a prepackaged bankruptcy?**
A situation where the firm and most of all creditors agree to a private reorganization before bankruptcy takes place. After the private agreement, the firm files for formal bankruptcy.

• **What is the main benefit of prepackaged bankruptcy?**
Revco's complicated capital structure.

• **What are some of the costs of the Revco D.S. Bankruptcy?**
The direct and indirect costs of financial distress indicating a costly change in management and structural direction.

CONCEPT QUESTIONS - CHAPTER 32

32.1 • **What is the difference between a Eurobond and a foreign bond?**
A Eurobond is issued by a foreign country, denominated in the currency of its country of origin and sold in a different country. A foreign bond is denominated in the currency of the country in which it is sold, although it is issued by a company from another country.

32.3 • **What is the law of one price? What is purchasing-power parity?**
The law of one price is the simplest version of PPP. It states that a commodity will cost the same regardless of what currency is used to purchase it. PPP says that different currencies represent different purchasing powers, and the exchange rate adjusts to keep the purchasing power constant.

• **What is the relationship between inflation and exchange-rate movements?**
This relationship is called "relative purchasing power parity" and states that the rate of inflation in one country relative to the inflation rate in another country determines the rate of change of the exchange rate of the currencies of the two countries.

32.4 • **What is the interest-rate-parity theorem?**
It is a theorem that implies that if interest rates are higher in one country than another, the latter country's currency will sell at a premium in the forward market In this way money earns the same regardless of what currency it is invested in.

- **Why is the forward rate related to the expected future spot rate?**
  The trading in forward rates is based on what traders expect the spot rate to be in the future. If the expectation for the spot rate is $X/DM in three months, disregarding risk aversion, the three month forward rate should also be $X/DM.

- **How can one offset foreign exchange risk through a transaction in the forward markets?**
  Through the purchase or sale of a forward contract in a position offsetting that of the firm's liability or promised payment.

32.5 • **What problems do international projects pose for the use of net present value techniques?**
  1. Foreign exchange conversion. What exchange rate should one use, the company's projection or the market's.
  2. Repatriation of funds. Some countries place restrictions on remittance of funds to the investing country.
  3. The appropriate discount rate may be lower than the domestic rate if the firm can diversify in ways that its shareholders cannot. Foreign political risk may raise the required return in some cases.

32.8 • **What issues arise when reporting foreign operations?**
  1. What exchange rate should you use if the exchange rate has changed during the period?
  2. How do you handle unrealized accounting gains or losses from foreign currency?

Chapter 2: Accounting Statements and Cash Flow

2.1

Assets

Current assets

Cash	$ 4,000
Accounts receivable	8,000
Total current assets	$ 12,000

Fixed assets

Machinery	$ 34,000
Patents	82,000
Total fixed assets	$116,000
Total assets	$128,000

Liabilities and equity

Current liabilities

Accounts payable	$ 6,000
Taxes payable	2,000
Total current liabilities	$ 8,000

Long-term liabilities

Bonds payable	$7,000

Stockholders equity

Common stock ($100 par)	$ 88,000
Capital surplus	19,000
Retained earnings	6,000
Total stockholders equity	$113,000
Total liabilities and equity	$128,000

2.2

	One year ago	Today
Long-term debt	$50,000,000	$50,000,000
Preferred stock	30,000,000	30,000,000
Common stock	100,000,000	110,000,000
Retained earnings	20,000,000	22,000,000
Total	$200,000,000	$212,000,000

2.3

Income Statement

Total operating revenues		$500,000
Less: Cost of goods sold	$200,000	
Administrative expenses	100,000	300,000
Earnings before interest and taxes		$200,000
Less: Interest expense		50,000
Earnings before Taxes		$150,000
Taxes		51,000
Net income		$99,000

2.4

a.

<u>Income Statement</u>
<u>The Flying Lion Corporation</u>

	<u>19X1</u>	<u>19X2</u>
Net sales	$800,000	$500,000
Cost of goods sold	(560,000)	(320,000)
Operating expenses	(75,000)	(56,000)
Depreciation	(300,000)	(200,000)
Earnings before taxes	$(135,000)	$(76,000)
Taxes*	40,500	22,800
Net income	$(94,500)	$(53,200)

* The problem states that Flying Lion has other profitable operations. Flying Lion can take advantage of tax losses by deducting the tax liabilities in the other operations that have taxable profits. If Flying Lion did not have other operations and tax losses could not be carried forward or backward, then taxes in each of these years would have been zero.

b. Cash flow during 19X2 = -$94,500 + $300,000 = $205,500
   Cash flow during 19X1 = -$53,200 + $200,000 = $146,800

2.5   The main difference between accounting profit and cash flow is that non-cash costs, such as depreciation expense, are included in accounting profits. Cash flows do not consider costs that do not represent actual expenditures. Cash flows deduct the entire cost of an investment at the time the cash flow occurs.

2.6   a. Net operating income = Sales - Cost of goods sold - Selling expenses - Depreciation
                              = $1,000,000 - $300,000 - $200,000 - $100,000
                              = $400,000
      b. Earnings before taxes = Net operating income - Interest expense
                              = $400,000 - 0.1 ($1,000,000)
                              = $300,000
      c. Net income = Earnings before taxes - Taxes
                              = $300,000 - 0.35 ($300,000)
                              = $195,000
      d. Cash flow = Net income + Depreciation + Interest expense
                              = $195,000 + $100,000 + $100,000
                              = $395,000

2.7

Statement of Cash Flows
The Stancil Company

Cash flows from the firm

Capital spending	$(1,000)
Additions to working capital	(4,000)
Total	$(5,000)

Cash flows to investors of the firm

Short-term debt	$(6,000)
Long-term debt	(20,000)
Equity (Dividend - Financing)	21,000
Total	$(5,000)

2.8   a.   The changes in net working capital can be computed from:

Sources of net working capital

Net income	$100
Depreciation	50
Increases in long-term debt	75
Total sources	$225

Uses of net working capital

Dividends	$50
Increases in fixed assets*	150
Total uses	$200
Additions to net working capital	$25

*Includes $50 of depreciation.

b.

Cash flow from the firm

Operating cash flow	$150
Capital spending	(150)
Additions to net working capital	(25)
Total	$(25)

Cash flow to the investors

Debt	$(75)
Equity	50
Total	$(25)

Chapter 3: Financial Markets and Net Present Value: First Principles of Finance (Advanced)

3.1 $120,000 - ($150,000 - $100,000) (1.1) = $65,000

3.2 $40,000 + ($50,000 - $20,000) (1.12) = $73,600

3.3   Financial markets arise to facilitate borrowing and lending between individuals. By borrowing and lending, people can adjust their pattern of consumption over time to fit their particular preferences. This allows corporations to accept all positive NPV projects, regardless of the inter-temporal consumption preferences of the shareholders.

3.4   a.   Since the PV of labor income is $60, and $60 = $40 + $22 / (1 + r), r must be equal to 10%.
       b.   NPV = $75 - $60 = $15
       c.   Her wealth is $75. Letting C denote consumption, she wants $75 = C + C/(1 + r) where r = 0.10. Solve for C; C = $39.29.

3.5   a. $90,000 / $80,000 - 1 = 0.125 = 12.5%
       b.   Harry will invest $10,000 in financial assets and $30,000 in productive assets today.
       c.   NPV = -$30,000 + $56,250 / 1.125
             = $20,000

3.6   a.   Consume $60,000 and put the remaining $40,000 into the financial market. At a 10% rate, the $40,000 will be $44,000 next year.
       b.   Borrow $30,000; consume $60,000. Invest $70,000 in the land. Next year she will have to repay $33,000 (=$30,000 x 1.1) for the loan.
       c.   If she follows the optimal strategy, she should invest in the land when the land investment is worth $80,000.
       d.   In the first case, she will then be able to consume $144,000 [= $100,000 + $44,000]. In the second case, she will be able to consume $147,000 (= $100,000 + $80,000 - $33,000).

3.7   a.   If shareholders and firms have equal access to perfect capital markets (the same risk-adjusted borrowing and lending rates for all parties), then the only way that managers can make shareholders better off is to increase their wealth. Increasing shareholder wealth is accomplished by accepting positive NPV projects. This maximizes (i.e. pushes out) the opportunity set available to shareholders.
       b.   A perfect capital market is the necessary assumption.

3.8   a.   ($7 million + $3 million) (1.10) = $11.0 million
       b.

             i. They could spend $10 million by borrowing $5 million today.
             ii. They will have to spend $5.5 million [= $11 million - ($5 million x 1.1)] at t=1.

3.9   a.   AE.
       b.   CF / BD. The equity will appreciate to BE on the announcement.
       c.   AF / AB.

Chapter 4: Net Present Value

4.1   a. $\$1,000 \times 1.05^{10} = \$1,628.89$
       b. $\$1,000 \times 1.07^{10} = \$1,967.15$
       c. $\$1,000 \times 1.05^{20} = \$2,653.30$
       d.   Interest compounds on the interest already earned. Therefore, the interest earned in part c, $\$1,653.30$, is more than double the amount earned in part a, $\$628.89$.

4.2   a. $\$1,000 / 1.1^{7} = \$513.16$
       b. $\$2,000 / 1.1 = \$1,818.18$
       c. $\$500 / 1.1^{8} = \$233.25$

4.3   You can make your decision by computing either the present value of the $\$2,000$ that you can receive in ten years, or the future value of the $\$1,000$ that you can receive now.
              Present value: $\$2,000 / 1.08^{10} = \$926.39$
              Future value: $\$1,000 \times 1.08^{10} = \$2,158.93$
   Either calculation indicates you should take the $\$1,000$ now.

4.4   Since this bond has no interim coupon payments, its present value is simply the present value of the $\$1,000$ that will be received in 25 years. Note: As will be discussed in the next chapter, the present value of the payments associated with a bond is the price of that bond.
              $PV = \$1,000 / 1.1^{25} = \$92.30$

4.5 $PV = \$1,500,000 / 1.08^{27} = \$187,780.23$

4.6   a.   At a discount rate of zero, the future value and present value are always the same. Remember, $FV = PV(1 + r)^{t}$. If $r = 0$, then the formula reduces to $FV = PV$. Therefore, the values of the options are $\$10,000$ and $\$20,000$, respectively. You should choose the second option.
       b.   Option one: $\$10,000 / 1.1 = \$9,090.91$
             Option two: $\$20,000 / 1.1^{5} = \$12,418.43$
             Choose the second option.
       c.   Option one: $\$10,000 / 1.2 = \$8,333.33$
             Option two: $\$20,000 / 1.2^{5} = \$8,037.55$
             Choose the first option.
       d.   You are indifferent at the rate that equates the PVs of the two alternatives. You know that rate must fall between 10% and 20% because the option you would choose differs at these rates. Let r be the discount rate that makes you indifferent between the options.
             $\$10,000 / (1 + r) = \$20,000 / (1 + r)^{5}$
             $(1 + r)^{4} = \$20,000 / \$10,000 = 2$
             $1 + r = 1.18921$
             $r = 0.18921 = 18.921\%$

4.7   PV of Joneses' offer $= \$150,000 / (1.1)^{3} = \$112,697.22$
       Since the PV of Joneses' offer is less than Smiths' offer, $\$115,000$, you should choose Smiths' offer.

4.8   a. $P_0 = \$1,000 / 1.08^{20} = \$214.55$
      b. $P_{10} = P_0 (1.08)^{10} = \$463.20$
      c. $P_{15} = P_0 (1.08)^{15} = \$680.59$

4.9   The \$1,000 that you place in the account at the end of the first year will earn interest for six
      years. The \$1,000 that you place in the account at the end of the second year will earn
      interest for five years, etc. Thus, the account will have a balance of
               $\$1,000 (1.12)^6 + \$1,000 (1.12)^5 + \$1,000 (1.12)^4 + \$1,000 (1.12)^3$
               $= \$6,714.61$

4.10 $PV = \$5,000,000 / 1.12^{10} = \$1,609,866.18$

4.11 a.   The cost of investment is \$900,000.
              PV of cash inflows $= \$120,000 / 1.12 + \$250,000 / 1.12^2 + \$800,000 / 1.12^3$
                              $= \$875,865.52$
              Since the PV of cash inflows is less than the cost of investment, you should not
              make the investment.
      b.   NPV $= -\$900,000 + \$875,865.52$
                    $= -\$24,134.48$
      c.   NPV $= -\$900,000 + \$120,000 / 1.11 + \$250,000 / 1.11^2 + \$800,000 / 1.11^3$
                    $= \$-4,033.18$
              Since the NPV is still negative, you should not make the investment.

4.12 NPV $= -(\$340,000 + \$10,000) + (\$100,000 - \$10,000) / 1.1$
            $+ \$90,000 / 1.1^2 + \$90,000 / 1.1^3 + \$90,000 / 1.1^4 + \$100,000 / 1.1^5$
            $= -\$2,619.98$
      Since the NPV is negative, you should not buy it.

      If the relevant cost of capital is 9 percent,
              NPV $= -\$350,000 + \$90,000 / 1.09 + \$90,000 / 1.09^2 + \$90,000 / 1.09^3$
                    $+ \$90,000 / 1.09^4 + \$100,000 / 1.09^5$
                    $= \$6,567.93$
              Since the NPV is positive, you should buy it.

4.13 a.   Profit = PV of revenue - Cost = NPV
              NPV $= \$90,000 / 1.1^5 - \$60,000 = -\$4,117.08$
              No, the firm will not make a profit.
      b.   Find r that makes zero NPV.
              $\$90,000 / (1+r)^5 - \$60,000 = \$0$
              $(1+r)^5 = 1.5$
              $r = 0.08447 = 8.447\%$

4.14 The future value of the decision to own your car for one year is the sum of the trade-in
      value and the benefit from owning the car. Therefore, the PV of the decision to own the
      car for one year is
               $\$3,000 / 1.12 + \$1,000 / 1.12 = \$3,571.43$
      Since the PV of the roommate's offer, \$3,500, is lower than the aunt's offer, you should
      accept aunt's offer.

4.15 a. $\$1.000 (1.08)^3 = \$1,259.71$

b. $\$1,000 [1 + (0.08 / 2)]^{2 \times 3} = \$1,000 (1.04)^6 = \$1,265.32$

c. $\$1,000 [1 + (0.08 / 12)]^{12 \times 3} = \$1,000 (1.00667)^{36} = \$1,270.24$

d. $\$1,000\ e^{0.08 \times 3} = \$1,271.25$

e. The future value increases because of the compounding. The account is earning interest on interest. Essentially, the interest is added to the account balance at the end of every compounding period. During the next period, the account earns interest on the new balance. When the compounding period shortens, the balance that earns interest is rising faster.

4.16 a. $\$1,000\ e^{0.12 \times 5} = \$1,822.12$

b. $\$1,000\ e^{0.1 \times 3} = \$1,349.86$

c. $\$1,000\ e^{0.05 \times 10} = \$1,648.72$

d. $\$1,000\ e^{0.07 \times 8} = \$1,750.67$

4.17 $PV = \$5,000 / [1+ (0.1 / 4)]^{4 \times 12} = \$1,528.36$

4.18 Effective annual interest rate of Bank America
$$= [1 + (0.041 / 4)]^4 - 1 = 0.0416 = 4.16\%$$
Effective annual interest rate of Bank USA
$$= [1 + (0.0405 / 12)]^{12} - 1 = 0.0413 = 4.13\%$$
You should deposit your money in Bank America.

4.19 The price of the consol bond is the present value of the coupon payments. Apply the perpetuity formula to find the present value. $PV = \$120 / 0.15 = \$800$

4.20 Quarterly interest rate $= 12\% / 4 = 3\% = 0.03$
Therefore, the price of the security $= \$10 / 0.03 = \$333.33$

4.21 The price at the end of 19 quarters (or 4.75 years) from today $= \$1 / (0.15 \div 4) = \$26.67$
The current price $= \$26.67 / [1+ (.15 / 4)]^{19} = \$13.25$

4.22 a. $\$1,000 / 0.1 = \$10,000$

b. $\$500 / 0.1 = \$5,000$ is the value one year from now of the perpetual stream. Thus, the value of the perpetuity is $\$5,000 / 1.1 = \$4,545.45$.

c. $\$2,420 / 0.1 = \$24,200$ is the value two years from now of the perpetual stream. Thus, the value of the perpetuity is $\$24,200 / 1.1^2 = \$20,000$.

4.23 The value at $t = 8$ is $\$120 / 0.1 = \$1,200$.
Thus, the value at $t = 5$ is $\$1,200 / 1.1^3 = \$901.58$.

4.24 $P = \$3 (1.05) / (0.12 - 0.05) = \$45.00$

4.25 $P = \$1 / (0.1 - 0.04) = \$16.67$

4.26 The first cash flow will be generated 2 years from today.
The value at the end of 1 year from today $= \$200,000 / (0.1 - 0.05) = \$4,000,000$.
Thus, $PV = \$4,000,000 / 1.1 = \$3,636,363.64$.

4.27 A zero NPV

$- \$100{,}000 + \$50{,}000 / r = 0$

$r = 0.5$

4.28 Apply the NPV technique. Since the inflows are an annuity you can use the present value of an annuity factor.

$$
\begin{aligned}
\text{NPV} &= -\$6{,}200 + \$1{,}200 \; A_{0.1}^{8} \\
&= -\$6{,}200 + \$1{,}200 \; (5.3349) \\
&= \$201.88
\end{aligned}
$$

Yes, you should buy the asset.

4.29 Use an annuity factor to compute the value two years from today of the twenty payments. Remember, the annuity formula gives you the value of the stream one year before the first payment. Hence, the annuity factor will give you the value at the end of year two of the stream of payments. Value at the end of year two $= \$2{,}000 \; A_{0.08}^{20}$

$$
\begin{aligned}
&= \$2{,}000 \; (9.8181) \\
&= \$19{,}636.20
\end{aligned}
$$

The present value is simply that amount discounted back two years.

$PV = \$19{,}636.20 / 1.08^2 = \$16{,}834.88$

4.30 The value of annuity at the end of year five

$$= \$500 \; A_{0.15}^{15} = \$500 \; (5.84737) = \$2{,}923.69$$

The present value $= \$2{,}923.69 / 1.12^5 = \$1{,}658.98$

4.31 The easiest way to do this problem is to use the annuity factor. The annuity factor must be equal to $\$12{,}800 / \$2{,}000 = 6.4$; remember $PV = C \; A_{r}^{t}$. The annuity factors are in the appendix to the text. To use the factor table to solve this problem, scan across the row labeled 10 years until you find 6.4. It is close to the factor for 9%, 6.4177. Thus, the rate you will receive on this note is slightly more than 9%.

You can find a more precise answer by interpolating between nine and ten percent.

$$
a \begin{bmatrix} 10\% \\ r \\ 9\% \end{bmatrix} b
\qquad
c \begin{bmatrix} 6.1446 \\ 6.4 \\ 6.4177 \end{bmatrix} d
$$

By interpolating, you are presuming that the ratio of a to b is equal to the ratio of c to d.

$(9 - r) / (9 - 10) = (6.4177 - 6.4) / (6.4177 - 6.1446)$

$r = 9.0648\%$

The exact value could be obtained by solving the annuity formula for the interest rate. Sophisticated calculators can compute the rate directly as 9.0626%.

4.32 a.   The annuity amount can be computed by first calculating the PV of the $25,000 which you need in five years. That amount is $17,824.65 [= $25,000 / 1.07^5]. Next compute the annuity which has the same present value.

$17,824.65 $= C \, A_{0.07}^5$

$17,824.65 $= C \, (4.1002)$

        C $= \$4,347.26$

Thus, putting $4,347.26 into the 7% account each year will provide $25,000 five years from today.

       b.   The lump sum payment must be the present value of the $25,000, i.e., $25,000 / 1.07^5 = $17,824.65

The formula for future value of any annuity can be used to solve the problem (see footnote 14 of the text).

4.33 The amount of loan is $120,000 × 0.85 = $102,000.

$CA_{0.10}^{20} = \$102,000$

The amount of equal installments is

$C = \$102,000 / A_{0.10}^{20} = \$102,000 / 8.513564 = \$11,980.88$

4.34 The present value of salary is $5,000 $A_{0.01}^{36} = \$150,537.53$

The present value of bonus is $10,000 $A_{0.1268}^{3} = \$23,740.42$ (EAR = 12.68% is used since bonuses are paid annually.)

The present value of the contract = $150,537.53 + $23,740.42 = $174,277.94

4.35 The amount of loan is $15,000 × 0.8 = $12,000.

$C \, A_{0.0067}^{48} = \$12,000$

The amount of monthly installments is

$C = \$12,000 / A_{0.0067}^{48} = \$12,000 / 40.96191 = \$292.96$

4.36 Option one: This cash flow is an annuity due. To value it, you must use the after-tax amounts. The after-tax payment is $160,000 (1 - 0.28) = $115,200. Value all except the first payment using the standard annuity formula, then add back the first payment of $115,200 to obtain the value of this option.

        Value $= \$115,200 + \$115,200 \, A_{0.10}^{30}$

               $= \$115,200 + \$115,200 \, (9.4269)$

               $= \$1,201,178.88$

Option two: This option is valued similarly. You are able to have $446,000 now; this is already on an after-tax basis. You will receive an annuity of $101,055 for each of the next thirty years. Those payments are taxable when you receive them, so your after-tax payment is $72,759.60 [= $101,055 (1 - 0.28)].

        Value $= \$446,000 + \$72,759.60 \, A_{0.10}^{30}$

               $= \$446,000 + \$72,759.60 \, (9.4269)$

               $= \$1,131,897.47$

Since option one has a higher PV, you should choose it.

4.37 The amount of loan is $9,000. The monthly payment C is given by solving the equation:
$$C \; A^{60}_{0.008} = \$9,000$$
$$C = \$9,000 \; / \; 47.5042 = \$189.46$$
In October 2000, Susan Chao has 35 (= 12 × 5 - 25) monthly payments left, including the one due in October 2000.
Therefore, the balance of the loan on November 1, 2000
$$= \$189.46 + \$189.46 \; A^{34}_{0.008}$$
$$= \$189.46 + \$189.46 \; (29.6651)$$
$$= \$5,809.81$$
Thus, the total amount of payoff = 1.01 ($5,809.81) = $5,867.91

4.38 Let r be the rate of interest you must earn.
$$\$10,000(1 + r)^{12} = \$80,000$$
$$(1 + r)^{12} = 8$$
$$r \qquad = 0.18921 = 18.921\%$$

4.39 First compute the present value of all the payments you must make for your children's education. The value as of one year before matriculation of one child's education is
$$\$21,000 \; A^{4}_{0.15} = \$21,000 \; (2.8550) = \$59,955.$$
This is the value of the elder child's education fourteen years from now. It is the value of the younger child's education sixteen years from today. The present value of these is
$$PV \quad = \$59,955 \; / \; 1.15^{14} + \$59,955 \; / \; 1.15^{16}$$
$$= \$14,880.44$$
You want to make fifteen equal payments into an account that yields 15% so that the present value of the equal payments is $14,880.44.
$$\text{Payment} = \$14,880.44 \; / \; A^{15}_{0.15} = \$14,880.44 \; / \; 5.8474 = \$2,544.80$$

4.40 The NPV of the policy is
$$NPV \quad = -\$750 \; A^{3}_{0.06} - \$800 \; A^{3}_{0.06} \; / \; 1.06^{3} + \$250,000 \; / \; [(1.06^{6}) \; (1.07^{59})]$$
$$= -\$2,004.76 - \$1,795.45 + \$3,254.33$$
$$= -\$545.88$$
Therefore, you should not buy the policy.

4.41 The NPV of the lease offer is
$$NPV \quad = \$120,000 - \$15,000 - \$15,000 \; A^{9}_{0.08} - \$25,000 \; / \; 1.08^{10}$$
$$= \$105,000 - \$93,703.32 - \$11,579.84$$
$$= -\$283.16$$
Therefore, you should not accept the offer.

4.42 This problem applies the growing annuity formula. The first payment is
$$\$50,000(1.04)^{2}(0.02) = \$1,081.60.$$
$$PV \quad = \$1,081.60 \; [1 \; / \; (0.08 - 0.04) - \{1 \; / \; (0.08 - 0.04)\} \{1.04 \; / \; 1.08\}^{40}]$$
$$= \$21,064.28$$
This is the present value of the payments, so the value forty years from today is
$$\$21,064.28 \; (1.08^{40}) = \$457,611.46$$

4.43 Use the discount factors to discount the individual cash flows. Then compute the NPV of the project. Notice that the four $1,000 cash flows form an annuity. You can still use the factor tables to compute their PV. Essentially, they form cash flows that are a six year annuity less a two year annuity. Thus, the appropriate annuity factor to use with them is 2.6198 (= 4.3553 - 1.7355).

Year	Cash Flow	Factor	PV
1	$700	0.9091	$636.37
2	900	0.8264	743.76
3	1,000		
4	1,000	2.6198	2,619.80
5	1,000		
6	1,000		
7	1,250	0.5132	641.50
8	1,375	0.4665	641.44
		Total	$5,282.87

$$\text{NPV} = -\$5,000 + \$5,282.87$$
$$= \$282.87$$

Purchase the machine.

4.44 Weekly inflation rate = 0.039 / 52 = 0.00075
Weekly interest rate = 0.104 / 52 = 0.002
$$\text{PV} = \$5 \, [1 / (0.002 - 0.00075)] \, \{1 - [(1 + 0.00075) / (1 + 0.002)]^{52 \times 30}\}$$
$$= \$3,429.38$$

4.45 Engineer:
$$\text{NPV} = -\$12,000 \, A_{0.05}^4 + \$20,000 / 1.05^5 + \$25,000 / 1.05^6 - \$15,000 / 1.05^7$$
$$- \$15,000 / 1.05^8 + \$40,000 \, A_{0.05}^{25} / 1.05^8$$
$$= \$352,533.35$$

Accountant:
$$\text{NPV} = -\$13,000 \, A_{0.05}^4 + \$31,000 \, A_{0.05}^{30} / 1.05^4$$
$$= \$345,958.81$$

Become an engineer.

After your brother announces that the appropriate discount rate is 6%, you can recalculate the NPVs. Calculate them the same way as above except using the 6% discount rate.
Engineer NPV = $292,419.47
Accountant NPV = $292,947.04
Your brother made a poor decision. At a 6% rate, he should study accounting.

4.46 Since Goose receives his first payment on July 1 and all payments in one year intervals from July 1, the easiest approach to this problem is to discount the cash flows to July 1 then use the six month discount rate (0.044) to discount them the additional six months.

$$\text{PV} = \$875,000 / (1.044) + \$650,000 / (1.044)(1.09) + \$800,000 / (1.044)(1.09^2)$$

$$+ \$1,000,000 / (1.044)(1.09^3) + \$1,000,000/(1.044)(1.09^4) + \$300,000 / (1.044)(1.09^5)$$

$$+ \; \$240{,}000 \; A^{17}_{0.09} \, / \, (1.044)(1.09^5) \; + \; \$125{,}000 \; A^{10}_{0.09} \, / \, (1.044)(1.09^{22})$$

$$= \; \$5{,}051{,}150$$

Remember that the use of annuity factors to discount the deferred payments yields the value of the annuity stream one period prior to the first payment. Thus, the annuity factor applied to the first set of deferred payments gives the value of those payments on July 1 of 1989. Discounting by 9% for five years brings the value to July 1, 1984. The use of the six month discount rate (4.4%) brings the value of the payments to January 1, 1984. Similarly, the annuity factor applied to the second set of deferred payments yields the value of those payments in 2006. Discounting for 22 years at 9% and for six months at 4.4% provides the value at January 1, 1984.

The equivalent five-year, annual salary is the annuity that solves:

$$\$5{,}051{,}150 \; = \; C \, A^5_{0.09}$$
$$C \; = \; \$5{,}051{,}150/3.8897$$
$$C \; = \; \$1{,}298{,}596$$

The student must be aware of possible rounding errors in this problem. The difference between 4.4% semiannual and 9.0% and for six months at 4.4% provides the value at January 1, 1984.

4.47 PV $= \$10{,}000 + (\$35{,}000 + \$3{,}500) \, [1 \, / \, (0.12 - 0.04)] \, [1 - (1.04 \, / \, 1.12)^{25}]$
$= \$415{,}783.60$

4.48 NPV $= -\$40{,}000 + \$10{,}000 \, [1 \, / \, (0.10 - 0.07)] \, [1 - (1.07 \, / \, 1.10)^5]$
$= \$3{,}041.91$
Revise the textbook.

4.49 The amount of the loan is $\$400{,}000 \, (0.8) = \$320{,}000$
The monthly payment is $C = \$320{,}000 \, / \; A^{360}_{0.0067} \;\; = \$2{,}348.10$
Thirty years of payments $\$2{,}348.10 \, (360) = \$845{,}316.00$
Eight years of payments $\$2{,}348.10 \, (96) = \$225{,}417.60$
The difference is the balloon payment of $\$619{,}898.40$

4.50 The lease payment is an annuity in advance
$C + C \; A^{23}_{0.01} = \$4{,}000$
$C \, (1 + 20.4558) = \$4{,}000$
$C = \$186.42$

4.51 The effective annual interest rate is
$[\, 1 + (0.08 \, / \, 4) \,]^4 - 1 = 0.0824$
The present value of the ten-year annuity is
$PV = 900 \; A^{10}_{0.0824} \;\; = \$5{,}974.24$
Four remaining discount periods
$PV = \$5{,}974.24 \, / \, (1.0824)^4 = \$4{,}352.43$

4.52 The present value of Ernie's retirement income

$$PV = \$300{,}000 \ A_{0.07}^{20} \ / \ (1.07)^{30} = \$417{,}511.54$$

The present value of the cabin
$$PV = \$350{,}000 \ / \ (1.07)^{10} = \$177{,}922.25$$
The present value of his savings
$$PV = \$40{,}000 \ A_{0.07}^{10} = \$280{,}943.26$$

In present value terms he must save an additional \$313,490.53
In future value terms
$$FV = \$313{,}490.53 \ (1.07)^{10} = \$616{,}683.32$$
He must save
$$C = \$616.683.32 \ / \ A_{0.07}^{20} = \$58{,}210.54$$

Chapter 5: How to Value Bonds and Stocks

5.1 a. $\$1,000 / 1.05^{10} = \$613.91$
     b. $\$1,000 / 1.10^{10} = \$385.54$
     c. $\$1,000 / 1.15^{10} = \$247.18$

5.2 The amount of the semi-annual interest payment is $40 (=$1,000 \times 0.08 / 2$). There are a total of 40 periods; i.e., two half years in each of the twenty years in the term to maturity. The annuity factor tables can be used to price these bonds. The appropriate discount rate to use is the semi-annual rate. That rate is simply the annual rate divided by two. Thus, for part b the rate to be used is 5% and for part c is it 3%.
     a. $\$40 \,(19.7928) + \$1,000 / 1.04^{40} = \$1,000$
         Notice that whenever the coupon rate and the market rate are the same, the bond is priced at par.
     b. $\$40 \,(17.1591) + \$1,000 / 1.05^{40} = \$828.41$
         Notice that whenever the coupon rate is below the market rate, the bond is priced below par.
     c. $\$40 \,(23.1148) + \$1,000 / 1.03^{40} = \$1,231.15$
         Notice that whenever the coupon rate is above the market rate, the bond is priced above par.

5.3 Semi-annual discount factor $= (1.12)^{1/2} - 1 = 0.05830 = 5.83\%$
     a. Price $= \$40 \ A_{0.0583}^{40} + \$1,000 / 1.0583^{40}$
                $= \$614.98 + \$103.67$
                $= \$718.65$
     b. Price $= \$50 \ A_{0.0583}^{30} + \$1,000 / 1.0583^{30}$
                $= \$700.94 + \$182.70$
                $= \$883.64$

5.4 Effective annual rate of 10%:
     Semi-annual discount factor $= (1.1)^{0.5} - 1 = 0.04881 = 4.881\%$
     Price $= \$40 \ A_{0.04881}^{40} + \$1,000 / 1.04881^{40}$
            $= \$846.33$

5.5 $\$923.14 = C \, A_{0.05}^{30} + \$1,000 / 1.05^{30}$
            $= (15.37245) \, C + \$231.38$
     $C = \$45$
     The annual coupon rate $= \$45 \times 2 / \$1,000 = 0.09 = 9\%$

5.6 a. The semi-annual interest rate is $60 / $1,000 = 0.06$. Thus, the effective annual rate is $1.06^2 - 1 = 0.1236 = 12.36\%$.
     b. Price $= \$30 \ A_{0.06}^{12} + \$1,000 / 1.06^{12}$
              $= \$748.48$
     c. Price $= \$30 \ A_{0.04}^{12} + \$1,000 / 1.04^{12}$
              $= \$906.15$

Note: In parts b and c we are implicitly assuming that the yield curve is flat. That is, the yield in year 5 applies for year 6 as well.

5.7　a.　$P_A = \$100\ A_{0.10}^{20} + \$1,000\ /\ 1.10^{20} = \$1,000$

$P_B = \$100\ A_{0.10}^{10} + \$1,000\ /\ 1.10^{10} = \$1,000$

b.　$P_A = \$100\ A_{0.12}^{20} + \$1,000\ /\ 1.12^{20} = \$850.61$

$P_B = \$100\ A_{0.12}^{10} + \$1,000\ /\ 1.12^{10} = \$887.00$

c.　$P_A = \$100\ A_{0.08}^{20} + \$1,000\ /\ 1.08^{20} = \$1,196.36$

$P_B = \$100\ A_{0.08}^{10} + \$1,000\ /\ 1.08^{10} = \$1,134.20$

5.8　a.　The price of long-term bonds should fall. The price is the PV of the cash flows associated with the bond. As the interest rate rises, the PV of those flows falls. This can be easily seen by looking at a one-year, pure discount bond.

Price = $\$1,000\ /\ (1 + i)$

As i. increases, the denominator rises. This increase causes the price to fall.

b.　The effect upon stocks is not as certain as that upon the bonds. The nominal interest rate is a function of both the real interest rate and the inflation rate; i.e.,

$(1 + i) = (1 + r)\ (1 + \text{inflation})$

From this relationship it is easy to conclude that as inflation rises, the nominal interest rate rises. Stock prices are a function of dividends and future prices as well as the interest rate. Those dividends and future prices are determined by the earning power of the firm. When inflation occurs, it may increase or decrease firm earnings. Thus, the effect of a rise in the level of general prices upon the level of stock prices is uncertain.

5.9　a.　$\$1,200 = \$80\ A_r^{20} + \$1,000\ /\ (1 + r)^{20}$

$r = 0.0622 = 6.22\%$

b.　$\$950 = \$80\ A_r^{10} + \$1,000\ /\ (1 + r)^{10}$

$r = 0.0877 = 8.77\%$

5.10　$P_A = (\$2,000\ A_{0.06}^{16})\ /\ (1.06)^{12} + (\$2,500\ A_{0.06}^{12})\ /\ (1.06)^{28} + \$40,000\ /\ (1.06)^{40}$

$= \$18,033.86$

$P_B = \$\ 40,000\ /\ (1.06)^{40} = \$3,888.89$

5.11　a.　True
　　b.　True
　　c.　False
　　d.　False
　　e.　True

5.12　a.　True
　　b.　False
　　c.　True
　　d.　False

5.13　Price = $\$2\ (1.08)\ /\ 1.12 + \$2\ (1.08^2)\ /\ 1.12^2 + \$2\ (1.08^3)\ /\ 1.12^3$
　　　　$+ \{\$2\ (1.08^3)(1.04)\ /\ (0.12 - 0.04)\}\ /\ 1.12^3$
　　　　$= \$28.89$

5.14   a.   False
        b.   True
        c.   False
        d.   False
        e.   True

5.15 $98.125 = 1.30\ (1.07)\ /\ r - 0.07$
        $r = 8.4175\ \%$

5.16   Price = $\$2\ (0.72)\ /\ 1.15 + \$4\ (0.72)\ /\ 1.15^2 + \$50\ /\ 1.15^3$
                            $= \$36.31$
        The number of shares you own = $\$100,000\ /\ \$36.31 = 2,754$ shares

5.17   a. $P = \$2\ /\ (0.12 - 0.05) = \$28.57$
        b. $P_{10} = D_{11}\ /\ (r - g)$
                    $= \$2\ (1.05^{10})\ /\ (0.12 - 0.05)$
                    $= \$46.54$

5.18   Value = $-\$5,000,000 + \$2,000,000\ /\ \{0.14 - (-0.02)\}$
                $= \$7,500,000$

5.19   Price = $\$1.15\ (1.18)\ /\ 1.12 + \$1.15\ (1.18^2)\ /\ 1.12^2 + \$1.15^2\ (1.18^2)\ /\ 1.12^3$
                    $+\ \{\$1.15^2\ (1.18^2)(1.06)\ /\ (0.12 - 0.06)\}\ /\ 1.12^3$
                $= \$26.95$

5.20 $\$30 = D\ /\ 1.12 + D\ /\ 1.12^2 + \{D\ (1 + 0.04)\ /\ (0.12 - 0.04)\}\ /\ 1.12^2$
                $= 12.053571\ D$
        $D = \$2.49$

5.21   Dividend one year from now = $\$5\ (1 - 0.10) = \$4.50$
        Price = $\$5 + \$4.50\ /\ \{0.14 - (-0.10)\}$
                $= \$23.75$
        Since the current $5 dividend has not yet been paid, it is still included in the stock price.

5.22   Price $= \$1\ A^{12}_{0.025} + \{\$1\ (1 + 0.005)\ /\ (0.025 - 0.005)\}\ /\ 1.025^{12}$
                $= \$10.26 + \$37.36$
                $= \$47.62$

5.23   Growth rate $g = 0.6 \times 0.14 = 0.084 = 8.4\%$
        Next year earnings = $\$20$ million $\times\ 1.084$
                            $= \$21.68$ million

5.24   g = retention ratio × ROE
        = 0.75 × 0.12
        = 0.09 = 9%
        Dividend per share = $10 million × (1 - 0.75) / 1.25 million
                           = $2
        The required rate of return = $2 (1.09) / $30 + 0.09
                                    = 0.1627 = 16.27%

5.25   a.   Price   = ($3 - $1.5) × 1.05 / (0.15 - 0.05)
                       = $15.75

        b.   NPVGO = -$15,000,000 - $5,000,000 / 1.15 + ($6,000,000 / 0.15) / 1.15
                    = $15,434,783
        The price increases by $15.43 per share.

5.26   a.   Price = EPS / r
                    = {$100 million / 20 million} / 0.15
                    = $33.33
        b.   NPV = -$15 million - $5 million / 1.15 + ($10 million / 0.15) / 1.15
                  = $38,623,188
        c.   Price = $33.33 + $38,623,188 / 20,000,000
                    = $35.26

5.27   Price = 1.40 (1.05) / 0.10 - 0.05
        Price = $29.40

5.28   Price = 2 / (1.16)^3 + 2 / (1.16)^4 + 2.12 / 0.16 - 0.06
                = 1.28 + 1.10 + 21.20
                = $23.58

5.29   a.   g = 0.4 × 0.15 = 0.06 = 6%
        b.   Dividend per share = $1.5 million × 0.6 / 300,000
                                 = $3
              Price   = $3 (1.06) / (0.13 - 0.06)
                       = $45.43
        c.   Assuming the additional earnings generated are all paid out as cash dividends.
              NPV   = -$1.2 million + $0.3 million {1 / (0.13 - 0.10)} {1 - (1.10 / 1.13)^{10}}
                     = $1,159,136.93
        d.   Price = $45.43 + $1,159,136.93 / 300,000
                     = $49.29

5.30   Price = 3 / 1.15 + 4.5 / (1.15)^2 + 4.725 / 0.15- 0.05
                = 2.61 + 3.40 + 47.52
                = $53.53

Answers to End-of-Chapter Problems

5.31   a.   P/E of Pacific Energy Company:
EPS = ($800,000 / 500,000) = $1.6
NPVGO = {$100,000 / 500,000} / 0.15 = $1.33
P/E = 1 / 0.15 + 1.33 / 1.6 = 7.50

       b.   P/E of U. S. Bluechips, Inc.:
NPVGO = {$200,000 / 500,000} / (0.15 - 0.10) = $8
P/E = 1 / 0.15 + 8 / 1.6 = 11.67

5.32   a.   Price = $4 / 0.14 = $28.57

       b.   Price = $28.57 + \dfrac{(-1 + 0.40 / 0.14) / 0.04}{(1.14)^3}$

$$= 28.57 + 31.33$$
$$= \$59.90$$

       c.   The expected return of 14% less the dividend yield of 5% provides a capital gain yield of 9%. If there is no investment the yield is 14%.

       d. $3 / $59.90 = .05 and $4 / $28.57 = .14 without the investment.

Appendix to Chapter 5

5A.1 a. $P = \$60 / 1.10 + \$1{,}060 / (1.11)^2$
          $= \$54.55 + \$860.32$
          $= \$914.87$

      b. $\$914.87 = \$60 / (1 + y) + \$1{,}060 / (1 + y)^2$
          $y = YTM = 10.97\%$

5A.2 $P = \$50 / 1.10 + \$1{,}050 / (1.08)^2$
          $= \$45.45 + \$900.21$
          $= \$945.66$

5A.3 $(1 + r_1)(1 + f_2) = (1 + r_2)^2$
          $(1.09)(1 + f_2) = (1.10)^2$
          $f_2 = .1101$

5A.4 $(1 + r_2)^2 = (1 + r_1)(1 + f_2)$
          $(1.07)^2 = (1.05)(1 + f_2)$
          $f_2 = .0904$, one-year forward rate over the 2nd year is 9.04%.

          $(1 + r_3)^3 = (1 + r_2)^2(1 + f_3)$
          $(1.10)^3 = (1.07)^2(1 + f_3)$
          $f_3 = .1625$, one-year forward rate over the 3rd year is 16.25%.

Chapter 6: Some Alternative Investment Rules

6.1   a.   Payback period of Project A = $1 + (\$7,500 - \$4,000) / \$3,500 = 2$ years
Payback period of Project B = $2 + (\$5,000 - \$2,500 - \$1,200) / \$3,000 = 2.43$ years
Project A should be chosen.

      b. $NPV_A = -\$7,500 + \$4,000 / 1.15 + \$3,500 / 1.15^2 + \$1,500 / 1.15^3 = -\$388.96$
$NPV_B = -\$5,000 + \$2,500 / 1.15 + \$1,200 / 1.15^2 + \$3,000 / 1.15^3 = \$53.83$
Project B should be chosen.

6.2   a.   Payback period = $6 + \{\$1,000,000 - (\$150,000 \times 6)\} / \$150,000 = 6.67$ years
Yes, the project should be adopted.

      b. $\$150,000 \, A_{0.10}^{11} = \$974,259$

The discounted payback period = $11 + (\$1,000,000 - \$974,259) / (\$150,000 / 1.1^{12})$
$= 11.54$ years

      c. $NPV = -\$1,000,000 + \$150,000 / 0.10 = \$500,000$

6.3   a.   Average Investment:
$(\$16,000 + \$12,000 + \$8,000 + \$4,000 + 0) / 5 = \$8,000$
Average accounting return:
$\$4,500 / \$8,000 = 0.5625 = 56.25\%$

      b.   1.   AAR does not consider the timing of the cash flows, hence it does not consider the time value of money.
            2.   AAR uses an arbitrary firm standard as the decision rule.
            3.   AAR uses accounting data rather than net cash flows.

6.4   Average Investment = $(\$2,000,000 + 0) / 2 = \$1,000,000$
Average net income = $[\$100,000 \{(1 + g)^5 - 1\} / g] / 5$
$= \{\$100,000 A (1.07^5 - 1) / 0.07\} / 5$
$= \$115,014.78$
AAR = $\$115,014.78 / \$1,000,000 = 11.50\%$
No, since the machine's AAR is less than the firm's cutoff AAR.

6.5   a

6.6   PI = $\$40,000 \, A_{0.15}^7 / \$160,000 = 1.04$

Since the PI exceeds one accept the project.

6.7   The IRR is the discount rate at which the NPV = 0.
$-\$3,000 + \$2,500 / (1 + IRR_A) + \$1,000 / (1 + IRR_A)^2 = 0$
By trial and error, $IRR_A = 12.87\%$
Since project B's cash flows are two times of those of project A, the $IRR_B = IRR_A = 12.87\%$

6.8   a.   Solve x by trial and error:
$-\$4,000 + \$2,000 / (1 + x) + \$1,500 / (1 + x)^2 + \$1,000 / (1 + x)^3 = 0$
$x = 6.93\%$

      b.   No, since the IRR (6.93%) is less than the discount rate of 8%.

6.9   Find the IRRs of project A analytically. Since the IRR is the discount rate that makes the NPV equal to zero, the following equation must hold.

$$-\$200 + \$200 / (1 + r) + \$800 / (1 + r)^2 - \$800 / (1 + r)^3 = 0$$
$$\$200 [-1 + 1 / (1 + r)] - \{\$800 / (1 + r)^2\}[-1 + 1 / (1 + r)] = 0$$
$$[-1 + 1 / (1 + r)] [\$200 - \$800 / (1 + r)^2] = 0$$

For this equation to hold, either $[-1 + 1 / (1 + r)] = 0$ or $[\$200 - \$800 / (1 + r)^2] = 0$. Solve each of these factors for the r that would cause the factor to equal zero. The resulting rates are the two IRRs for project A. They are either $r = 0\%$ or $r = 100\%$.

Note: By inspection you should have known that one of the IRRs of project A is zero. Notice that the sum of the un-discounted cash flows for project A is zero. Thus, not discounting the cash flows would yield a zero NPV. The discount rate which is tantamount to not discounting is zero.

Here are some of the interactions used to find the IRR by trial and error. Sophisticated calculators can compute this rate without all of the tedium involved in the trial-and-error method.

NPV	$= -\$150 + \$50 / 1.3 + \$100 / 1.3^2 + \$150 / 1.3^3 = \$15.91$
NPV	$= -\$150 + \$50 / 1.4 + \$100 / 1.4^2 + \$150 / 1.4^3 = -\$8.60$
NPV	$= -\$150 + \$50 / 1.37 + \$100 / 1.37^2 + \$150 / 1.37^3 = -\$1.89$
NPV	$= -\$150 + \$50 / 1.36 + \$100 / 1.36^2 + \$150 / 1.36^3 = \$0.46$
NPV	$= -\$150 + \$50 / 1.36194 + \$100 / 1.36194^2 + \$150 / 1.36194^3$ $= \$0.0010$
NPV	$= -\$150 + \$50 / 1.36195 + \$100 / 1.36195^2 + \$150 / 1.36195^3$ $= -\$0.0013$
NPV	$= -\$150 + \$50 / 1.361944 + \$100 / 1.361944^2 + \$150 / 1.361944^3$ $= \$0.0000906$

Thus, the IRR is approximately 36.1944%.

6.10 a.   Solve r in the equation:
$$\$5,000 - \$2,500 / (1 + r) - \$2,000 / (1 + r)^2 - \$1,000 / (1 + r)^3$$
$$- \$1,000 / (1 + r)^4 = 0$$
By trial and error,
IRR $= r = 13.99\%$

       b.   Since this problem is the case of financing, accept the project if the IRR is less than the required rate of return.
IRR $= 13.99\% > 10\%$
Reject the offer.

       c.   IRR $= 13.99\% < 20\%$
Accept the offer.

       d.   When $r = 10\%$:
NPV $= \$5,000 - \$2,500 / 1.1 - \$2,000 / 1.1^2 - \$1,000 / 1.1^3 - \$1,000 / 1.1^4$
$= -\$359.95$
When $r = 20\%$:
NPV $= \$5,000 - \$2,500 / 1.2 - \$2,000 / 1.2^2 - \$1,000 / 1.2^3 - \$1,000 / 1.2^4$
$= \$466.82$
Yes, they are consistent with the choices of the IRR rule since the signs of the cash flows change only once.

6.11 a.   Project A:

$$NPV = -\$5{,}000 + \$3{,}500 / (1 + r) + \$3{,}500 / (1 + r)^2 = 0$$

IRR = r = 25.69%

Project B:

$$NPV = -\$100{,}000 + \$65{,}000 / (1 + r) + \$65{,}000 / (1 + r)^2 = 0$$

IRR = r = 19.43%

b.   Choose project A because it has a higher IRR.

c.   The difference in scale is ignored.

d.   Apply the incremental IRR method.

e.

	C_0	C_1	C_2
B - A	-$95,000	$61,500	$61,500

$$NPV = -\$95{,}000 + \$61{,}500 / (1 + r) + \$61{,}500 / (1 + r)^2 = 0$$

Incremental IRR = r = 19.09%

f.   If the discount rate is less than 19.09%, choose project B. Otherwise, choose project A.

g. $NPV_A = -\$5{,}000 + \$3{,}500 / 1.15 + \$3{,}500 / 1.15^2 = \$689.98$

$NPV_B = -\$100{,}000 + \$65{,}000 / 1.15 + \$65{,}000 / 1.15^2 = \$5{,}671.08$

Choose project B.

6.12 a. $PV_A = \{\$5{,}000 / (0.12 - 0.04)\} / 1.12^2 = \$49{,}824.61$

$PV_B = (-\$6{,}000 / 0.12) / 1.12 = -\$44{,}642.86$

b.   The IRR for project C must solve

$$\{\$5{,}000 / (x - 0.04)\} / (1 + x)^2 + (-\$6{,}000 / x) / (1 + x) = 0$$

$$\$5{,}000 / (x - 0.04) - \$6{,}000 (1 + x) / x = 0$$

$$25 x^2 + 3.17 x - 1 = 0$$

$$x = \{-3.17 - (110.0489)^{0.5}\} / 50 \ \text{ or } \ \{-3.17 + (110.0489)^{0.5}\} / 50$$

The relevant positive root is IRR = x = 0.1464 = 14.64%

c. To arrive at the appropriate decision rule, we must graph the NPV as a function of the discount rate. At a discount rate of 14.64% the NPV is zero. To determine if the graph is upward or downward sloping, check the NPV at another discount rate. At a discount rate of 10% the NPV is $14,325.07 [= $68,870.52 - $54,545.54]. Thus, the graph of the NPV is downward sloping. From the discussion in the text, if an NPV graph is downward sloping, the project is an investing project. The correct decision rule for an investing project is to accept the project if the discount rate is below 14.64%.

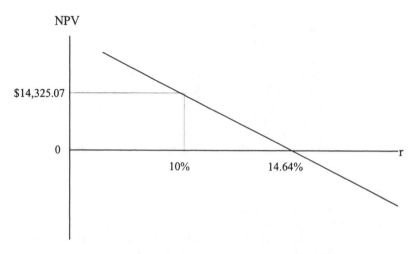

6.13 Generally, the statement is false. If the cash flows of project B occur early and the cash flows of project A occur late, then for a low discount rate the NPV of A can exceed the NPV of B. Examples are easy to construct.

	C_0	C_1	C_2	IRR	NPV @ 0%
A:	-$1,000,000	$0	$1,440,000	0.20	$440,000
B:	-2,000,000	2,400,000	0	0.20	400,000

In one particular case, the statement is true for equally risky projects. If the lives of the two projects are equal and in every time period the cash flows of the project B are twice the cash flows of project A, then the NPV of project B will be twice as great as the NPV of project A for any discount rate between 0% and 20%.

6.14 a. $NPV_\alpha = \$756.57 - \$500 = \$256.57$
      $NPV_\beta = \$2,492.11 - \$2,000 = \$492.11$
      b. Choose project beta.

6.15 Although the profitability index is higher for project B than for project A, the NPV is the increase in the value of the company that will occur if a particular project is undertaken. Thus, the project with the higher NPV should be chosen because it increases the value of the firm the most. Only in the case of capital rationing could the pension fund manager be correct.

6.16 a. $PI_A = (\$70,000 / 1.12 + \$70,000 / 1.12^2) / \$100,000 = 1.183$
$PI_B = (\$130,000 / 1.12 + \$130,000 / 1.12^2) / \$200,000 = 1.099$
$PI_C = (\$75,000 / 1.12 + \$60,000 / 1.12^2) / \$100,000 = 1.148$

b. $NPV_A = -\$100,000 + \$118,303.57 = \$18,303.57$
$NPV_B = -\$200,000 + \$219,706.63 = \$19,706.63$
$NPV_C = -\$100,000 + \$114,795.92 = \$14,795.92$

c. Accept all three projects because PIs of all the three projects are greater than one.

d. Based on the PI rule, project C can be eliminated because its PI is less than the one of project A, while both have the same amount of the investment. We can compute the PI of the incremental cash flows between the two projects,

Project	C_0	C_1	C_2	PI
B - A	-$100,000	$60,000	$60,000	1.014

We should take project B since the PI of the incremental cash flows is greater than one.

e. Project B has the highest NPV, while A has the next highest NPV.
Take both projects A and B.

6.17 a. The payback period is the time it takes to recoup the initial investment of a project. Accept any project that has a payback period that is equal to or shorter than the company's standard payback period. Reject all other projects.

b. The average accounting return (AAR) is defined as
Average project earnings ÷ Average book value of the investment.
Accept projects for which the AAR is equal to or greater than the firm's standard. Reject all other projects.

c. The internal rate of return (IRR) is the discount rate which makes the net present value (NPV) of the project zero. The accept / reject criteria is:

If $C_0 < 0$ and all future cash flows are positive, accept the project if IRR ≥ discount rate.
If $C_0 < 0$ and all future cash flows are positive, reject the project if IRR < discount rate.
If $C_0 > 0$ and all future cash flows are negative, accept the project if IRR ≤ discount rate.
If $C_0 > 0$ and all future cash flows are negative, reject the project if IRR > discount rate.

If the project has cash flows that alternate in sign, there is likely to be more than one positive IRR. In that situation, there is no valid IRR accept / reject rule.

d. The profitability index (PI) is defined as:
(The present value of the cash flows subsequent to the initial investment ÷ The initial investment)
Accept any project for which the profitability index is equal to or greater than one. Reject project for which that is not true.

e. The net present value (NPV) is the sum of the present values of all project cash flows. Accept those projects with NPVs which are equal to or greater than zero. Rejects proposals with negative NPVs.

6.18 Let project A represent New Sunday Early Edition; and let project B represent New Saturday Late Edition.

a. Payback period of project A = 2 + ($1,200 - $1,150) / $450 = 2.11 years
Payback period of project B = 2 + ($2,100 - $1,900) / $800 = 2.25 years
Based on the payback period rule, you should choose project A.

b. Project A:
Average investment = ($1,200 + $0) / 2 = $600
Depreciation = $400 / year
Average income = [($600 - $400) + ($550 - $400) + ($450 - $400)] / 3
= $133.33
AAR = $133.33 / $600 = 22.22%

Project B:
Average investment = ($2,100 + $0) / 2 = $1,050
Depreciation = $700 / year
Average income = [($1,000 - $700) + ($900 - $700) + ($800 - $700)] / 3
= $200
AAR = $200 / $1,050 = 19.05%

c. IRR of project A:
-$1,200 + $600 / (1 + r) + $550 / (1 + r)^2 + $450 / (1 + r)^3 = 0
IRR = r = 16.76%

IRR of project B:
-$2,100 + $1,000 / (1 + r) + $900 / (1 + r)^2 + $800 / (1 + r)^3 = 0
IRR = r = 14.29%

Project A has a greater IRR.

d. IRR of project B-A:
Incremental cash flows

Year	0	1	2	3
B - A	-$900	$400	$350	$350

-$900 + $400 / (1 + r) + $350 / (1 + r)^2 + $350 / (1 + r)^3 = 0
Incremental IRR = r = 11.02%

If the required rate of return is greater than 11.02%, then choose project A.
If the required rate of return is less than 11.02%, then choose project B.

6.19 Let project A be Deepwater Fishing; let project B be New Submarine Ride.

a. Project A:

Year	Discounted CF	Cumulative CF
0	-$600,000	-$600,000
1	234,783	-365,217
2	264,650	-100,567
3	197,255	

Discounted payback period of project A = 2 + $100,567 / $197,255
= 2.51 years

Project B:

Year	Discounted CF	Cumulative CF
0	-$1,800,000	-$1,800,000
1	869,565	-930,435
2	529,301	-401,134
3	591,765	

Discounted payback period of project B = 2 + $401,134 / $591,765
= 2.68 years

Project A should be chosen.

b.   IRR of project A:

$-\$600,000 + \$270,000 / (1 + r) + \$350,000 / (1 + r)^2 + \$300,000 / (1 + r)^3 = 0$

IRR $= r = 24.30\%$

IRR of project B:

$-\$1,800,000 + \$1,000,000 /(1 + r) + \$700,000 / (1 + r)^2 + \$900,000 / (1 + r)^3$
$= 0$

IRR $= r = 21.46\%$

Based on the IRR rule, project A should be chosen since it has a greater IRR.

c.   Incremental IRR:

Year	0	1	2	3
B - A	-$1,200,000	$730,000	$350,000	$600,000

$-\$1,200,000 + \$730,000 / (1 + r) + \$350,000 / (1 + r)^2 + \$600,000 / (1 + r)^3 = 0$

Incremental IRR $= r = 19.92\%$

Since the incremental IRR is greater than the required rate of return, 15%, choose project B.

d. $NPV_A = -\$600,000 + \$270,000 / 1.15 + \$350,000 / 1.15^2 + \$300,000 / 1.15^3$
     $= \$96,687.76$

$NPV_B = -\$1,800,000 + \$1,000,000 / 1.15 + \$700,000 / 1.15^2 + \$900,000 / 1.15^3$
     $= \$190,630.39$

Since $NPV_B > NPV_A$, choose project B.

Yes, the NPV rule is consistent with the incremental IRR rule.

6.20 a.   The IRR is the discount rate at which the NPV = 0

$$-\$600,000 + \frac{\$100,000}{(r - 8\%)}\left[1 - \left(\frac{1 + 8\%}{1 + r}\right)^{11}\right] - \frac{\$50,000}{(1 + r)^{11}} = 0$$

IRR $\approx 18.56\%$

b.   Yes, the mine should be opened since its IRR exceeds its required return of 10%.

Chapter 7: Net Present Value and Capital Budgeting

7.1   a.   Yes, the reduction in the sales of the company's other products is an incremental cash flow. Include these lost sales because they are a cost (a revenue reduction) which the firm must bear if it chooses to produce the new product.

        b.   Yes, the expenditures on plant and equipment are incremental cash flows. These are direct costs of the new product line.

        c.   No, the research and development costs are not included. The costs of research and development undertaken on the product during the past 3 years are sunk costs and should not be included in the evaluation of the project. The sunk costs must be borne whether or not the firm chooses to produce the new product; thus, they should have no bearing on the acceptability of the project.

        d.   Yes, the annual depreciation charge is part of the incremental cash flows. The depreciation charge is considered when computing the cash flows of the project. Remember, though, that it is the **depreciation tax shield** that is actually the cash flow.

        e.   No, the dividend payments are not incremental cash flows. Dividend payments are not a cost of the project. The choice of whether or not to pay a dividend is a decision of the firm, which is separate from the decision of choosing investment projects. Dividend will be discussed thoroughly in a later chapter.

        f.   Yes, the resale value is an important cash flow at the end of the life of a project. Yet, be careful with the resale value of plant and equipment. The price at which the firm sells the equipment is a cash inflow. If that price is different from the book value of the asset at the time of sale, tax consequence will arise. Remember that after an asset has been fully depreciated under current depreciation code, its book value is equal to zero. The difference between the book value and the sale price creates losses or gains which in turn create a tax credit or liability.

        g.   Yes, salary and medical costs for production employees on leave are incremental cash flows of the project. The salaries of all personnel connected to the project must be included as costs of that project. Thus, the costs of employees who are on leave for a portion of the project life must be included as costs of that project.

7.2   c

7.3

		Year 0	Year 1	Year 2	Year 3	Year 4
(1)	Sales revenue	-	$7,000	$7,000	$7,000	$7,000
(2)	Operating costs	-	2,000	2,000	2,000	2,000
(3)	Depreciation	-	2,500	2,500	2,500	2,500
(4)	Income before tax	-	2,500	2,500	2,500	2,500
(5)	Taxes at 34%	-	850	850	850	850
(6)	Net income	0	1,650	1,650	1,650	1,650
(7)	Cash flow from operation [(1)-(2)-(5)]	0	4,150	4,150	4,150	4,150
(8)	Investment	-10,000	-	-	-	-
(9)	Changes in net working capital	-200	-50	-50	100	200
(10)	Total cash flow from investment	-10,200	-50	-50	100	200
(11)	Total cash flow	-10,200	4,100	4,100	4,250	4,350

a. Net income [from (6)]:

    0   1,650   1,650   1,650   1,650

b. Incremental cash flow [from (11)]:

   -10,200   4,100   4,100   4,250   4,350

c. NPV = -$10,200 + $4,100 / 1.12 + $4,100 / 1.12^2 + $4,250 / 1.12^3 + $4,350 / 1.12^4

    = $2,518.78

7.4 Since there is uncertainty surrounding the bonus payments, which McRae might receive, you must use the expected value of McRae's salary in the computation of the PV of his contract. The expected value of McRae's salary in years one through three is

$$\$250,000 + 0.6 \times \$75,000 + 0.4 \times \$0 = \$295,000.$$
$$PV = \$400,000 + \$295,000 \,[(1 - 1 / 1.1236^3) / 0.1236]$$
$$+ \{\$125,000 / 1.1236^3\} \,[(1 - 1 / 1.1236^{10} / 0.1236]$$
$$= \$1,594,825.68$$

7.5 To evaluate Benson's alternatives, compute the after-tax net cash flows (A/T-NCF). First, note that the building left and depreciation are not incremental and should not be included in the analysis of these two alternatives.

Product A:	t = 0	t = 1 - 14	t = 15	
Revenues		$105,000	$105,000	
-Foregone rent		12,000	12,000	
-Expenditures		60,000	63,750	**
-Depreciation*		12,000	12,000	
Earnings before taxes		$21,000	$17,250	
-Taxes (34%)		7,140	5,865	
Net income		$13,860	$11,385	
+Depreciation		12,000	12,000	
Capital investment	-$180,000			
A/T-NCF	-$180,000	$25,860	$23,385	

*Depreciation = ($144,000 + $36,000) / 15 = $12,000
**Cash expenditures + Restoration costs

$$NPV_A = -\$180,000 + \$25,860 \; A^{14}_{0.12} + \$23,385 / 1.12^{15}$$
$$= -\$180,000 + \$25,860 \,(6.6282) + \$23,385 / 1.12^{15}$$
$$= -\$4,322.40$$

The cash flows in year 1 - 14 could have been computed using the simplification demonstrated in the text.

    A/T-NCF = Revenue (1 - T) - Expenses (1 - T) + Depreciation (T)
        = $105,000 (0.66) - $72,000 (0.66) + $12,000 (0.34)
        = $25,860

The cash flows for the final year could have been computed by adjusting for the after-tax value of the restoration costs.

    $25,860 - $3,750 (0.66) = $23,385

Product B:	t = 0	t = 1 - 14	t = 15	
Revenues		$127,500	$127,500	
-Foregone rent		12,000	12,000	
-Expenditures		75,000	103,125	**
-Depreciation*		14,400	14,400	
Earnings before taxes		$26,100	-$2,025	
-Taxes (34%)		8,874	-689	
Net income		$17,226	-$1,336	
+Depreciation		14,400	14,400	
Capital investment	-$216,000			
A/T-NCF	-$216,000	$31,626	$13,064	

*Depreciation = ($162,000 + $54,000) / 15 = $14,400

    **Cash expenditures + Restoration costs

$$NPV_B = -\$216,000 + \$31,626 \ A^{14}_{0.12} + \$13,064 / 1.12^{15}$$
$$= -\$216,000 + \$31,626 \ (6.6282) + \$13,064 / 1.12^{15}$$
$$= -\$3,989.80$$

The cash flows in year 1 - 14 could have been computed using the simplification demonstrated the text.

$$A/T\text{-}NCF = Revenue \ (1 - T) - Expenses \ (1 - T) + Depreciation \ (T)$$
$$= \$127,500 \ (0.66) - \$87,000 \ (0.66) + \$14,400 \ (0.34)$$
$$= \$31,626$$

The cash flows for the final year could have been computed by adjusting for the after-tax value of the restoration costs.

$$\$31,626 - \$28,125 \ (0.66) = \$13,064$$

Benson should continue to rent the building.

7.6   EPS = $800,000 / 200,000 = $4
      NPVGO = (-$400,000 + $1,000,000) / 200,000 = $3
      Price = EPS / r + NPVGO
          = $4 / 0.12 + $3
          =$36.33

7.7

	Year 0	Year 1	Year 2	Year 3	Year 4	Year 5
Sales revenue		$400,000	$420,000	$441,000	$463,050	$486,200
Operating costs		200,000	220,000	242,000	266,200	292,820
Depreciation		80,000	80,000	80,000	80,000	80,000
Income before tax		120,000	120,000	119,000	116,850	113,380
Taxes at 34%		40,800	40,800	40,460	39,729	38,549
Net income		79,200	79,200	78,540	77,121	74,831
Cash flow from operation (Sales Revenue – Operating Costs – Taxes)		159,200	159,200	158,540	157,121	154,831
Investment	-$400,000					

$$NPV = -\$400,000 + \$159,200 / 1.15 + \$159,200 / 1.15^2 + \$158,540 / 1.15^3$$
$$+ \$157,121 / 1.15^4 + \$154,831 / 1.15^5$$
$$= \$129,868.29$$

7.8

		Year 0	Year 1	Year 2	Year 3	Year 4	Year 5
1.	Annual Salary Savings		$120,000	$120,000	$120,000	$120,000	$120,000
2.	Depreciation		100,000	160,000	96,000	57,600	57,600
3.	Taxable Income		20,000	-40,000	24,000	62,400	62,400
4.	Taxes		6,800	-13,600	8,160	21,216	21,216
5.	Operating Cash Flow (line 1-4)		113,200	133,600	111,840	98,784	98,784
6.	Δ Net working capital	$100,000					-100,000
7.	Investment	$500,000					75,792*
8.	Total Cash Flow	-$400,000	$113,200	$133,600	$111,840	$98,784	$74,576

*75,792 = $100,000 - 0.34 ($100,000 - $28,800)
$$NPV = -\$400,000 + \$113,200 / 1.12 + \$133,600 / 1.12^2 + \$111,840 / 1.12^3$$
$$+ \$98,784 / 1.12^4 + \$74,576 / 1.12^5$$
$$= -\$7,722.52$$

7.9

	t = 0	t = 1- 2	t = 3
Revenues		$600,000	$600,000
- Expenses		150,000	150,000
- Depreciation		150,000	150,000
Earnings Before Taxes		$300,000	$300,000
- Taxes (35%)		105,000	105,000
Net Income		$195,000	$195,000
+ Depreciation		150,000	150,000
Capital Investment	- $750,000		+ $40,000
Working Capital	- 25,000		+ $25,000
Capital Loss			- $260,000
A / T - NCF	- $775,000	$345,000	$150,000

The capital loss reflects $300,000 in book value of the asset less the sale of $ 40,000.
The cash flows in year 1-2 could have been calculated by
A/T - NCF = Revenue (1 - T) - Expenses (1 - T) + Depreciation (0.35)
$$= \$600,000 (0.65) - \$150,000 (0.65) + \$150,000(0.35)$$
$$= \$345,000$$

$$NPV = -\$775,000 + \$345,000 \, A^2_{0.17} + \$150,000 / (1.17)^3$$
$$= -\$134.445.45$$

7.10 $A/T - NCF = \$200,000\,(1.03)^5\,(1 - 0.35) - \$50,000\,(1.03)^5\,(1 - 0.35)$
$+ \$50,000\,(0.35) + \$30,000\,(1 - 0.35) + \$10,000$
$= \$184,032.7$

7.11   This is an annuity due (or annuity in advance) problem.
PV of lease revenue after tax
$= 0.66\,L\,[1 / (0.13 - 0.03) - \{1 / (0.13 - 0.03)\}\,(1.03 / 1.13)^{20}](1.13)$
$= 6.28904\,L$
Where L = the first year lease payment.

PV of depreciation tax shield for annual depreciation of $200,000
$= 0.34 \times \$200,000\; A^{20}_{0.09} = \$620,741.11$

Solve the equation:
$NPV = -\$4,000,000 + 6.28904\,L + \$620,741.11 = 0$
$L = \$537,325.08$

7.12

	t = 0	t = 1 – 3	t = 4
Revenues		$1,200,000	$1,200,000
- Expenses		300,000	300,000
- Depreciation		400,000	400,000
Earnings Before Taxes		$500,000	$500,000
- Taxes (35%)		175,000	175,000
Net Income		$325,000	$325,000
+ Depreciation		400,000	400,000
Capital Investment	- $2,000,000		+$150,000
NWC	- 100,000		+$100,000
Capital Loss			- $250,000
A / T – NCF	-$2,100,000	$725,000	$725,000

$NPV = -\$2,100,000 + \$725,000\; A^{4}_{0.1655}$
$= -\$93,391$

7.13   Real interest rate $= (1.15 / 1.04) - 1 = 10.58\%$
$NPV_A = -\$40,000 + \$20,000 / 1.1058 + \$15,000 / 1.1058^2 + \$15,000 / 1.1058^3$
$= \$1,446.76$
$NPV_B = -\$50,000 + \$10,000 / 1.15 + \$20,000 / 1.15^2 + \$40,000 / 1.15^3$
$= \$119.17$
Choose project A.

7.14   After-tax revenues
$= \{\$50,000\,(1 - 0.34) / 1.05\}\; A^{7}_{0.14} = \$31,428.57\; A^{7}_{0.14}$

$= \$134,775.29$
Assume production costs grow at a nominal rate of 7% a year, the real growth rate of the
production costs $= [(1 + 7\%) / (1 + 5\%)] - 1 = 1.905\%$

After-tax expenses
$$= -\{\$20,000\ (1 - 0.34) / 1.05\}\ \{1 / (0.14 - 0.01905)\}\ [1 - (1.01905 / 1.14)^7]$$
$$= -\$56,535.24$$
Depreciation tax shield [from table 7.5]
$$= \$120,000 \times 0.34 \times 0.7214$$
$$= \$29,433.12$$
$$\text{NPV} = -\$120,000 + \$134,775.29 - \$56,535.24 + \$29,433.12$$
$$= -\$12,326.83$$
Do not accept the suggestion.

7.15   PV = $120,000 / {0.11 - (-0.06)}
        = $705,882.35

7.16 a.   The only mistake that Gultekin made was to discount at the risk-free rate of interest. The bankruptcy risk adjustment to the cash flows was correct, but these should have been discounted by a risk-adjusted rate. Given that Gultekin's portfolio is un-diversified (all of his money would be in the restaurant), he should have used a higher discount rate. The deduction of the managerial wage was appropriate since the opportunity to earn that amount elsewhere is Gultekin's opportunity cost of working in the restaurant.

     b.   You should have chosen a higher discount rate and recomputed the value of the restaurant. For example, with a discount rate of 10%, the value is $28,000 / [0.10 - (-0.06)] = $175,000. Notice that the restaurant's cash flows form a growing (actually declining) perpetuity.

7.17   The simplest approach to this problem is to discount the real cash flows. Since the revenues and costs are growing perpetuities, the formula for computing the PV of such a stream can be used. The first year amounts of the revenues and costs are stated in nominal terms. Since the growth rate and discount rate are real rates, adjust the initial amounts. For revenues, labor costs and the other costs, those amounts are $150,000 / 1.06, $80,000 / 1.06 and $40,000 / 1.06, respectively.

PV (revenue) = ($150,000 / 1.06) / (0.10 - 0.05) = $2,830,189
PV (labor costs) = ($80,000 / 1.06) / (0.10 - 0.03) = $1,078,167
PV (other costs) = ($40,000 / 1.06) / {0.10 - (-0.01)} = $343,053

The lease payment is given in nominal terms and it should be discounted by the nominal rate which is 0.1342 [= (1.07 × 1.06) - 1]. Thus, the present value of the lease payments is $20,000 / 0.1342 = $149,031. The lease payments are constant in nominal terms, but not in real terms. This can be seen that by computing the real value of the first few lease payments.

Year	Nominal	Real
1	$20,000	$20,000 / 1.06 = $18,868
2	$20,000	$20,000 / 1.06² = $17,800
3	$20,000	$20,000 / 1.06³ = $16,792

The real payments form a declining perpetuity. You can apply the growing perpetuity formula to compute their PV in real terms, but be careful about which growth rate you use. The growth rate is not 6% as the inflation rate would imply. The growth rate is (1 / 1.06) - 1 = -0.0566. Using this growth rate, the PV of the real lease payments is $18,868 / [0.07 - (-0.0566)] = $149,036. You can use either method for computing the PV of the lease payments, but you are wise to use whichever method is easiest and most straight-forward.

In this case, it would be easy to use the wrong growth rate or the wrong initial cash flow in the calculation of the real nominal flows. Note, both methods must give you the same amount in PV terms. (The difference in this case is due to rounding.) To find the NPV of BICC's toad ranch, add the present values of the revenues and the costs. Recall, the start-up costs are negligible.

$$\text{NPV} = \$2,830,189 - \$1,078,167 - \$343,053 - \$149,031$$
$$= \$1,259,938.$$

7.18

	Year 1	Year 2	Year 3	Year 4
Revenues	40,000,000	80,000,000	80,000,000	60,000,000
Labor Costs	30,600,000	31,212,000	31,836,240	32,472,965
Energy Costs	1,030,000	1,060,900	1,092,727	1,125,509
(Revenues-Costs)	8,370,000	47,727,100	47,071,033	26,401,526
After-tax (Revenues-Costs)	5,524,200	31,499,886	31,066,882	17,425,007

$$\text{NPV} = -\$32,000,000 + (\$5,524,200/1.08 + \$31,499,886/1.08^2 + \$31,066,882/1.08^3$$
$$+ \$17,425,007/1.08^4) + \$8,000,000(34\%)\,A_{0.04}^4$$
$$= \$43,464,183$$

where $8,000,000 is the amount of depreciation each year.

7.19   Initial revenues = $2.5 × 2,000,000
$$= \$5,000,000$$

Initial expenses = $0.7 × 2,000,000
$$= \$1,400,000$$

PV after tax = $5,000,000 (1 - 0.34) / (0.10 - 0.07) - $1,400,000 (1 - 0.34) / (0.10 - 0.05)
$$= \$110,000,000 - \$18,480,000$$
$$= \$91,520,000$$

7.20   The analysis of the NPV of this project is most easily accomplished by separating the depreciation costs from the project's other cash flows. Those costs should be discounted at a riskless rate. The riskless nominal rate is given. The revenues and variable costs are given in nominal terms, but their growth rates are real growth rates. Hence, they are most easily discounted using the real rate for risky cash flows. Remember that you can use different types of discount rates (real vs. nominal) in a problem as long as you are careful to discount real cash flows with the real rate and nominal cash flows with the nominal rate.

First, determine the net income from the revenues and expenses not including depreciation.

Note that the nominal price of a buckeye during the first year was $3.15. The inflation rate during the period was 5%. Therefore, the real price of a buckeye was $3.00 [= 3.15 / 1.05]. Similarly, the nominal variable cost for a buckeye was $0.2625; the real variable cost is $0.25 [= $0.2625 / 1.05].

	t = 1	t = 2	t = 3	t = 4	t = 5
Revenue	$3,000,000	$3,150,000	$3,307,500	$3,472,875	$3,646,519
- Variable cost	250,000	255,000	260,100	265,302	270,608
Pre-tax earnings	2,750,000	2,895,000	3,047,400	3,207,573	3,375,911
- Taxes (34%)	935,000	984,300	1,036,116	1,090,575	1,147,810
Net income	1,815,000	1,910,700	2,011,284	2,116,998	2,228,101
After-tax sale*					330,000
	1,815,000	1,910,700	2,011,284	2,116,998	2,558,101

*After-tax proceeds = $500,000 × 0.66
              = $330,000
Since these cash flows are in real terms, you must use the real discount rate to find the PV of the flows.

$\qquad$ Real discount rate = 1.20 / 1.05 - 1 = 0.1429 = 14.29%

The PV of the annual net incomes using the real discount rate of 14.29% is $6,950,673. (Note: Although the actual real discount rule is 14.2857143..., we round to 14.29 to computational conventional.)
The NPV of the project is the present value of the net income in each year plus the present value of the depreciation tax shield.

The depreciation per year: $6,000,000 / 5 = $1,200,000
The depreciation tax shield per year: $1,200,000 × 0.34 = $408,000

Again, the depreciation tax shield is in nominal terms, so discount it using the nominal riskless rate.

$\qquad$ NPV $= -\$6,000,000 + \$6,950,673 + \$408,000 \ A^5_{0.11}$

$\qquad$ $= \$2,458,600$

7.21 Let I be the maximum price the Majestic Mining Company should be willing to pay for the equipment. Examine the incremental cash flows from purchasing the new equipment.

Incremental C_0:

Cost of the new equipment	-I
Sale of the old equipment	$20,000
Tax effect of the sale*	0
Total	$20,000 - I

*Tax savings $\quad$ = T (Book value - Sale price)
$\qquad\qquad$ = 0.34 ($20,000 - $20,000)
$\qquad\qquad$ = $0
Book value $\quad$ = Cost - Accumulated depreciation
$\qquad\qquad$ = $40,000 - 5($40,000 / 10)
$\qquad\qquad$ = $20,000

Incremental C_1 - C_5 :
$\quad$ After-tax savings: $10,000 × 0.66 = $6,600
$\quad$ Depreciation tax shield: [I / 5 - $4,000] × 0.34

Incremental C_6 - C_8 :
    After-tax savings: $\$10,000 \times 0.66 = \$6,600$
    Depreciation tax shield*: $\$0$
*At the end of year five, both pieces of equipment have been fully depreciated.
Thus, Majestic Mining will no longer get a depreciation tax shield.

Additional cash flows in t = 8:
Sale of equipment	$5,000
Tax effect*	-1,700
Total	$3,300

*Tax savings = T (Book value - Sale price)
          = 0.34 ($0 - $5,000)
          = -$1,700

Book value: Since the equipment was depreciated to a zero value over five years, its book value is zero at the end of year eight.

$$NPV = -I + \$20,000 + \$6,600 \ A^8_{0.08}$$
$$+ [I / 5 - \$4,000] \ (0.34) \ A^5_{0.08} + \$3,300 / 1.08^8$$
$$= -I + \$20,000 + \$6,600 \ (5.7466)$$
$$+ [I / 5 - \$4,000] \ (0.34) \ (3.9927) + \$3,300 / 1.08^8$$
$$= \$0$$
$$0.7285 \ I = \$54,280.3753$$
$$I = \$74,510$$

7.22 <u>Headache only</u>
    After-tax operating income
      = [($4 × 5,000,000) - ($1.50 × 5,000,000)] (1 - 0.34)
      = $8,250,000

Depreciation tax shield	t = 1	t = 2	t = 3
Nominal depreciation	$3,400,000	$3,400,000	$3,400,000
Real depreciation	3,238,095	3,083,900	2,937,048
Tax shields (Real)	1,100,952	1,048,526	998,596

$$NPV = -\$10,200,000 + \$8,250,000 \ A^3_{0.13} + \$1,100,952 / 1.13$$
$$+ \$1,048,526 / 1.13^2 + \$998,596 / 1.13^3$$
$$= \$11,767,030$$

<u>Headache and Arthritis</u>
    After-tax operating income
        = [($4 × 10,000,000) - ($1.70 × 10,000,000)] (1 - 0.34)
        = $15,180,000

Depreciation tax shield	t = 1	t = 2	t = 3
Nominal depreciation	$4,000,000	$4,000,000	$4,000,000
Real depreciation	3,809,524	3,628,118	3,455,350
Tax shields (Real)	1,295,238	1,233,560	1,174,819

After-tax cash flow from sale of machinery = $1,000,000 (1-.34) = $660,000.

$$\text{NPV} = -\$12,000,000 + \$15,180,000\ A^3_{0.13} + \$1,295,238 / 1.13$$
$$+ \$1,233,560 / 1.13^2 + \$1,174,819 / 1.13^3 + \$660,000 / 1.13^3$$
$$= \$27,226,204$$

The firm should choose to manufacture Headache and Arthritis.

7.23   Assume the tax rate is zero.

t = 0	t = 1	t = 2	t = 3	t = 4	t = 5	t = 6	
$12,000	$6,000	$6,000	$6,000	$4,000			...
				$12,000	$6,000	$6,000	...

The present value of one cycle is:

$$\text{PV} = \$12,000 + \$6,000\ A^3_{0.06} + \$4,000 / 1.06^4$$
$$= \$12,000 + \$6,000 (2.6730) + \$4,000 / 1.06^4$$
$$= \$31,206.37$$

The cycle is four years long, so use a four year annuity factor to compute the equivalent annual cost (EAC).

$$\text{EAC} = \$31,206.37 / A^4_{0.06}$$
$$= \$31,206.37 / 3.4651$$
$$= \$9,006$$

The present value of such a stream in perpetuity is
$$\$9,006 / 0.06 = \$150,100$$

7.24   PV of cash outflows

$$\text{PV} = \$60,000 + (1 - 0.34)\ \$5,000\ A^3_{0.14} - (0.34)\ \$20,000\ A^3_{0.14}$$
$$= \$51,874.29$$
$$= \text{EAC}\ (A^3_{0.14})$$
$$\text{EAC} = \$22,343.89$$

7.25 PV of cash outflows

$$\text{PV} = \$60,000 + (1 - 0.35)\ \$2,000\ A^5_{0.18} - (0.35)\ \$12,000\ A^5_{0.18}$$
$$= \$50,931.20$$
$$= \text{EAC}\ (A^5_{0.18})$$
$$\text{EAC} = \$16,286.67$$

7.26 PV of cash outflows

$$PV = \$45,000 + (1 - 0.34) \$5,000 \ A_{0.12}^{3} - (0.34) \$15,000 \ A_{0.12}^{3} - \$10,000 / (1.12)^{3}$$

$$= \$22,030.11$$

$$= EAC \ (A_{0.12}^{3})$$

$$EAC = \$9,172.22$$

7.27 Real discount rate $= (1.14 / 1.05) - 1 = 8.57\%$

PV of cash outflow from XX40

$$= \$700 + \$100 / 1.0857 + \$100 / 1.0857^{2} + \$100 / 1.0857^{3}$$

$$= \$955.08$$

$$= EAC \ A_{0.0857}^{3} = (2.55082) \ EAC$$

$$EAC = \$374.42$$

PV of cash outflow from RH45

$$= \$900 + \$110 / 1.0857 + \$110 / 1.0857^{2} + \$110 / 1.0857^{3}$$

$$+ \$110 / 1.0857^{4} + \$110 / 1.0857^{5}$$

$$= \$1,332.68$$

$$= EAC \ (A_{0.0857}^{5}) = (3.93344) \ EAC$$

$$EAC = \$338.81$$

Choose RH45.

7.28 <u>Facility I</u>

After-tax maintenance costs

$$= (1 - 0.34) \$60,000 \ A_{0.10}^{7} = \$192,789.39$$

Depreciation tax shield

$$= (0.34) \$300,000 \ A_{0.10}^{7} = \$496,578.72$$

PV of cash outflow

$$= \$2,100,000 + \$192,789.39 - \$496,578.72$$

$$= \$1,796,210.67$$

$$= EAC \ (A_{0.10}^{7})$$

$$EAC \ = \$368,951.55$$

<u>Facility II</u>

After-tax maintenance costs

$$= (1 - 0.34) \$100,000 \ A_{0.10}^{10} = \$405,541.43$$

Depreciation tax shield

$$= (0.34) \$280,000 \ A_{0.10}^{10} = \$584,962.79$$

PV of cash outflow

$$= \$2,800,000 + \$405,541.43 - \$584,962.79$$

$$= \$2,620,578.64$$

$$= EAC \ (A_{0.10}^{10})$$

$$EAC \ = \$426,487.11$$

Choose facility I.

7.29   New Machine
        PV of cash outflow

$$= \$3,000,000 + (1 - 0.34) \$500,000 \ A_{0.12}^5$$

$$- (0.34) \$600,000 \ A_{0.12}^5 - \$500,000 (1 - 0.34) / 1.12^5$$

$$= \$3,266,950.94$$

$$= EAC \ (A_{0.12}^5) = (3.60478) \ EAC$$

EAC $= \$906,283.98$

Old Machine
(1) If replace in year 1.
        Opportunity cost of selling (after-tax)
            $= \$2,000,000 - 0.34 (\$2,000,000 - \$1,000,000)$
            $= \$1,660,000$
        After-tax maintenance cost (Present value)
            $= \$400,000 (1 - 0.34) / 1.12$
            $= \$235,714.29$
        PV of salvage value after tax
            $= \{\$1,200,000 - 0.34 (\$1,200,000 - \$800,000)\} / 1.12$
            $= \$950,000$
        PV of depreciation tax shield
            $= 0.34 \times \$200,000 / 1.12$
            $= \$60,714.29$
        Thus, PV of cash outflow
            $= \$1,660,000 + \$235,714.29 - \$950,000 - \$60,714.29$
            $= \$885,000$
        Thus, PV in year 1 $= \$991,200 >$ EAC of new machine.
Replace right now.

* We can check whether PV of old machine in year 2 has still higher cash outflow than EAC of new machine.
(2) Year 2
        PV in year 1
            $= \{\$1,200,000 - 0.34 (\$1,200,000 - \$800,000)\}$
            $+ \$1,500,000 (1 - 0.34) / 1.12$
            $- \{\$800,000 - 0.34 (\$800,000 - \$600,000)\} / 1.12$
            $- 0.34 \times \$200,000 / 1.12$
            $= \$1,233,642.85$
        Thus, PV in year 2
            $= \$1,233,642.85 \times 1.12$
            $= \$1,381,680.00$
        Even much greater than the cost in (1).
Replace right now.

7.30   10 SALs
        PV $= \$3,750 \times 10 + (\$500 \times 10) \ A_{0.11}^8 - (\$500 \times 10) / 1.11^8$
                $= \$61,060.98$
                $= EAC \ (A_{0.11}^8)$
        EAC $= \$11,865.43$

8 DETs

PV $= \$5,250 \times 8 + (\$700 \times 8) \; A_{0.11}^{6} - (\$600 \times 8) / 1.11^{6}$

$= \$63,124.74$

$= EAC \, (A_{0.11}^{6})$

EAC $= \$14,921.21$

Gold star should buy 10 SALs.

7.31   To evaluate the word processors, compute their equivalent annual costs (EAC).

Bang

PV(costs) $= (10 \times \$8,000) + (10 \times \$2,000) \; A_{0.14}^{4}$

$= \$80,000 + \$20,000 \, (2.9137)$

$= \$138,274$

EAC $= \$138,274 / 2.9137$

$= \$47,456$

IOU

PV(costs) $= (11 \times \$5,000) + (11 \times \$2,500) \; A_{0.14}^{3}$

$- (11 \times \$500) / 1.14^{3}$

$= \$55,000 + \$27,500 \, (2.3216) - \$5,500 / 1.14^{3}$

$= \$115,132$

EAC $= \$115,132 / 2.3216$

$= \$49,592$

BYO should purchase the Bang word processors.

7.32   Mixer X

NPV $= -\$400,000 + \$120,000 \; A_{0.11}^{5}$

$= \$43,507.64$

EAC $= \$43,507.64 / A_{0.11}^{5} = \$11,771.88$

Mixer Y

NPV $= -\$600,000 + \$130,000 \; A_{0.11}^{8}$

$= \$68,995.96$

EAC $= \$68,995.96 / A_{0.11}^{8} = \$13,407.37$

Choose Mixer Y.

7.33   a.   Tamper A

PV $= \$600,000 + \$110,000 \; A_{0.12}^{5}$

$= \$996,525.38$

EAC $= \$996,525.38 / A_{0.12}^{5}$

$= \$276,445.84$

<u>Tamper B</u>

$$PV = \$750,000 + \$90,000 \ A_{0.12}^{7}$$
$$= \$1,160,738.09$$
$$EAC = \$1,160,738.09 \ / \ A_{0.12}^{7}$$
$$= \$254,338.30$$

Choose Tamper B.

b.   The two assumptions behind replacement chains are:
   1.   The time horizon is long.
   2.   Replacement at the end of each cycle is possible.

7.34   First compute the equivalent annual cost (EAC) of the new machine.

$$PV(\text{costs}) = \$3,000 + \$20 \ A_{0.10}^{6} - \$1,200 \ / \ 1.10^{6}$$
$$= \$3,000 + \$20 \ (4.3553) - \$1,200 \ / \ 1.10^{6}$$
$$= \$2,410$$
$$EAC = \$2,410 \ / \ 4.3553$$
$$= \$553$$

Compute the cost of keeping the old autoclave for an additional year. Those costs include the foregone resale value for the previous year and maintenance for the current year. The costs are reduced by the resale value at the end of the current year.

PV of keeping the old autoclave through year one:
$$PV = \$900 + \$200 \ / \ 1.10 - \$850 \ / \ 1.10$$
$$= \$309$$

The value of these costs at the end of year one is:
$$\$309 \times 1.10 = \$340$$
It is cheaper to operate the old autoclave than to purchase the new one.

Cost at the end of year one of keeping the old autoclave through year two:
$$PV = \$850 + \$275 \ / \ 1.10 - \$775 \ / \ 1.10$$
$$= \$395$$
The value of these costs at the end of year two is:
$$\$395 \times 1.10 = \$435$$
It is cheaper to operate the old autoclave than to purchase the new one.

Cost at the end of year two of keeping the old autoclave through year three:
$$PV = \$775 + \$325 \ / \ 1.10 - \$700 \ / \ 1.10$$
$$= \$434$$
The value of these costs at the end of year three is:
$$\$434 \times 1.10 = \$477$$
It is cheaper to operate the old autoclave than to purchase the new one.

Cost at the end of year three of keeping the old autoclave through year four:
$$PV = \$700 + \$450 \ / \ 1.10 - \$600 \ / \ 1.10$$
$$= \$564$$
The value of these costs at the end of year four is:
$$\$564 \times 1.10 = \$620$$

It would be cheaper to purchase the new autoclave than to operate the old one in year four. Hence, Philben should purchase the new machine at the end of year three.

To be certain that future costs of the old autoclave do not make it more economical to operate, you should compute the annual cost of each of the additional years.
Cost at the end of year four of keeping the old autoclave through year five:

$$PV = \$600 + \$500 / 1.10 - \$500 / 1.10$$
$$= \$600$$

The value of these costs at the end of year five is:

$$\$600 \times 1.10 = \$660$$

The decision to replace after year three was correct.

7.35

	Net Present Value	$3i,968,128	
	IRR	80%	76.94%
	PI	2.97	

New Equipment		**Old Equipment**	
New Equip. Value	28,000,000	Book Value	12,000,000
Useful Life	3	Market Value	20,000,000
		Increase in Working Cap	5,000,000

Year	Depreciation	Balance		
			Growth	12%
1	9,333,333	18,666,667		
2	12,444,444	6,222,222	Dep./yr (old)	3,000,000
3	4,148,148	2,074,074	Tax Rate	40%
4	2,074,074	0	Discount rate	10%

Half-year convention in first year; switch to straight in year 3

	0	1	2	3	4
Purchase New Equip.	(28,000,000)				
Sell Old Equip.	20,000,000				
Tax on Old Equip.	(3,200,000)				
Change in W/C	(5,000,000)				5,000,000
Pre-tax CF Savings		17,500,000	19,600,000	21,952,000	24,586,240
Depreciation (old)		3,000,000	3,000,000	3,000,000	3,000,000
Depreciation (new)		(9,333,333)	(12,444,444)	(4,148,148)	(2,074,074)
Taxable Income		11,166,667	10,155,556	20,803,852	25,512,166
Taxes		(4,466,667)	(4,062,222)	(8,321,541)	(10,204,866)
Net Income		6,700,000	6,093,333	12,482,311	15,307,300
Depreciation Add-back		6,333,333	9,444,444	1,148,148	(925,926)
Cash Flow (after-tax)	-16,200,000	13,033,333	15,537,778	13,630,459	19,381,374

Mini Case: Goodweek Tires, Inc.

Assumptions

PP&E Investment			120,000,000
Useful life of PP&E Investment (years)			7
Salvage Value of PP&E Investment			60,000,000

Annual Depreciation Expense (7 year MACRS)

Year		MACRS %	Depreciation	Ending Book Value
	1	14.29%	17,148,000	102,852,000
	2	24.49%	29,388,000	73,464,000
	3	17.49%	20,988,000	52,476,000
Last year of project	4	12.49%	14,988,000	37,488,000
	5	8.93%	10,716,000	26,772,000
	6	8.93%	10,716,000	16,056,000
	7	8.93%	10,716,000	5,340,000
	8	4.45%	5,340,000	0

SuperTread price/unit in OEM market (year 1)	36.00
SuperTread price/unit in Replacement market (year 1)	59.00
SuperTread cost/unit (year 1)	18.00

Year 1 marketing and admin costs	25,000,000
Annual inflation rate	3.25%
Corporate Tax rate	40.00%

Beta (1/24/97 Valueline)	1.30
Rf (30 year U.S. Treasury Bond)	5.50%
Rm (S&P 500 30 year average)	13.50%
Re (from CAPM) $R_e = R_f + \beta_e[\, R_M - R_f \,] = 0.055 + 1.3[\, 0.135 - 0.055 \,] = 15.90\%$	15.90%

Year 1 OEM Market for SuperTread (2 million new cars x 4 tires/car)	8,000,000
OEM Market growth	2.50%
SuperTread share of OEM market	11.00%

Year 1 Replacement Market for SuperTread	14,000,000
Replacement Market growth	2.00%
SuperTread share of Replacement market	8.00%

Year	0	1	2	3	4
Sales					
OEM Market					
Units		880,000	902,000	924,550	947,664
Price		36.00	37.53	39.13	40.79
Total OEM Market		31,680,000	33,852,060	36,173,042	38,653,156
Replacement Market					
Units		1,120,000	1,142,400	1,165,248	1,188,553
Price		59.00	61.51	64.12	66.85
Total Replacement Market		66,080,000	70,266,168	74,717,530	79,450,885
Total Sales		97,760,000	104,118,228	110,890,572	118,104,041
Variable Costs					
Units (OEM + Replacement)		2,000,000	2,044,400	2,089,798	2,136,217
Cost		18.00	18.77	19.56	20.39
Total Variable Costs		36,000,000	38,363,166	40,881,699	43,565,831
SG&A		25,000,000	25,812,500	26,651,406	27,517,577
Depreciation		17,148,000	29,388,000	20,988,000	14,988,000
EBIT		19,612,000	10,554,562	22,369,466	32,032,633
Interest		0	0	0	0
Tax (40%)		7,844,800	4,221,825	8,947,786	12,813,053
Net Income		11,767,200	6,332,737	13,421,680	19,219,580
EBIT + Dep - Taxes		28,915,200	35,720,737	34,409,680	34,207,580
Less: Change in NWC	11,000,000	3,664,000	953,734	1,015,852	(16,633,586)
Less: Captial Spending	120,000,000				(50,995,200)
CF from Assets:	(131,000,000)	25,251,200	34,767,003	33,393,828	101,836,366
Discounted CF from Assets		21,787,058	25,882,152	21,449,437	56,437,679
Total Discounted CF from Assets	125,556,326				
Less: Investment	(131,000,000)				
Net Present Value	$(5,443,674)				

Results

Payback	3.37 years
Discounted Payback	>4 never pays back
AAR	16.42%
IRR	14.22%
NPV	$ (5,443,674)
PI	0.96

Chapter 8: Strategy and Analysis in Using Net Present Value

8.1   Go directly:

$$NPV = 0.5 \times \$20 \text{ million} + 0.5 \times \$5 \text{ million}$$
$$= \$12.5 \text{ million}$$

Test marketing:

$$NPV = -\$2 \text{ million} + (0.75 \times \$20 \text{ million} + 0.25 \times \$5 \text{ million}) / 1.15$$
$$= \$12.13 \text{ million}$$

Go directly to the market.

8.2   Focus group: $-\$120,000 + 0.70 \times \$1,200,000 = \$720,000$
        Consulting firm: $-\$400,000 + 0.90 \times \$1,200,000 = \$680,000$
        Direct marketing: $0.50 \times \$1,200,000 = \$600,000$
        The manager should conduct a focus group.

8.3   Price more aggressively:

$$-\$1,300,000 + (0.55 \times 0) + 0.45 \times (-\$550,000)$$
$$= -\$1,547,500$$

Hire lobbyist:

$$-\$800,000 + (0.75 \times 0) + 0.25 \times (-\$2,000,000)$$
$$= -\$1,300,000$$

Tandem should hire the lobbyist.

8.4   Let sales price be x.
        Depreciation $= \$600,000 / 5 = \$120,000$
        BEP: $(\$900,000 + \$120,000) / (x - \$15) = 20,000$
        $x = \$66$

8.5   The accounting break-even

$$= (120,000 + 20,000) / (1,500 - 1,100)$$
$$= 350 \text{ units}$$

8.6   a.   The accounting break-even

$$= 340,000 / (2.00 - 0.72)$$
$$= 265,625 \text{ abalones}$$

        b. $[(\$2.00 \times 300,000) - (340,000 + 0.72 \times 300,000)] (0.65)$
                $= \$28,600$
                This is the after tax profit.

8.7   EAC $= \$140,000 / A_{0.15}^{7} = \$33,650$

        Depreciation $= \$140,000 / 7 = \$20,000$
        BEP $= \{\$33,650 + \$340,000 \times 0.65 - \$20,000 \times 0.35\} / \{(\$2 - \$0.72) \times 0.65\}$
              $= 297,656.25$
              $\approx 297,657 \text{ units}$

8.8   Depreciation = $200,000 / 5 = $40,000

$$\text{EAC} = \$200,000 / A_{0.12}^{5} = \$200,000 / 3.60478$$

$$= \$55,482$$

$$\text{BEP} = \{\$55,482 + \$350,000 \times 0.75 - \$40,000 \times 0.25\} / \{(\$25 - \$5) \times 0.75\}$$

$$= 20,532.13$$

$$\approx 20533 \text{ units}$$

8.9   Let I be the break-even purchase price.

<u>Incremental C_0</u>

Sale of the old machine	$20,000
Tax effect	3,400
Total	$23,400

Depreciation per period
$$= \$45,000 / 15$$
$$= \$3,000$$

Book value of the machine
$$= \$45,000 - 5 \times \$3,000$$
$$= \$30,000$$

Loss on sale of machine
$$= \$30,000 - \$20,000$$
$$= \$10,000$$

Tax credit due to loss
$$= \$10,000 \times 0.34$$
$$= \$3,400$$

<u>Incremental cost savings:</u>
$$\$10,000 (1 - 0.34) = \$6,600$$

<u>Incremental depreciation tax shield:</u>
$$[I / 10 - \$3,000] (0.34)$$

The break-even purchase price is the Investment (I), which makes the NPV be zero.

$$\text{NPV} = 0$$

$$= -I + \$23,400 + \$6,600 \; A_{0.15}^{10}$$

$$+ [I / 10 - \$3,000] (0.34) \; A_{0.15}^{10}$$

$$= -I + \$23,400 + \$6,600 \, (5.0188)$$

$$+ I \, (0.034) \, (5.0188) - \$3,000 \, (0.34) \, (5.0188)$$

$$I = \$61,981$$

8.10   Pessimistic:

$$\text{NPV} = -\$420,000 + \sum_{t=1}^{7} \frac{\{23,000(\$38-\$21)-\$320,000\} \times 0.65 + \$60,000 \times 0.35}{1.13^t}$$

$$= -\$123,021.71$$

Expected:

$$\text{NPV} = -\$420,000 + \sum_{t=1}^{7} \frac{\{25,000(\$40-\$20)-\$300,000\} \times 0.65 + \$60,000 \times 0.35}{1.13^t}$$

$$= \$247,814.17$$

Optimistic:

$$\text{NPV} = -\$420,000 + \sum_{t=1}^{7} \frac{\{27,000(\$42-\$19)-\$280,000\}\times0.65+\$60,000\times0.35}{1.13^t}$$

$$= \$653,146.42$$

Even though the NPV of pessimistic case is negative, if we change one input while all others are assumed to meet their expectation, we have all positive NPVs like the one before. Thus, this project is quite profitable.

Pessimistic		NPV
Unit sales	23,000	$132,826.30
Price	$38	$104,079.33
Variable costs	$21	$175,946.75
Fixed costs	$320,000	$190,320.24

8.11 Pessimistic:

$$\text{NPV} = -\$1,500,000$$
$$+ \sum_{t=1}^{5} \frac{\{110,000 \times 0.22(\$115-\$72)-\$850,000\} \times 0.60 + \$300,000 \times 0.40}{1.13^t}$$
$$= -\$675,701.68$$

Expected:

$$\text{NPV} = -\$1,500,000$$
$$+ \sum_{t=1}^{5} \frac{\{120,000 \times 0.25(\$120-\$70)-\$800,000\} \times 0.60 + \$300,000 \times 0.40}{1.13^t}$$
$$= \$399,304.88$$

Optimistic:

$$\text{NPV} = -\$1,500,000$$
$$+ \sum_{t=1}^{5} \frac{\{130,000\times0.27(\$125-\$68)-\$750,000\}\times0.60+\$300,000\times0.40}{1.13^t}$$
$$= \$1,561,468.43$$

The expected present value of the new tennis racket is $428,357.21. (Assuming there are equal chances of the 3 scenarios occurring.)

8.12 $$\text{NPV} = -1,500,000 + \sum_{t=1}^{5} \frac{\{130,000\times0.22(\$120-\$70)-\$800,000\}\times0.60+\$300,000\times0.40}{1.13^t}$$
$$= \$251,581.17$$

The 3% drop in market share hurt significantly more than the 10,000 increase in market size helped. However, if the drop were only 2%, the effects would be about even. Market size is going up by over 8%, thus it seems market share is more important than market size.

8.13 a. $\text{NPV} = -\$10,000,000 + (\$750,000 \times A_{.10}^{10}) = -\$5,391,574.67$

b. $\text{Revised NPV} = -\$10,000,000 + \$750,000 / 1.10 + [(.5 \times \$1,500,000 \times A_{.10}^{9})$
$+ (.5 \times \$200,000)] / 1.10$
$= -\$5,300,665.58$

$\text{Option value of abandonment} = -\$5,300,665.58 - (-\$5,391,574.67)$
$= \$90,909.09$

8.14 a. $\text{NPV} = -\$100M + (\$100 \times 2M \times A_{.20}^{10}) = \$738.49\text{Million}$

b. $\$50M = C\,A_{.20}^{9}$
$C = \$12.40 \text{ Million (or 1.24 Million units)}$

Chapter 9: Capital Market Theory: An Overview

9.1 a. Capital gains = $38 - $37 = $1 per share

b. Total dollar returns = Dividends + Capital Gains
$$= \$1,000 + (\$1*500) = \$1,500$$
On a per share basis, this calculation is $2 + $1 = $3 per share

c. On a per share basis, $3/$37 = 0.0811 = 8.11%
On a total dollar basis, $1,500/(500*$37) = 0.0811 = 8.11%

d. No, you do not need to sell the shares to include the capital gains in the computation of the returns. The capital gain is included whether or not you realize the gain. Since you could realize the gain if you choose, you should include it.

9.2 Purchase Price = $10,400/200 = $52.00
  a. Total dollar return = $600 + 200($54.25 - $52) =$1,050
  b. Capital gain = 200($54.25-52) = $450
  c. Percentage Return = $1050/$10400 = 10.10%
  d. Dividend Yield = $600/(200*52) = 5.77%

9.3 $[2.40+(\$31-\$42)]/42=-\$8.60/\$42=-0.2048=-20.48\%$

9.4 The expected holding period return is:
$$[\$5.50+(\$54.75-\$52)]/\$52=0.15865=15.865\%$$

9.5 You can find the nominal returns, I, on each of the securities in the text. The inflation rate, π, for the period is also in the text. It is 3.2%. The real return, r, is $(1+I)/(1+\pi)-1$. An approximation for the real rate is $r = i - \pi$. Notice that the approximation is good when the nominal interest rate is close to the inflation rate.

	Nominal	Real	Approximation
a. Common Stocks	12.2%	8.7%	9.2%
b. L/T Corp. Bonds	5.7%	2.4%	2.5%
c. L/T Govt. Bonds	5.2%	1.9%	2.0%
d. U.S. T-Bills	3.7%	0.5%	0.5%

9.6 E(R) = T-Bill rate + Average Excess Return
$$= 6.2\% + (12.4\% - 3.9\%)$$
$$= 14.7\%$$

9.7 Suppose the two companies' stock price 2 years ago were P_0

	2 years ago	1 year ago	Today
Koke	P_0	$1.1\,P_0$	$1.1*0.9* P_0 = 0.99\,P_0$
Pepsee	P_0	$0.9\,P_0$	$0.9*1.1* P_0 = 0.99\,P_0$

Both stocks have the same prices, but their prices are lower than 2 years ago.

9.8 Five-year Holding Period Return
$$= (1-0.0491) \times (1+0.2141) \times (1+0.2251) \times (1+0.0627) \times (1+0.3216)-1$$
$$= 98.64\%$$

9.9 Risk Premium = 6.1 - 3.8 = 2.3%
Expected Return on the market long term corporate bonds
$$= 4.36\% + 2.3\% = 6.96\%$$

9.10 a. $\overline{R} = \dfrac{-0.026 - 0.01 + 0.438 + 0.047 + 0.164 + 0.301 + 0.199}{7} = 0.159$

b.

R	$R - \overline{R}$	$(R - \overline{R})^2$
-0.026	-0.185	0.03423
-0.010	-0.169	0.02856
0.438	0.279	0.07784
0.047	-0.112	0.01254
0.164	0.005	0.00003
0.301	0.142	0.02016
0.199	0.040	0.00160
	Total	0.17496

$$\sigma^2 = 0.17496 / (7 - 1) = 0.02916$$

$$\sigma = \sqrt{0.02916} = 0.1708 = 17.08\%$$

Note, because the data are historical data, the appropriate denominator in the calculation of the variance is N-1.

9.11 a.

	Common Stocks	Treasury Bills	Realized Risk Premium
-7	32.4%	11.2%	21.2%
-6	-4.9	14.7	-19.6
-5	21.4	10.5	10.9
-4	22.5	8.8	13.7
-3	6.3	9.9	-3.6
-2	32.2	7.7	24.5
Last	18.5	6.2	12.3

b. The average risk premium is 8.49%.

$$\frac{21.2 - 19.6 + 10.9 + 13.7 - 3.6 + 24.5 + 12.3}{7} = 8.49$$

c. Yes, it is possible for the observed risk premium to be negative. This can happen in any single year. The average risk premium over many years should be positive.

9.12   a.

Economic State	Prob. (P)	Return if State Occurs	P×Return
Recession	0.2	0.05	0.010
Moderate Growth	0.6	0.08	0.048
Rapid Expansion	0.2	0.15	0.030
		Expected Return =	0.088

b.

Return if State Occurs	$R - \overline{R}$	$(R - \overline{R})^2$	$P \times (R - \overline{R})^2$
0.05	-0.038	0.001444	0.0002888
0.08	-0.008	0.000064	0.0000384
0.15	0.062	0.003844	0.0007688
		Variance =	0.0010960

Standard deviation = $\sqrt{0.001096} = 0.03311$

9.13   a.

Economic State	Prob.(P)	Return if State occurs	P×Return
Recession	0.3	0.02	0.006
Moderate Growth	0.4	0.05	0.020
Rapid Expansion	0.3	0.10	0.030
		Expected Return =	0.056

b.

Return if State occurs	$R - \overline{R}$	$(R - \overline{R})^2$	$P \times (R - \overline{R})^2$
0.02	-0.036	0.001296	0.0003888
0.05	-0.006	0.000036	0.0000144
0.10	0.044	0.001936	0.0005808
		Variance =	0.0009840

Standard deviation = $\sqrt{0.000984} = 0.03137 = 3.137\%$

9.14   a.
$$\overline{R}_m = 0.12 \times 0.23 + 0.40 \times 0.18 + 0.25 \times 0.15 + 0.15 \times 0.09 + 0.08 \times 0.03$$
$$= 0.153 = 15.3\%$$

b.
$$\overline{R}_T = 0.12 \times 0.12 + 0.40 \times 0.09 + 0.25 \times 0.05 + 0.15 \times 0.01 + 0.08 \times (-0.02)$$
$$= 0.0628 = 6.28\%$$

9.15   a.

$$\overline{R}_p = (0.04 + 0.06 + 0.09 + 0.04) / 4 = 0.0575$$

$$\overline{R}_Q = (0.05 + 0.07 + 0.10 + 0.14) / 4 = 0.09$$

b.

$R_p - \overline{R}_p$	$(R_p - \overline{R}_p)^2$
-0.0175	0.00031
-0.0025	0.00001
+0.0325	0.00106
-0.0175	0.00031
	0.00169

Variance of $R_p = 0.00169 / 4 = 0.00042$

Standard Deviation of $R_p = \sqrt{0.00042} = 0.02049$

$R_Q - \overline{R}_Q$	$\left(R_Q - \overline{R}_Q\right)^2$
-0.04	0.0016
-0.02	0.0004
0.01	0.0001
0.05	0.0025
	0.0046

Variance of $R_Q = 0.0046 / 4 = 0.00115$

Standard Deviation of $R_Q = \sqrt{0.00115} = 0.03391$

9.16 R_S = Average Return on the Small Company Stocks.

$\overline{R}_m$ = Average Return on the Market Index.

S_S^2 = Variance in the Returns of the Small Company Stocks.

S_S = Standard Deviation in the Returns of the Small Company Stocks.

S_m^2 = Variance in the Returns of the Market Index.

S_m = Standard Deviation in the Returns of the Market Index.

a. $$\overline{R}_S = \frac{0.477 + 0.339 - 0.350 - 0.005}{5} = 0.1542$$

$$\overline{R}_m = \frac{0.402 + 0.648 - 0.580 + 0.328 + 0.004}{5} = 0.1604$$

b.

Small Company Stocks			Market Index		
$R_s - \overline{R}_s$	$\left(R_s - \overline{R}_s\right)^2$		$R_m - \overline{R}_m$	$\left(R_m - \overline{R}_m\right)^2$	
0.3228	0.10419984		0.2416	0.05837056	
0.1848	0.03415104		0.4876	0.23775376	
-0.5042	0.25421764		-0.7404	0.54819216	
0.1558	0.02427364		0.1676	0.02808976	
-0.1592	0.02534464		-0.1564	0.02446096	
			Total =	0.89686720	

$$s^2_s = 0.44218680/4 \quad s^2_m = 0.89686720/4$$

$$= 0.1105467 \quad\quad = 0.2242168$$

$$s_s = \sqrt{0.1105467} \quad s_m = \sqrt{0.2242168}$$

$$= 0.33249 \quad\quad = 0.47352$$

Note, because the data are historical returns, the appropriate denominator in the calculation of the variance is N-1.

9.17   Let R_{cs} = The Returns on Common Stocks (in %)
Let R_{ss} = The Returns on Small Stocks (in %)
Let R_{cb} = The Returns on Long-term Corporate Bonds (in %)
Let R_{gb} = The Returns on Long- term Government Bonds (in %)
Let R_{tb} = The Returns on Treasury Bills (in %)
Let – over a variable denote its average value

Year	R_{cs}	R_{ss}	$R_{ch-0.1405}$	R_{gb}	R_{tb}
1980	0.3242	0.3988	-0.0262	-0.0395	0.1124
1981	-0.0491	0.1388	-0.0096	0.0185	0.1471
1982	0.2141	0.2801	0.4379	0.4035	0.1054
1983	0.2251	0.3967	0.0470	0.0068	0.0880
1984	0.0627	-0.0667	0.1639	0.1543	0.0985
1985	0.3216	0.2466	0.3090	0.3097	0.0772
1986	0.1847	0.0685	0.1985	0.2444	0.0616
Total	1.2833	1.4628	1.1205	1.0977	0.6902
Average	0.1833	0.2090	0.1601	0.1568	0.0986

Year	$R_{cs} - \overline{R}_{cs}$	$R_{ss} - \overline{R}_{ss}$	$R_{ch} - \overline{R}_{ch}$	$R_{gb} - \overline{R}_{gb}$	$R_{tb} - \overline{R}_{tb}$
1980	0.1409	0.1898	-0.1863	-0.1963	0.0138
1981	-0.2324	-0.0702	-0.1697	-0.1383	0.0485
1982	0.0308	0.0711	0.2778	0.2467	0.0068
1983	0.0418	0.1877	-0.1131	-0.1500	-0.0106
1984	-0.1206	-0.2757	0.0038	-0.0025	-0.0001
1985	0.1383	0.0376	0.1489	0.1529	-0.0214
1986	0.0014	-0.1405	0.0384	0.0876	-0.0370

Year	$(R_{cs} - \overline{R}_{cs})^2$	$(R_{ss} - \overline{R}_{ss})^2$	$(R_{ch} - \overline{R}_{ch})^2$	$(R_{gb} - \overline{R}_{gb})^2$	$(R_{tb} - \overline{R}_{tb})^2$
1980	0.0198	0.0360	0.0347	0.0385	0.0002
1981	0.0540	0.0049	0.0288	0.0191	0.0024
1982	0.0009	0.0051	0.0772	0.0609	0.0000
1983	0.0017	0.0352	0.0128	0.0225	0.0001
1984	0.0146	0.0760	0.0000	0.0000	0.0000
1985	0.0191	0.0014	0.0222	0.0234	0.0005
1986	0.0000	0.0197	0.0015	0.0077	0.0014
Total	0.1102	0.1784	0.1771	0.1721	0.0045

Because these data are historical data, the proper divisor for computing the variance is N-1. Thus, the variance of the returns of each security is the sum of the squared deviations divided by six.

$$\text{Var} (R_{cs}) = 0.018372 \qquad \text{SD} (R_{cs}) = 0.1355$$
$$\text{Var} (R_{ss}) = 0.029734 \qquad \text{SD} (R_{ss}) = 0.1724$$
$$\text{Var} (R_{cb}) = 0.029522 \qquad \text{SD} (R_{cb}) = 0.1718$$
$$\text{Var} (R_{gb}) = 0.02868 \qquad \text{SD} (R_{gb}) = 0.16935$$
$$\text{Var} (R_{tb}) = 0.00075 \qquad \text{SD} (R_{tb}) = 0.02747$$

9.18   a.   The average return on small company stocks is
$$\overline{R}_s = (6.85-9.30+22.87+10.18-21.56+44.63)\%/6 = 8.95\%$$
The average return on T-bills is:
$$\overline{R}_T = (6.16 + 5.47 + 6.35 + 8.37 + 7.81 + 5.60) / 6 = 6.63\%$$

b.

Small Company Stock			T-Bills		
R_s	$R_s - \overline{R}_s$	$\left(R_s - \overline{R}_s\right)^2$	R_T	$R_T - \overline{R}_T$	$\left(R_T - \overline{R}_T\right)^2$
0.0685	-0.020950	0.000439	0.0616	-0.004667	0.000022
-0.0930	-0.182450	0.033288	0.0547	-0.011567	0.000134
0.2287	0.139250	0.019391	0.0635	-0.002767	0.000008
0.1018	0.012350	0.000153	0.0837	0.017433	0.000304
-0.2156	-0.305050	0.093056	0.0781	0.011833	0.000140
0.4463	0.356850	0.127342	0.0560	-0.010267	0.000105
	Total	0.273667		Total	0.000713
	Var =	5.47%		Var =	0.01%
	Std. =	23.40%		Std. =	1.19%

c. Returns on T-bills are lower than small stock returns but their variance is much smaller.

9.19 The range with 95% probability is: $\left[\text{Mean} - 2\sigma, \quad \text{Mean} + 2\sigma\right]$

$\Rightarrow$ [17.5-2× 8.5, 17.5+2×8.5]

$\Rightarrow$ [0.5%, 34.5%]

9.20 a. Expected Return on the Market:

= 0.25(-8.2%)+0.5(12.3%)+0.25(25.8%)

= 10.55%

Expected Return on T-Bills: = 3.5%

b. Expected Premium = 0.25(-8.2-3.5)+0.5(12.3-3.5)+0.25(25.8-3.5) = 7.05%

Chapter 10: Return and Risk: The Capital-Asset-Pricing Model (CAPM)

10.1 a. $\overline{R}$ = 0.1 (− 4.5%) + 0.2 (4.4%) + 0.5 (12.0%) + 0.2 (20.7%)
            = 10.57%

      b. σ^2 = 0.1 (−0.045 − 0.1057)^2 + 0.2 (0.044 − 0.1057)^2 + 0.5 (0.12 − 0.1057)^2
            + 0.2 (0.207 − 0.1057)^2
            = 0.0052

           σ = (0.0052)$^{1/2}$ = 0.072 = 7.20%

10.2 a. $\overline{R}_A$ = (6.3 + 10.5 + 15.6) / 3 = 10.8%
           $\overline{R}_B$ = (-3.7 + 6.4 + 25.3) / 3 = 9.3%

      b. σ_A^2 = {(0.063 − 0.108)^2 + (0.105 − 0.108)^2 + {(0.156 − 0.108)^2} / 3
            = 0.001446

           σ_A = (0.001446)$^{1/2}$ = 0.0380 = 3.80%
           σ_B^2 = {(− 0.037 − 0.093)^2 + (0.064 − 0.093)^2 + (0.253 − 0.093)^2} / 3
            = 0.014447

           σ_B = (0.014447)$^{1/2}$ = 0.1202 = 12.02%

      c.   Cov(R_A,R_B) = [(.063 − .108) (− .037 − .093) + (.105 − .108) (.064 − .093)
            + (.156 − .108) (.253 − .093)] / 3
            = .013617 / 3 = .004539
           Corr(R_A,R_B) = .004539 / (.0380 x .1202) = .9937

10.3 a. $\overline{R}_{HB}$ = 0.25 (−2.0) + 0.60 (9.2) + 0.15 (15.4)
            = 7.33%

           $\overline{R}_{SB}$ = 0.25 (5.0) + 0.60 (6.2) + 0.15 (7.4)
            = 6.08%

      b. σ_{HB}^2 = 0.25 (− 0.02 − 0.0733)^2 + 0.60 (0.092 − 0.0733)^2
            + 0.15 (0.154 − 0.0733)^2
            = 0.003363

           σ_{HB} = (0.003363)$^{1/2}$ = 0.05799 = 5.80%
           σ_{SB}^2 = 0.25 (0.05 − 0.0608)^2 + 0.60 (0.062 − 0.0608)^2
            + 0.15 (0.074 − 0.0608)^2
            = 0.000056

           σ_{SB} = (0.000056)$^{1/2}$ = 0.00749 = 0.75%

      c.   Cov (R_{HB}, R_{SB})
            = 0.25 (− 0.02 − 0.0733) (0.05 − 0.0608)
            + 0.60 (0.092 − 0.0733) (0.062 − 0.0608)
            + 0.15 (0.154 − 0.0733) (0.074 − 0.0608)
            = 0.000425286

           Corr (R_{HB}, R_{SB})
            = 0.000425286 / (0.05799 × 0.00749)
            = 0.9791

10.4 Holdings of Atlas stock = 120 × $50 = $6,000
      Holdings of Babcock stock = 150 × $20 = $3,000

      Weight of Atlas stock = $6,000 / $9,000 = 2 / 3
      Weight of Babcock stock = $3,000 / $9,000 = 1 / 3

10.5   a. R_P $= 0.3\,(0.12) + 0.7\,(0.18) = 0.162 = 16.2\%$

       b. σ_P^2 $= 0.3^2\,(0.09)^2 + 0.7^2\,(0.25)^2 + 2\,(0.3)\,(0.7)\,(0.09)\,(0.25)\,(0.2)$

                         $= 0.033244$

               σ_P $= (0.033244)^{1/2} = 0.1823 = 18.23\%$

10.6   a. $\overline{R}_P$ $= 0.4\,(0.15) + 0.6\,(0.25) = 0.21 = 21\%$

               σ_P^2 $= 0.4^2\,(0.1)^2 + 0.6^2\,(0.2)^2 + 2\,(0.4)\,(0.6)\,(0.1)\,(0.2)\,(0.5)$

                         $= 0.0208$

               σ_P $= (0.0208)^{1/2} = 0.1442 = 14.42\%$

       b. σ_P^2 $= 0.4^2\,(0.1)^2 + 0.6^2\,(0.2)^2 + 2\,(0.4)\,(0.6)\,(0.1)\,(0.2)\,(-0.5)$

                         $= 0.0112$

               σ_P $= (0.0112)^{1/2} = 0.1058 = 10.58\%$

       c.   As the stocks are more negatively correlated, the standard deviation of the portfolio decreases.

10.7   Macrosoft: $100 \times \$80 = \$8,000$
Intelligent: $300 \times \$40 = \$12,000$

Weight: Macrosoft: $\$8,000 / \$20,000 = 0.4$
                 Intelligent: $\$12,000 / \$20,000 = 0.6$

       a. $\overline{R}_P$ $= 0.4\,(0.15) + 0.6\,(0.20) = 0.18 = 18\%$

               σ_P^2 $= 0.4^2\,(0.08)^2 + 0.6^2\,(0.2)^2 + 2\,(0.4)\,(0.6)\,(0.38)\,(0.08)\,(0.20)$

                         $= 0.0183424$

               σ_P $= (0.0183424)^{1/2} = 0.1354 = 13.54\%$

       b.   New weight:

                 Macrosoft: $\$8,000 / \$12,000 = 0.667$
                 Intelligent: $\$4,000 / \$12,000 = 0.333$

               $\overline{R}_P$ $= 0.667\,(0.15) + 0.333\,(0.20) = 0.1666 = 16.66\%$

               σ_P^2 $= 0.667^2\,(0.08)^2 + 0.333^2\,(0.2)^2 + 2\,(0.667)\,(0.333)\,(0.38)\,(0.08)\,(0.20)$

                         $= 0.009984$

               σ_P $= (0.009984)^{1/2} = 0.09992 = 9.99\%$

10.8   a. $\overline{R}_U$ $= 7\%$

               $\overline{R}_V$ $= 0.2\,(-0.05) + 0.5\,(0.10) + 0.3\,(0.25) = 0.115 = 11.5\%$

               σ_U^2 $= \sigma_U = 0$

               σ_V^2 $= 0.2\,(-0.05 - 0.115)^2 + 0.5\,(0.10 - 0.115)^2 + 0.3\,(0.25 - 0.115)^2$

                         $= 0.0110$

               σ_V $= (0.0110)^{1/2} = 0.105 = 10.5\%$

       b. $\text{Cov}\,(R_U, R_V)$

                     $= 0.2\,(-0.05 - 0.115)\,(0.07 - 0.07)$

                       $+\; 0.5\,(0.10 - 0.115)\,(0.07 - 0.07)$

                       $+\; 0.3\,(0.25 - 0.115)\,(0.07 - 0.07)$

                     $= 0$

         $\text{Corr}\,(R_U, R_V) = 0$

       c. $\overline{R}_P$ $= 0.5\,(0.115) + 0.5\,(0.07) = 0.0925 = 9.25\%$

               σ_P^2 $= 0.5^2\,(0.0110) = 0.00275$

               σ_P $= (0.00275)^{1/2} = 0.0524 = 5.24\%$

10.9   a. R_P $= 0.3\,(0.10) + 0.7\,(0.20) = 0.17 = 17.0\%$

σ_P^2 $= 0.3^2\,(0.05)^2 + 0.7^2\,(0.15)^2 = 0.01125$

σ_P $= (0.01125)^{1/2} = 0.10607 = 10.61\%$

b. $\overline{R}_P$ $= 0.9\,(0.10) + 0.1\,(0.20) = 0.11 = 11.0\%$

σ_P^2 $= 0.9^2\,(0.05)^2 + 0.1^2\,(0.15)^2 = 0.00225$

σ_P $= (0.00225)^{1/2} = 0.04743 = 4.74\%$

c.   No, I would not hold 100% of stock A because the portfolio in b has higher expected return but less standard deviation than stock A.

I may or may not hold 100% of stock B, depending on my preference.

10.10   The expected return on any portfolio must be less than or equal to the return on the stock with the highest return. It cannot be greater than this stock's return because all stocks with lower returns will pull down the value of the weighted average return.

Similarly, the expected return on any portfolio must be greater than or equal to the return of the asset with the lowest return. The portfolio return cannot be less than the lowest return in the portfolio because all higher earning stocks will pull up the value of the weighted average.

10.11   a. $\overline{R}_A$ $= 0.4\,(0.03) + 0.6\,(0.15) = 0.102 = 10.2\%$

$\overline{R}_B$ $= 0.4\,(0.065) + 0.6\,(0.065) = 0.065 = 6.5\%$

σ_A^2 $= 0.4\,(0.03 - 0.102)^2 + 0.6\,(0.15 - 0.102)^2$

   $= 0.003456$

σ_A $= (0.003456)^{1/2} = 0.05878 = 5.88\%$

$\sigma_B^2 = \sigma_B = 0$

b. X_A $= \$2{,}500\,/\,\$6{,}000 = 0.417$

X_B $= 1 - 0.417 = 0.583$

$\overline{R}_P$ $= 0.417\,(0.102) + 0.583\,(0.065) = 0.0804 = 8.04\%$

σ_P^2 $= X_A^2\,\sigma_A^2 = 0.0006$

σ_P $= (0.0006)^{1/2} = 0.0245 = 2.45\%$

c.   Amount borrowed $= -40 \times \$50 = -\$2{,}000$

$X_A = \$8{,}000\,/\,\$6{,}000 = 4\,/\,3$

$X_B = 1 - X_A = -1\,/\,3$

$\overline{R}_P$ $= (4\,/\,3)\,(0.102) + (-1\,/\,3)\,(0.065) = 0.1143 = 11.43\%$

σ_P^2 $= (4\,/\,3)^2\,(0.003456) = 0.006144$

σ_P $= (0.006144)^{1/2} = 0.07838 = 7.84\%$

10.12   The wide fluctuations in the price of oil stocks do not indicate that oil is a poor investment. If oil is purchased as part of a portfolio, what matters is only its beta. Since the price captures beta plus idiosyncratic risks, observing price volatility is not an adequate measure of the appropriateness of adding oil to a portfolio. Remember that total variability should not be used when deciding whether or not to put an asset into a large portfolio.

10.13 a.
$$R_1 = 0.1 (0.25) + 0.4 (0.20) + 0.4 (0.15) + 0.1 (0.10)$$
$$= 0.175 = 17.5\%$$

$$\overline{R}_2 = 0.1 (0.25) + 0.4 (0.15) + 0.4 (0.20) + 0.1 (0.10)$$
$$= 0.175 = 17.5\%$$

$$\overline{R}_3 = 0.1 (0.10) + 0.4 (0.15) + 0.4 (0.20) + 0.1 (0.25)$$
$$= 0.175 = 17.5\%$$

R_1 if State occurs	$R_1 - \overline{R}_1$	$(R_1 - \overline{R}_1)^2$	$P \times (R_1 - \overline{R}_1)^2$
0.25	0.075	0.005625	0.0005625
0.20	0.025	0.000625	0.0002500
0.15	-0.025	0.000625	0.0002500
0.10	-0.075	0.005625	0.0005625
		Variance	0.0016250

Standard deviation $= \sqrt{0.001625}$
$= 0.0403$

R_2 if State occurs	$R_2 - \overline{R}_2$	$(R_2 - \overline{R}_2)^2$	$P \times (R_2 - \overline{R}_2)^2$
0.25	0.075	0.005625	0.0005625
0.15	-0.025	0.000625	0.0002500
0.20	0.025	0.000625	0.0002500
0.10	-0.075	0.005625	0.0005625
		Variance	0.0016250

Standard deviation $= \sqrt{0.001625}$
$= 0.0403$

R_3 if State occurs	$R_3 - \overline{R}_3$	$(R_3 - \overline{R}_3)^2$	$P \times (R_3 - \overline{R}_3)^2$
0.10	-0.075	0.005625	0.0005625
0.15	-0.025	0.000625	0.0002500
0.20	0.025	0.000625	0.0002500
0.25	0.075	0.005625	0.0005625
		Variance	0.0016250

Standard deviation $= \sqrt{0.001625}$
$= 0.0403$

b. Cov(1,2) = .10 (.25 - .175) (.25 - .175) + .40 (.20 - .175) (.15 - .175) + .40 (.15 - .175)
(.20 - .175) + .10 (.10 - .175) (.10 - .175)
= 0.000625

Cov(1,3) = .10 (.25 - .175) (.10 - .175) + .40 (.20 - .175) (.15 - .175) + .40 (.15 - .175)
(.20 - .175) + .10 (.10 - .175) (.25 - .175)
= - 0.001625

Cov(2,3) = .10 (.25 - .175) (.10 - .175) + .40 (.15 - .175) (.15 - .175) + .40 (.20 - .175)
(.20 - .175) + .10 (.10 - .175) (.25 - .175)
= - 0.000625

Corr(1,2) = 0.000625 / (0.0403 x 0.0403) = 0.385
Corr(1,3) = - 0.001625 / (0.0403 x 0.0403) = - 1
Corr(2,3) = - 0.000625 / (0.0403 x 0.0403) = - 0.385

c. $E(R) = .5 \times .175 + .5 \times .175 = .175$
$Var = .5 \times .5 \times .0403 \times .0403 + .5 \times .5 \times .0403 \times .0403 + 2 \times .5 \times .5 \times .000625$
$= 0.0011245$
$\sigma = 0.0335$

d. $E(R) = .5 \times .175 + .5 \times .175 = .175$
$Var = .5 \times .5 \times .0403 \times .0403 + .5 \times .5 \times .0403 \times .0403 + 2 \times .5 \times .5 \times (-.001625)$
$= 0$
$\sigma = 0$

e. $E(R) = .5 \times .175 + .5 \times .175 = .175$
$Var = .5 \times .5 \times .0403 \times .0403 + .5 \times .5 \times .0403 \times .0403 + 2 \times .5 \times .5 \times (-.000625)$
$= 0.0004995$
$\sigma = 0.0224$

f. Portfolio with negatively correlated stocks can achieve higher degree of diversification than portfolio with positively correlated stocks, holding expected return for each stock constant. Applying proper weights on perfectly negatively correlated stocks can reduce portfolio variance to 0. As long as the correlation is not 1, there is benefit of diversification.

10.14 a.

State	Return on A	Return on B	Probability
1	15%	35%	$0.4 \times 0.5 = 0.2$
2	15%	-5%	$0.4 \times 0.5 = 0.2$
3	10%	35%	$0.6 \times 0.5 = 0.3$
4	10%	-5%	$0.6 \times 0.5 = 0.3$

b. $\overline{R}_P = 0.2 [0.5 (0.15) + 0.5 (0.35)] + 0.2[0.5 (0.15) + 0.5 (-0.05)]$
$+ 0.3 [0.5 (0.10) + 0.5 (0.35)] + 0.3 [0.5 (0.10) + 0.5 (-0.05)]$
$= 0.135$
$= 13.5\%$

10.15 a. $\overline{R}_P = \Sigma \overline{R}_i / N = \{N (0.10)\} / N = 0.10 = 10\%$
$\sigma_P^2 = \Sigma\Sigma Cov (R_i, R_j) / N^2 + \Sigma \sigma_i^2 / N^2$
$= N (N - 1) (0.0064) / N^2 + N (0.0144) / N^2$
$= (0.0064) (N - 1) / N + (0.0144) / N$

b. As $N \to \infty$, $\sigma_P^2 \to 0.0064 = Cov (R_i, R_j)$

c. The covariance of the returns of the securities is the most important factor to consider when placing securities in a well-diversified portfolio.

10.16 The statement is false. Once the stock is part of a well-diversified portfolio, the important factor is the contribution of the stock to the variance of the portfolio. In a well-diversified portfolio, this contribution is the covariance of the stock with the rest of the portfolio.

10.17   The covariance is a more appropriate measure of risk in a well-diversified portfolio because it reflects the effect of the security on the variance of the portfolio. Investors are concerned with the variance of their portfolios and not the variance of the individual securities. Since covariance measures the impact of an individual security on the variance of the portfolio, covariance is the appropriate measure of risk.

10.18   If we assume that the market has not stayed constant during the past three years, then the low volatility of Southern Co.'s stock price only indicates that the stock has a beta that is very near to zero. The high volatility of Texas Instruments' stock price does not imply that the firm's beta is high. Total volatility (the price fluctuation) is a function of both systematic and unsystematic risk. The beta only reflects the systematic risk. Observing price volatility does not indicate whether it was due to systematic factors, or firm specific factors. Thus, if you observe a high price volatility like that of TI, you cannot claim that the beta of TI's stock is high. All you know is that the total risk of TI is high.

10.19   Note: The solution to this problem requires calculus.
Specifically, the solution is found by minimizing a function subject to a constraint. Calculus ability is not necessary to understand the principles behind a minimum variance portfolio.

$$\text{Min } \{ X_A^2 \sigma_A^2 + X_B^2 \sigma_B^2 + 2 X_A X_B \text{Cov}(R_A, R_B)\}$$
$$\text{subject to } X_A + X_B = 1$$

Let $X_A = 1 - X_B$. Then,
$$\text{Min } \{(1 - X_B)^2 \sigma_A^2 + X_B^2 \sigma_B^2 + 2(1 - X_B) X_B \text{Cov}(R_A, R_B)\}$$
Take a derivative with respect to X_B.
$$d\{\bullet\} / dX_B = (2 X_B - 2) \sigma_A^2 + 2 X_B \sigma_B^2 + 2 \text{Cov}(R_A, R_B) - 4 X_B \text{Cov}(R_A, R_B)$$
Set the derivative equal to zero, cancel the common 2 and solve for X_B.
$$X_B \sigma_A^2 - \sigma_A^2 + X_B \sigma_B^2 + \text{Cov}(R_A, R_B) - 2 X_B \text{Cov}(R_A, R_B) = 0$$

$$X_B = \{\sigma_A^2 - \text{Cov}(R_A, R_B)\} / \{\sigma_A^2 + \sigma_B^2 - 2 \text{Cov}(R_A, R_B)\}$$
and
$$X_A = \{\sigma_B^2 - \text{Cov}(R_A, R_B)\} / \{\sigma_A^2 + \sigma_B^2 - 2 \text{Cov}(R_A, R_B)\}$$
Using the data from the problem yields,
    $X_A = 0.8125$ and
    $X_B = 0.1875$.

a.   Using the weights calculated above, the expected return on the minimum variance portfolio is
    $E(R_P)$ $= 0.8125 \, E(R_A) + 0.1875 \, E(R_B)$
        $= 0.8125 \, (5\%) + 0.1875 \, (10\%)$
        $= 5.9375\%$

b.   Using the formula derived above, the weights are
    $X_A = 2 / 3$ and
    $X_B = 1 / 3$

c.   The variance of this portfolio is zero.
    σ_P^2 $= X_A^2 \sigma_A^2 + X_B^2 \sigma_B^2 + 2 X_A X_B \text{Cov}(R_A, R_B)$
        $= (4 / 9) (0.01) + (1 / 9) (0.04) + 2 (2 / 3) (1 / 3) (-0.02)$
        $= 0$
    This demonstrates that assets can be combined to form a risk-free portfolio.

10.20   The slope of the capital market line is

$$(\bar{R}_M - R_f) / \sigma_M = (12 - 5) / 10 = 0.7$$

a. $\bar{R}_P = 5 + 0.7\,(7) = 9.9\%$

b. $\sigma_P = (\bar{R}_P - R_f) / 0.7 = (20 - 5) / 0.7 = 21.4\%$

10.21   The slope of the characteristic line of Fuji is

$$\frac{\bar{R}_{Fuji}(Bull) - \bar{R}_{Fuji}(Bear)}{\bar{R}_M(Bull) - \bar{R}_M(Bear)} = (12.8 - 3.4) / (16.3 - 2.5)$$

$$= 0.68$$

a.   Beta = slope of the characteristic line = 0.68
         The responsiveness to the market = 0.68

b.   Slope = 0.68 = {12.8 - $\bar{R}_{Fuji}$(Bear) } / {16.3 - (-4.0)}

         Thus, $\bar{R}_{Fuji}$(Bear)   = 12.8 - 0.68 (16.3 + 4.0)

                                           = -1.00%

10.22   Polonius' portfolio will be the market portfolio. He will have no borrowing or lending in his portfolio.

10.23   a. $\bar{R}_P$ = (0.10 + 0.14 + 0.20) / 3 = 0.1467 = 14.67%

         b. β_P = (0.7 + 1.2 + 1.8) / 3 = 1.23

         c.   To be in equilibrium, three securities should be located on a straight line (the Security Market Line).
                  Check the slopes.
                           Slope between A & B = (0.14 - 0.10) / (1.2 - 0.7) = 0.08
                           Slope between B & C = (0.20 - 0.14) / (1.8 - 1.2) = 0.10
                  Since the slopes are different, these securities are not in equilibrium.

10.24   Expected Return For Alpha = 6% + 1.2×8.5% =16.2%

10.25   Expected return for Ross = 6% + (0.8×8.5%) = 12.8%

10.26   Expected Return in Jordan = 8% + (1.5×7%) =18.5%

10.27   14.2%= 3.7%+β(7.5%)   ⇒ β = 1.4

10.28 $0.25 = R_f + 1.4\,[R_M - R_f]$ (I)
                  $0.14 = R_f + 0.7\,[R_M - R_f]$ (II)

                  (I) – (II)=$0.11 = 0.7\,[R_M - R_f]$ (III)
                           $[R_M - R_f] = 0.1571$

         Put (III) into (I) $0.25 = R_f + 1.4[0.1571]$
                                       $R_f = 3\%$

         $[R_M - R_f] = 0.1571$
                  $R_M = 0.1571 + 0.03$
                       = 18.71%

10.29 a. $E(R_A) = (0.25)(-0.1) + (0.5)(0.1) + (0.25)(0.2) = 0.075$
           $E(R_B) = (0.25)(-0.3) + (0.5)(0.05) + (0.25)(0.4) = 0.05$

       b.

           (I) $E(R_A) = R_f + \beta_A [E(R_M) - R_f] = 0.075$
           (II) $E(R_B) = R_f + \beta_B [E(R_M) - R_f] = 0.05$
           $(I) - (II) = 0.025 = (\beta_A - \beta_B)[E(R_M) - R_f]$
                $0.025 = 0.25[E(R_M) - R_f]$,
           so the market risk premium $= [E(R_M) - R_f] = 10\%$

10.30 a.

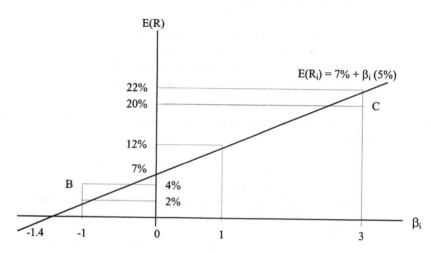

       b.   i.   See point B on the graph in part a.
            ii.   There does exist a mis-pricing of the security. According to the SML,
                  this asset should have a return of 2% [= 7% + (-1) (5%)]. Since the
                  return is too high, the price of this asset must be too low. (Remember,
                  asset prices and rates of return are inversely related!) Since the asset is
                  under-priced, you should buy it.
       c.   i.   See point C on the graph in part a.
            ii.   There does exist a mis-pricing of the security. According to the SML,
                  this asset should have a return of 22% [= 7% + (3) (5%)]. Since the
                  return is too low, the price of this asset must be too high. Since the asset
                  is overpriced, you should sell it.

10.31 Expected return $= 0.05 + 1.8 (0.08) = 0.194 = 19.4\%$
       The analyst expects only 18%, so he is pessimistic.
10.32 a. $\overline{R} = 6.4 + 1.2 (13.8 - 6.4) = 15.28\%$
       b. $\overline{R} = 3.5 + 1.2 (13.8 - 3.5) = 15.86\%$

Answers to End-of-Chapter Problems

10.33   Market excess return $= E(R_M) - R_f$
                    $= 20\% - 5\% = 15\%$
         Portfolio excess return $= E(R_E) - R_f$
                    $= 25\% - 5\% = 20\%$
         Portfolio beta $= \beta_E = 20\% / 15\% = 4/3$
                    $\beta_E = \{Corr(R_E, R_M) \sigma(R_E)\} / \sigma(R_M)$
         Therefore,
                    $4/3 = (1 \times 4\%) / \sigma(R_M)$
                    $\sigma(R_M) = 3\%$
         Note: $Corr(R_E, R_M) = 1$ because this portfolio is a combination of the riskless asset and
                 the market portfolio.

         For the security with $Corr(R_S, R_M) = 0.5$,
                    $\beta_S = \{Corr(R_S, R_M) \sigma(R_S)\} / \sigma(R_M)$
                        $= (0.5 \times 2\%) / 3\%$
                        $= 0.3333$
         Thus, $E(R_S)$ $= 5\% + \beta_S (15\%)$
                         $= 5\% + (0.3333) (15\%)$
                         $= 10\%$

10.34   a.   The risk premium $= \overline{R}_M - R_f$
                 Potpourri stock return:
                         $16.7 = 7.6 + 1.7 (\overline{R}_M - R_f)$
                         $\overline{R}_M - R_f = (16.7 - 7.6) / 1.7 = 5.353\%$
        b. $\overline{R}_{Mag} = 7.6 + 0.8 (5.353) = 11.88\%$
        c. $X_{Pot} \beta_{Pot} + X_{Mag} \beta_{Mag} = 1.07$
                 $1.7 X_{Pot} + 0.8 (1 - X_{Pot}) = 1.07$
                 $0.9 X_{Pot} = 0.27$
                 $X_{Pot} = 0.3$
                 $X_{Mag} = 0.7$
                 Thus invest \$3,000 in Potpourri stock and \$7,000 in Magnolia.
                 $\overline{R}_P = 7.6 + 1.07 (5.353) = 13.33\%$

                 Note: The other way to calculate $\overline{R}_P$ is
                         $\overline{R}_P = 0.3 (16.7) + 0.7 (11.88) = 13.33\%$

10.35 $\overline{R}_Z$ $= R_f + \beta_Z (\overline{R}_M - R_f)$
        β_Z $= Cov(R_Z, R_M) / \sigma_M^2 = Corr(R_Z, R_M) \sigma_Z \sigma_M / \sigma_M^2$
                    $= Corr(R_Z, R_M) \sigma_Z / \sigma_M$
                    $\sigma_Z = (0.0169)^{1/2} = 0.13$
                    $\sigma_M = (0.0121)^{1/2} = 0.11$

        Thus, $\beta_Z = 0.45 (0.13) / 0.11 = 0.5318$
        $\overline{R}_Z$ $= 0.063 + 0.5318 (0.148 - 0.063)$
                     $= 0.1082$
                     $= 10.82\%$

10.36 a. $R_i = 4.9\% + \beta_i (9.4\%)$

      b. $\beta_D = \mathrm{Cov}(R_D, R_M) / \sigma_M^2 = 0.0635 / 0.04326 = 1.468$
             $\bar{R}_D = 4.9 + 1.468 (9.4) = 18.70\%$

10.37 CAPM:

      Johnson $19 = R_f + 1.7 (\bar{R}_M - R_f)$
      Williamson $14 = R_f + 1.2 (\bar{R}_M - R_f)$
                       $5 = 0.5 (\bar{R}_M - R_f)$
             Thus $(\bar{R}_M - R_f) = 10\%$
      $19 = R_f + 1.7 (10)$
      $R_f = 2\%$
      $\bar{R}_M = 12\%$

10.38 The statement is false. If a security has a negative beta, investors would want to hold the asset to reduce the variability of their portfolios. Those assets will have expected returns that are lower than the risk free rate. To see this, examine the SML equation.
      $E(R_i) = R_f + \beta_i \{E(R_M) - R_f)\}$
      If $\beta_i < 0$, $E(R_i) < R_f$.

10.39 Weights:
      $X_A = 5 / 30 = 0.1667$
      $X_B = 10 / 30 = 0.3333$
      $X_C = 8 / 30 = 0.2667$
      $X_D = 1 - X_A - X_B - X_C = 0.2333$
      Beta of portfolio
      $= 0.1667 (0.75) + 0.3333 (1.10) + 0.2667 (1.36) + 0.2333 (1.88)$
      $= 1.293$
      $\bar{R}_P = 4 + 1.293 (15 - 4) = 18.22\%$

10.40 a.   (i) $\beta_A = \rho_{A,M} \sigma_A / \sigma_M$
                      $\rho_{A,M} = \beta_A \sigma_M / \sigma_A$
                      $= (0.9) (0.10) / 0.12$
                      $= 0.75$
             (ii) $\sigma_B = \beta_B \sigma_M / \rho_{B,M}$
                      $= (1.10) (0.10) / 0.40$
                      $= 0.275$
             (iii) $\beta_C = \rho_{C,M} \sigma_C / \sigma_M$
                      $= (0.75) (0.24) / 0.10$
                      $= 1.80$
             (iv) $\rho_{M,M} = 1$
             (v) $\beta_M = 1$
             (vi) $\sigma_f = 0$
             (vii) $\rho_{f,M} = 0$
             (viii) $\beta_f = 0$

      b.   SML:
                      $E(R_i) = R_f + \beta_i \{E(R_M) - R_f\}$
                      $= 0.05 + (0.10) \beta_i$

Security	$\overline{R}_i$	β_i	$E(R_i)$
A	0.13	0.90	0.14
B	0.16	1.10	0.16
C	0.25	1.80	0.23

Security A performed worse than the market, while security C performed better than the market. Security B is fairly priced.

c.   According to the SML, security A is overpriced while security C is under-priced. Thus, you could invest in security C while sell security A (if you currently hold it).

10.41   a.   The typical risk-averse investor seeks high returns and low risks. To assess the two stocks, find the risk and return profiles for each stock.

Returns:

State of economy	Probability	Return on A*
Recession	0.1	-0.20
Normal	0.8	0.10
Expansion	0.1	0.20

* Since security A pays no dividend, the return on A is simply $(P_1 / P_0) - 1$.

$\overline{R}_A$ $= 0.1 (-0.20) + 0.8 (0.10) + 0.1 (0.20)$
        $= 0.08$
$\overline{R}_B$ $= 0.09$ This was given in the problem.

Risk:

$R_A - \overline{R}_A$	$(R_A - \overline{R}_A)^2$	$P \times (R_A - \overline{R}_A)^2$
-0.28	0.0784	0.00784
0.02	0.0004	0.00032
0.12	0.0144	0.00144
	Variance	0.00960

Standard deviation $(R_A) = 0.0980$

$\beta_A = \{Corr(R_A, R_M)\ \sigma(R_A)\} / \sigma(R_M)$
     $= 0.8 (0.0980) / 0.10$
     $= 0.784$

$\beta_B = \{Corr(R_B, R_M)\ \sigma(R_B)\} / \sigma(R_M)$
     $= 0.2 (0.12) / 0.10$
     $= 0.24$

The return on stock B is higher than the return on stock A. The risk of stock B, as measured by its beta, is lower than the risk of A. Thus, a typical risk-averse investor will prefer stock B.

b. R_P $= (0.7)\ R_A + (0.3)\ R_B$
$= (0.7)\ (0.8) + (0.3)\ (0.09)$
$= 0.083$

$\sigma_P^{\ 2}$ $= 0.7^2\ \sigma_A^{\ 2} + 0.3^2\ \sigma_B^{\ 2} + 2\ (0.7)\ (0.3)\ Corr\ (R_A,\ R_B)\ \sigma_A\ \sigma_B$
$= (0.49)\ (0.0096) + (0.09)\ (0.0144) + (0.42)\ (0.6)\ (0.0980)\ (0.12)$
$= 0.0089635$

σ_P $= \sqrt{0.0089635}$
$= 0.0947$

c. The beta of a portfolio is the weighted average of the betas of the components of the portfolio.

β_P $= (0.7)\ \beta_A + (0.3)\ \beta_B$
$= (0.7)\ (0.784) + (0.3)\ (0.240)$
$= 0.621$

Chapter 11: An Alternative View of Risk and Return: The Arbitrage Pricing Theory

11.1   **Real GNP** was higher than anticipated. Since returns are positively related to the level of GNP, returns should rise based on this factor.
Inflation was exactly the amount anticipated. Since there was no surprise in this announcement, it will not affect Lewis-Striden returns.
Interest Rates are lower than anticipated. Since returns are negatively related to interest rates, the lower than expected rate is good news. Returns should rise due to interest rates.
The President's death is bad news. Although the president was expected to retire, his retirement would not be effective for six months. During that period he would still contribute to the firm. His untimely death mean that those contributions would not be made. Since he was generally considered an asset to the firm, his death will cause returns to fall.
The poor research results are also bad news. Since Lewis-Striden must continue to test the drug as early as expected. The delay will affect expected future earnings, and thus it will dampen returns now.
The research breakthrough is positive news for Lewis Striden. Since it was unexpected, it will cause returns to rise.
The competitor's announcement is also unexpected, but it is not a welcome surprise. this announcement will lower the returns on Lewis-Striden.
Systematic risk is risk that cannot be diversified away through formation of a portfolio. Generally, systematic risk factors are those factors that affect a large number of firms in the market. Note those factors do not have to equally affect the firms. The systematic factors in the list are real GNP, inflation and interest rates.
Unsystematic risk is the type of risk that can be diversified away through portfolio formation. Unsystematic risk factors are specific to the firm or industry. Surprises in these factors will affect the returns of the firm in which you are interested, but they will have no effect on the returns of firms in a different industry and perhaps little effect on other firms in the same industry. For Lewis-Striden, the unsystematic risk factors are the president's ability to contribute to the firm, the research results and the competitor.

11.2   a.   Systematic Risk $= 0.042(4,480 - 4,416) - 1.4(4.3\% - 3.1\%) - 0.67(11.8\% - 9.5\%)$
$\qquad = -0.53\%$
       b.   Unsystematic Risk $= -2.6\%$
       c.   Total Return $= 9.5\% - 0.53\% - 2.6\% = 6.37\%$

11.3
       a.   Systematic Risk $= 2.04(4.8\% - 3.5\%) - 1.90(15.2\% - 14.0\%) = 0.372\%$
       b.   Unsystematic Return $= 0.36(27 - 23) = 1.44\%$
       c.   Total Return $= 10.0 + 0.37 + 1.44 = 11.81\%$

11.4　a.　　Stock A:

$$R_A = \overline{R}_A + \beta_A \left(R_m - \overline{R}_m \right) + \varepsilon_A$$
$$= 10.5\% + 1.2 \left(R_m - 14.2\% \right) + \varepsilon_A$$

Stock B:

$$R_B = \overline{R}_B + \beta \left(R_m - \overline{R}_m \right) + \varepsilon_B$$
$$= 13.0\% + 0.98 \left(R_m - 14.2\% \right) + \varepsilon_B$$

Stock C:

$$R_C = \overline{R}_C + \beta_C \left(R_m - \overline{R}_m \right) + \varepsilon_C$$
$$= 15.7\% + 1.37 \left(R_m - 14.2\% \right) + \varepsilon_C$$

b.

$$R_P = 0.30 R_A + 0.45 R_B + 0.25 R_C$$
$$= 0.30 \left[10.5\% + 1.2 \left(R_m - 14.2\% \right) + \varepsilon_A \right]$$
$$+ 0.45 \left[13.0\% + 0.98 \left(R_m - 14.2\% \right) + \varepsilon_B \right]$$
$$+ 0.25 \left[15.7\% + 1.37 \left(R_m - 14.2\% \right) + \varepsilon_c \right]$$
$$= 0.30 \left(10.5\% \right) + 0.45 \left(13\% \right) + 0.25 \left(15.7\% \right)$$
$$+ \left[0.30 \left(1.2 \right) + 0.45 \left(0.98 \right) + 0.25 \left(1.37 \right) \right] \left(R_m - 14.2\% \right)$$
$$+ 0.30 \varepsilon_A + 0.45 \varepsilon_B + 0.25 \varepsilon_c$$
$$= 12.925\% + 1.1435 \left(R_m - 14.2\% \right)$$
$$+ 0.30 \varepsilon_A + 0.45 \varepsilon_B + 0.25 \varepsilon_C$$

c.　　i.

$$R_A = 10.5\% + 1.2 \left(15\% - 14.2\% \right)$$
$$= 11.46\%$$
$$R_B = 13\% + 0.98 \left(15\% - 14.2\% \right)$$
$$= 13.7\%$$
$$R_C = 15.7\% + 1.37 \left(15\% - 14.2\% \right)$$
$$= 16.8\%$$

ii.

$$R_P = 12.925\% + 1.1435 \left(15\% - 14.2\% \right)$$
$$= 13.8398\%$$

Answers to End-of-Chapter Problems

11.5

    a.   Since five stocks have the same expected returns and the same betas, the portfolio also has the same expected return and beta.

$$\overline{R}_p = 11.0 + 0.84F_1 + 1.69F_2 + \frac{1}{5}\left(E_1 + E_2 + E_3 + E_4 + E_5\right)$$

    b.

$$\overline{R}_p = 11.0 + 0.84F_1 + 1.69F_2 + \frac{E_1}{N} + \frac{E_2}{N} + \ldots + \frac{E_N}{N}$$

As $N \to \infty$, $\frac{1}{N} \to 0$, but E_js are finite,

Thus, $\overline{R}_p = 11.0 + 0.84F_1 + 1.69F_2$

11.6   To determine which investment investor would prefer, you must compute the variance of portfolios created by many stocks from either market. Note, because you know that diversification is good, it is reasonable to assume that once an investor chose the market in which he or she will invest, he or she will buy many stocks in that market.

    Known: $E_F = 0$ and $\sigma = 0.1$

                $E_\varepsilon = 0$ and $\sigma_{\varepsilon_i} = 0.2$ for all i.

    Assume: The weight of each stock is 1/N; that is, $X_i = 1/N$ for all i.

If a portfolio is composed of N stocks each forming 1/N proportion of the portfolio, the return on the portfolio is 1/N times the sum of the returns on the N stocks. Recall that the return on each stock is $0.1 + \beta F + \varepsilon$.

$$R_P = (1/N) \sum R_i$$
$$= ((1/N) \sum (0.1 + \beta F + \varepsilon))$$
$$= 0.1 + \beta F + (1/N) \sum \varepsilon$$

$$E(R_P) = E[0.1 + \beta F + (1/N) \sum \varepsilon]$$
$$= 0.1 + \beta E(F) + (1/N) \sum E(\varepsilon)$$
$$= 0.1 + \beta(0) + (1/N) \sum 0$$
$$= 0.1$$

$$Var(R_P) = E[R_P - E(R_P)]^2$$
$$= E[0.1 + \beta F + (0.1/N) \sum \varepsilon - 0.1]^2$$
$$= E[\beta F + (1/N) \sum \varepsilon]^2$$
$$= E[\beta^2 F^2 + 2\beta F(1/N) \sum \varepsilon + (1/N^2)(\sum \varepsilon)^2]$$
$$= \beta^2 s^2 + (1/N) s^2 \varepsilon_i + (1 - 1/N) Cov(\varepsilon_i, \varepsilon_j)$$

In the limit as $N \Rightarrow \infty$, the variance is
$$= \beta^2 s^2 + Cov(\varepsilon_i, \varepsilon_j)$$
$$= 0.01\beta^2 + 0.04 Corr(\varepsilon_i, \varepsilon_j)$$

Thus, $R_{1i} = 0.10 + 1.5F + \varepsilon_{1i}$
$$R_{2i} = 0.10 + 0.5f + \varepsilon_{2i}$$
$$E(R_{1p}) = E(R_{2P}) = 0.1$$
$$Var(R_{1p}) = 0.0225 + 0.04 Corr(\varepsilon_{1i}, \varepsilon_{1j})$$
$$Var(R_{2P}) = 0.0025 + 0.04 Corr(\varepsilon_{2i}, \varepsilon_{2j})$$

a.

$$Corr(\varepsilon_{1i}, \varepsilon_{1j}) = Corr(\varepsilon_{2i}, \varepsilon_{2j}) = 0$$
$$Var(R_{1p}) = 0.0225$$
$$Var(R_{2p}) = 0.00225$$

Since $Var(R_{1p}) \rangle Var(R_{2p})$, a risk averse investor will prefer to invest in the second market.

b. $\text{Corr}\left(\varepsilon_{1i},\varepsilon_{1j}\right) = 0.9$ and $\text{Corr}\left(\varepsilon_{2i},\varepsilon_{2j}\right) = 0$

$\text{Var}\left(R_{1p}\right) = 0.0585$

$\text{Var}\left(R_{2p}\right) = 0.0025$

Since $\text{Var}\left(R_{1p}\right) \rangle \text{Var}\left(R_{2p}\right)$, a risk averse investor will prefer to invest in the second market.

c. $\text{Corr}\left(\varepsilon_{1i},\varepsilon_{1j}\right) = 0$ and $\text{Corr}\left(\varepsilon_{2i},\varepsilon_{2j}\right) = 0.5$

$\text{Var}\left(R_{1p}\right) = 0.0225$

$\text{Var}\left(R_{2p}\right) = 0.0225$

Since $\text{Var}\left(R_{1p}\right) = \text{Var}\left(R_{2p}\right)$, a risk averse investor will be indifferent between investing in the two market.

d. Indifference implies that the variances of the portfolio in the two markets are equal.

$$\text{Var}\left(R_{1p}\right) = \text{Var}\left(R_{2p}\right)$$

$$0.0225 + 0.04\text{Corr}\left(\varepsilon_{1i},\varepsilon_{1j}\right) = 0.0025 + 0.04\text{Corr}\left(\varepsilon_{2i},\varepsilon_{2j}\right)$$

$$\text{Corr}\left(\varepsilon_{2i},\varepsilon_{2j}\right) = \text{Corr}\left(\varepsilon_{1i},\varepsilon_{1j}\right) + 0.5$$

This is exactly the relationship used in part c.

11.7

a. $Var\left(R_j\right)=\beta_i^2 Var\left(R_m\right)+Var\left(\varepsilon_i\right)$

$\therefore s^2_A = 0.7^2\left(1.21\right)+1.00 = 1.5929\%$

$\Rightarrow s_A = \sqrt{1.5929/100} = 12.62\%$

$s^2_B = 1.2^2\left(1.21\right)+1.44 = 3.1824\%$

$\Rightarrow s_B = \sqrt{3.1824/100} = 0.1784 = 17.84\%$

$s_C^2 = 1.5^2\left(1.21\right)+2.25 = 4.9725\%$

$\Rightarrow s_C = \sqrt{4.9725/100} = 0.2230 = 22.30\%$

b. i. As $N \to \infty$, $Var\left(\varepsilon_j\right)/N \to 0$

$\therefore Var\left(R_i\right)=\beta_i^2 Var\left(R_m\right)$

$s_A^2 = 0.7^2\left(1.21\right)= 0.5929\%$

$s_B^2 = 1.2^2\left(1.21\right)= 1.7424\%$

$s_C^2 = 1.5^2\left(1.21\right)= 2.7225\%$

ii. APT Model: $\overline{R}_i = R_F +\left(\overline{R}_m - R_F\right)\beta_i$

$\overline{R}_A = 3.3+(10.6-3.3)(0.7) = 8.41\%$

$\overline{R}_B = 3.3+(10.6-3.3)(1.2) = 12.06\%$

$\overline{R}_C = 3.3+(10.6-3.3)(1.5) = 14.25\%$

APT Model shows that assets A & B are accurately priced but asset C is overpriced. Thus, rational investors will not hold asset C.

iii. If short selling is allowed, all rational investors will sell short asset C so that the price of asset C will decrease until no arbitrage opportunity exists. In other words, price of asset C should decrease until the return become 14.25%.

11.8 a. Let X= the proportion of security of one in the portfolio and (1-X) = the proportion of security two in the portfolio.

$R_{pt} = XR_{1t} +\left(1-X\right)R_{2t}$

$= x\left[E\left(R_{1t}\right)+\beta_{11}F_{1t} +_{12} F_{2t}\right]+\left(1-x\right)\left[E\left(R_{2t}\right)+\beta_{21}F_{1t} +\beta_{22}F_{2t}\right]$

The condition that the return of the portfolio does not depend on F_1 implies:

$$X\beta_{11} + (1-X)\beta_{21} = 0$$
$$X + (1-X)0.5 = 0$$

Thus, P=(-1,2); i.e. sell short security one and buy security two.

$$E(R_p) = (-1)20\% + 2(20\%) = 20\%$$
$$\beta_{p2} = (-1)(1.5) + 2(2) = 2.5$$

b.   Follow the same logic as in part a, we have

$$X\beta_{31} + (1-X)\beta_{41} = 0$$
$$X + (1-X)1.5 = 0$$
$$X = 3$$

Where X is the proportion of security three in the portfolio. Thus, sell short security four and buy security three.

$$E(R_p) = 3(10\%) + (-2)(10\%) = 10\%$$
$$\beta_{p2} = 3(0.5) - 2(0.75) = 0$$

this is a risk free portfolio!

c.   The portfolio in part b provides a risk free return of 10% which is higher than the 5% return provided by the risk free security. To take advantage of this opportunity, borrow at the risk free rate of 5% and invest the funds in a portfolio built by selling short security four and buying security three with weights (3,-2).

d.   Assuming that the risk free security will not change. The price of security four (that everyone is trying to sell short) will decrease and the price of security three (that everyone is trying to buy) will increase. Hence the return of security four will increase and the return of security three will decrease.

The alternative is that the prices of securities three and four will remain the same, and the price of the risk-free security drops until its return is 10%.

Finally, a combined movement of all security prices is also possible. The prices of security four and the risk-free security will decrease and the price of security four will increase until the opportunity disappears.

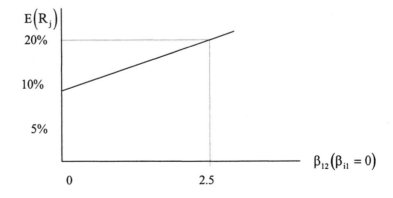

Chapter 12: Risk, Return, and Capital Budgeting

12.1 Cost of equity
$$R_s = 5 + 0.95\,(9) = 13.55\%$$
NPV of the project
$$= -\$1.2 \text{ million} + \sum_{t=1}^{5} \frac{\$340,000}{1.1355^t}$$
$$= -\$20,016.52$$
Do not undertake the project.

12.2 a. $\overline{R}_D = (-0.05 + 0.05 + 0.08 + 0.15 + 0.10) / 5 = 0.066$

$\overline{R}_M = (-0.12 + 0.01 + 0.06 + 0.10 + 0.05) / 5 = 0.02$

b.

$R_D - \overline{R}_D$	$R_M - \overline{R}_M$	$(R_M - \overline{R}_M)^2$	$(R_D - \overline{R}_D)(R_M - \overline{R}_M)$
-0.116	-0.14	0.0196	0.01624
-0.016	-0.01	0.0001	0.00016
0.014	0.04	0.0016	0.00056
0.084	0.08	0.0064	0.00672
0.034	0.03	0.0009	0.00102
		0.0286	0.02470

Beta of Douglas
$$= 0.02470 / 0.0286$$
$$= 0.864$$

12.3 R_s $= 6\% + 1.15 \times 10\% = 17.5\%$

R_B $= 6\% + 0.3 \times 10\% = 9\%$

a. Cost of equity $= R_s = 17.5\%$

b. $B / S = 0.25$

$B / (B + S) = 0.2$

$S / (B + S) = 0.8$

$\text{WACC} = 0.8 \times 17.5\% + 0.2 \times 9\% (1 - 0.35)$

$\qquad = 15.17\%$

12.4 $\sigma_C = (0.04225)^{\frac{1}{2}} = 0.065$

$\sigma_M = (0.01467)^{\frac{1}{2}} = 0.0383$

Beta of ceramics craftsman
$$= \rho_{CM}\,\sigma_C\,\sigma_M / \sigma_M^2 = \rho_{CM}\,\sigma_C / \sigma_M$$
$$= (0.675)\,(0.065) / 0.0383$$
$$= 1.146$$

12.5 a. To compute the beta of Mercantile Manufacturing's stock, you need the product of the deviations of Mercantile's returns from their mean and the deviations of the market's returns from their mean. You also need the squares of the deviations of the market's returns from their mean.

The mechanics of computing the means and the deviations were presented in an earlier chapter.

$$\overline{R}_T = 0.196 / 12 = 0.016333$$
$$\overline{R}_M = 0.236 / 12 = 0.019667$$
$$E(R_T - \overline{R}_T)(R_M - \overline{R}_M) = 0.038711$$
$$E(R_M - \overline{R}_M)^2 = 0.038588$$
$$\beta = 0.038711 / 0.038588$$
$$= 1.0032$$

b. The beta of the average stock is 1. Mercantile's beta is close to 1, indicating that its stock has average risk.

12.6 a. R_M can have three values, 0.16, 0.18 or 0.20. The probability that R_M takes one of these values is the sum of the joint probabilities of the return pair that include the particular value of R_M. For example, if R_M is 0.16, R_J will be 0.16, 0.18 or 0.22. The probability that R_M is 0.16 and R_J is 0.16 is 0.10. The probability that R_M is 0.16 and R_J is 0.18 is 0.06. The probability that R_M is 0.16 and R_J is 0.22 is 0.04. The probability that R_M is 0.16 is, therefore, 0.10 + 0.06 + 0.04 = 0.20. The same procedure is used to calculate the probability that R_M is 0.18 and the probability that R_M is 0.20. Remember, the sum of the probability must be one.

R_M	Probability
0.16	0.20
0.18	0.60
0.20	0.20

b. i. $\overline{R}_M = 0.16 (0.20) + 0.18 (0.60) + 0.20 (0.20)$
$$= 0.18$$

ii. $\sigma_M^2 = (0.16 - 0.18)^2 (0.20) + (0.18 - 0.18)^2 (0.60)$
$$+ (0.20 - 0.18)^2 (0.20)$$
$$= 0.00016$$

iii. $\sigma_M = (0.00016)^{\frac{1}{2}} = 0.01265$

c.
R_J	Probability
.16	.10
.18	.20
.20	.40
.22	.20
.24	.10

d. i. $\overline{E}_j = .16 (.10) + .18 (.20) + .20 (.40) + .22 (.20) + .24(.10) = .20$

ii. $\sigma_j^2 = (.16 - .20)^2 (.10) + (.18 - .20)^2 (.20) + (.20 - .20)^2 (.40)$
$$+ (.22 - .20)^2 (.20) + (.24 - .20)^2 (.10) = .00048$$

iii. $\sigma_j = (0.00048)^{\frac{1}{2}} = .02191$

e. $\text{Cov}_{mj} = (.16 - .18)(.16 - .20)(.10) + (.16 - .18)(.18 - .20)(.06)$
$\qquad + (.16 - .18)(.22 - .20)(.04) + (.20 - .18)(.18 - .20)(.02)$
$\qquad + (.20 - .18)(.22 - .20)(.04) + (.20 - .18)(.24 - .20)(.10)$
$\qquad = .000176$

$\text{Corr}_{mj} = (0.000176) / (0.01265)(0.02191) = 0.635$

f. $\beta_j = (.635)(.02191) / (.01265) = 1.10$

12.7 i. The risk of the new project is the same as the risk of the firm without the project.
ii. The firm is financed entirely with equity.

12.8 a. Pacific Cosmetics should use its stock beta in the evaluation of the project only if the risk of the perfume project is the same as the risk of Pacific Cosmetics.
b. If the risk of the project is the same as the risk of the firm, use the firm's stock beta. If the risk differs, then use the beta of an all-equity firm with similar risk as the perfume project. A good way to estimate the beta of the project would be to average the betas of many perfume producing firms.

12.9 $E(R_S) = 0.1 \times 3 + 0.3 \times 8 + 0.4 \times 20 + 0.2 \times 15 = 13.7\%$
$E(R_B) = 0.1 \times 8 + 0.3 \times 8 + 0.4 \times 10 + 0.2 \times 10 = 9.2\%$
$E(R_M) = 0.1 \times 5 + 0.3 \times 10 + 0.4 \times 15 + 0.2 \times 20 = 13.5\%$

State	$\{R_S - E(R_S)\}\{R_M - E(R_M)\}\text{Pr}$	$\{R_B - E(R_B)\}\{R_M - E(R_M)\}\text{Pr}$
1	$(0.03-0.137)(0.05-0.135)\times0.1$	$(0.08-0.092)(0.05-0.135)\times0.1$
2	$(0.08-0.137)(0.10-0.135)\times0.3$	$(0.08-0.092)(0.10-0.135)\times0.3$
3	$(0.20-0.137)(0.15-0.135)\times0.4$	$(0.10-0.092)(0.15-0.135)\times0.4$
4	$(0.15-0.137)(0.20-0.135)\times0.2$	$(0.10-0.092)(0.20-0.135)\times0.2$
Sum	0.002056	0.00038
	$= \text{Cov}(R_S, R_M)$	$= \text{Cov}(R_B, R_M)$

$\sigma_M{}^2 = 0.1(0.05 - 0.135)^2 + 0.3(0.10-0.135)^2$
$\qquad + 0.4(0.15-0.135)^2 + 0.2(0.20-0.135)^2$
$\qquad = 0.002025$

a. Beta of debt $= \text{Cov}(R_B, R_M) / \sigma_M{}^2 = 0.00038 / 0.002025$
$\qquad = 0.188$
b. Beta of stock $= \text{Cov}(R_S, R_M) / \sigma_M{}^2 = 0.002055 / 0.002025$
$\qquad = 1.015$
c. $B / S = 0.5$
Thus, $B / (S + B) = 1 / 3 = 0.3333$
$\qquad S / (S + B) = 2 / 3 = 0.6667$
Beta of asset $= 0.188 \times 0.3333 + 1.015 \times 0.6667$
$\qquad = 0.739$

12.10   The discount rate for the project should be lower than the rate implied by the use of the Security Market Line. The appropriate discount rate for such projects is the weighted average of the interest rate on debt and the cost of equity. Since the interest rate on the debt of a given firm is generally less than the firm's cost of equity, using only the stock's beta yields a discount rate that is too high. The concept and practical uses of a weighted average discount rate will be in a later chapter.

12.11
  i.   Revenues
        The gross income of the firm is an important factor in determining beta. Firms whose revenues are cyclical (fluctuate with the business cycle) generally have high betas. Firms whose revenues are not cyclical tend to have lower betas.
  ii.   Operating leverage
        Operating leverage is the percentage change in earnings before interest and taxes (EBIT) for a percentage change in sales, [(Change in EBIT / EBIT) (Sales / Change in sales)]. Operating leverage indicates the ability of the firm to service its debt and pay stockholders.
  iii. Financial leverage
        Financial leverage arises from the use of debt. Financial leverage indicates the ability of the firm to pay stockholders. Since debt holders must be paid before stockholders, the higher the financial leverage of the firm, the riskier its stock.

        The beta of common stock is a function of all three of these factors. Ultimately, the riskiness of the stock, of which beta captures a portion, is determined by the fluctuations in the income available to the stockholders. (As was discussed in the chapter, whether income is paid to the stockholders in the form of dividends or it is retained to finance projects are irrelevant as long as the projects are of similar risk as the firm.) The income available to common stock, the net income of the firm, depends initially on the revenues or sales of the firm. The operating leverage indicates how much of each dollar of revenue will become EBIT. Financial leverage indicates how much of each dollar of EBIT will become net income.

12.12 a.   Cost of equity for National Napkin
            $= 7 + 1.29 (13 - 7)$
            $= 14.74\%$
     b. $B / (S + B) = S / (S + B) = 0.5$
            $WACC = 0.5 \times 7 \times 0.65 + 0.5 \times 14.74$
                $= 9.645\%$

12.13 $B = \$60 \text{ million} \times 1.2 = \$72 \text{ million}$
      $S = \$20 \times 5 \text{ million} = \$100 \text{ million}$
      $B / (S + B) = 72 / 172 = 0.4186$
      $S / (S + B) = 100 / 172 = 0.5814$
      $WACC = 0.4186 \times 12\% \times 0.75 + 0.5814 \times 18\%$
            $= 14.23\%$

Answers to End-of-Chapter Problems

12.14 $S = \$25 \times 20$ million $= \$500$ million
  $B = 0.95 \times \$180$ million $= \$171$ million
  $B / (S + B) = 0.2548$
  $S / (S + B) = 0.7452$
  $\text{WACC} = 0.7452 \times 20\% + 0.2548 \times 10\% \times 0.60$
  $\qquad = 16.43\%$

12.15 $\qquad B / S = 0.75$
  $B / (S + B) = 3 / 7$
  $S / (S + B) = 4 / 7$
  $\text{WACC} = (4 / 7) \times 15\% + (3 / 7) \times 9\% \times (1 - 0.35)$
  $\qquad = 11.08\%$

  $\text{NPV} = -\$25 \text{ million} + \sum_{t=1}^{5} \frac{\$7\text{million}}{(1 + 0.1108)^{t}}$

  $\qquad = \$819,299.04$
  Undertake the project.

12.16 $\text{WACC} = (0.5) \times 28\% + (0.5) \times 10\% \times (1 - 0.35)$
  $\qquad = 17.25\%$
  $\text{NPV} = -\$1,000,000 + (1 - 0.35) \$600,000 \ A_{0.1725}^{5}$
  $\qquad = \$240,608.50$

Mini Case: Allied Products

Assumptions

PP&E Investment	42,000,000
Useful life of PP&E Investment (years)	7
Salvage Value of PP&E Investment	12,000,000

Annual Depreciation Expense (7 year MACRS)

	Year	MACRS %	Depreciation	Ending Book Value
	1	14.29%	6,001,800	35,998,200
	2	24.49%	10,285,800	25,712,400
	3	17.49%	7,345,800	18,366,600
	4	12.49%	5,245,800	13,120,800
Last year of project	5	8.93%	3,750,600	9,370,200
	6	8.93%	3,750,600	5,619,600
	7	8.93%	3,750,600	1,869,000
	8	4.45%	1,869,000	0

NEW GPWS price/unit (Year 1)	70,000
NEW GPWS variable cost/unit (Year 1)	50,000
UPGRADE GPWS price/unit (Year 1)	35,000
UPGRADE GPWS variable cost/unit (Year 1)	22,000
Year 1 marketing and admin costs	3,000,000
Annual inflation rate	3.00%
Corporate Tax rate	40.00%
Beta (9/27 Valueline)	1.20
Rf (30 year U.S. Treasury Bond)	6.20%
Rm (S&P 500 30 year average)	14.50%
Re (from CAPM) $R_S = 6.2\% + 1.2 (14.5\% - 6.2\%)$	16.16%
WACC $= 0.5(6.2\%)(1\text{-}40\%) + 0.5(16.16\%)$	9.9400%

New Aircraft Production (i.e. NEW GPWS Market)

	Probability	Year 1	Year 2	Year 3	Year 4	Year 5
Strong Growth	0.15	350	403	463	532	612
Moderate Growth	0.45	250	275	303	333	366
Mild Recession	0.30	150	159	169	179	189
Severe Recession	0.10	50	52	53	55	56
Expected New Airplane Production		215	237	261	289	319

NEW GPWS Market Growth (Strong Growth)	15.00%
NEW GPWS Market Growth (Moderate Growth)	10.00%
NEW GPWS Market Growth (Mild Recession)	6.00%
NEW GPWS Market Growth (Severe Recession state of economy)	3.00%
Total Annual Market for UPGRADE GPWS (units)	2,500
Allied Signal Market Share in each market	45.00%

Answers to End-of-Chapter Problems

Year	0	1	2	3	4	5
Sales						
NEW						
Units		97	107	118	130	144
Price		70,000	72,100	74,263	76,491	78,786
Total NEW		6,772,500	7,688,654	8,736,317	9,935,345	11,308,721
UPGRADE						
Units		1,125	1,125	1,125	1,125	1,125
Price		35,000	36,050	37,132	38,245	39,393
Total UPGRADE		39,375,000	40,556,250	41,772,938	43,026,126	44,316,909
Total Sales		46,147,500	48,244,904	50,509,254	52,961,470	55,625,630
Variable Costs						
NEW		4,837,500	5,491,896	6,240,226	7,096,675	8,077,658
UPGRADE		24,750,000	25,492,500	26,257,275	27,044,993	27,856,343
Total Variable Costs		29,587,500	30,984,396	32,497,501	34,141,668	35,934,001
SG&A		3,000,000	3,090,000	3,182,700	3,278,181	3,376,526
Depreciation		6,001,800	10,285,800	7,345,800	5,245,800	3,750,600
EBIT		7,558,200	3,884,708	7,483,253	10,295,821	12,564,503
Interest		0	0	0	0	0
Tax		3,023,280	1,553,883	2,993,301	4,118,329	5,025,801
Net Income		4,534,920	2,330,825	4,489,952	6,177,493	7,538,702
EBIT + Dep - Taxes		10,536,720	12,616,625	11,835,752	11,423,293	11,289,302
Less: Change in NWC	2,000,000	307,375	104,870	113,218	122,611	(2,648,074)
Less: Captial Spending	42,000,000					(10,948,080)
CF from Assets:	(44,000,000)	10,229,345	12,511,755	11,722,534	11,300,682	24,885,455
Discounted CF from Assets		9,304,480	10,351,583	8,821,741	7,735,381	15,494,120
Total Discounted CF from Assets		51,707,305				
Less: Investment		(44,000,000)				
Net Present Value		**$ 7,707,305**				

Results

Payback	3.93 years
Discounted Payback	4.50 years
AAR	20.81%
IRR	15.76%
NPV	$7,707,305
PI	1.18

Chapter 13: Corporate-Financing Decisions and Efficient Capital Markets

13.1 a.   Firms should accept financing proposals with positive net present values (NPVs).
    b.   Firms can create valuable financing opportunities through the use of subsidies and inside information, or by lowering their transaction costs.

13.2
Weak form: Prices reflect all information contained in historical data.
Semi-strong form: In addition to historical data, prices reflect all publicly available information.
Strong form: Prices reflect all information, public or private.

13.3 a.   False: Market efficiency implies prices reflect all available information, but it does not imply certain knowledge. Many pieces of information that are available and reflected in prices are somewhat uncertain. Efficiency of markets does not eliminate that uncertainty and therefore does not imply perfect forecasting ability.

    b.   True: Market efficiency exists when prices reflect all available information. To be weak form efficient, the market must incorporate all historical data into prices. Under the semi-strong form of the hypothesis, the market incorporates all publicly available information in addition to the historical data. In a strong form efficient market, prices reflect all publicly and privately available information.

    c.   False: Market efficiency implies that market participants are rational. Rational people will immediately act upon new information and they will bid prices up or down to reflect that information.

    d.   False: Since in efficient markets prices reflect all available information, prices will fluctuate whenever new information becomes available.

    e.   True: Without competition among investors, information could not be readily transmitted. Without quick transmission of information, prices would not reflect the information immediately and markets would not be efficient.

13.4
    a.   Aerotech's stock price should rise immediately after the announcement of this positive news.
    b.   Only scenario *ii* (the stock price jumps to $116 and remains there) indicates market efficiency. In that case, the price rose immediately to the level that eliminated all possibility of abnormal returns. In the other two scenarios, there are periods of time during which an investor could trade on the information and earn abnormal returns.

13.5 False. In an efficient market, the stock price would have adjusted before the founder's death only if investors had perfect forecasting ability. The 12.5% increase in the stock price after the founder's death indicates that either the market did not anticipate the death or it anticipated it imperfectly. Since the market reacted to new information, it was efficient. It is interesting that the stock rice rose after the announcement of the founder's death. This price behavior indicates that the market felt he was a liability to the firm.

13.6 Investors should not be deterred from buying UPC's stock because of the announcement. If the market is at least semi-strong form efficient, the stock price will have already reflected the present value of the payments that UPC must make. Buying the stock at the post-announcement price should provide the same return that the stock was providing before the announcement. (NOTE: UPC's current stockholders bear the burden of the loss. At the time of the announcement, returns would have been abnormally low. After the information was incorporated into the price, returns are normal again.)

13.7 The market is generally considered to be efficient up to the semi-strong form, which means that no systematic profit can be made by trading on publicly available information. The lead engineer of the device can profit from purchasing the firm's stock before the news release on the implementation of the new technology because she can trade on insider information. As the information on the new technology becomes publicly available, nobody can profit from rushing into the stock market based on Wall Street Journal articles.

13.8 Given that semi-strong form of market efficiency holds approximately in the real world, the stock price should stay the same. The accounting system changes are publicly available information. The investors would know that in essence, there is no change in the operational, and the financial state of the firm's current and future cash flows. So the stock price will not change after the announcement of increased earnings.

13.9 No, Alex cannot make money by investing in firms that just issued public stock based on the fact that these firms performed better than others. If they are considered better performing firms, the market's expectation of their current and future cash flows would already have been raised to a higher level and reflected in the current stock prices. No abnormal profit can be made since the purchasing prices of the stocks would have already been commensurate with the higher expected earning powers.

13.10 Because the number of subscribers has increased dramatically, the time it takes for information in the newsletters to be reflected in prices has shortened. With shorter adjustment periods, it becomes impossible to earn abnormal returns with the information provided by Sooners.

13.11 You should not agree with your broker. The performance ratings of the small manufacturing firms were published, and therefore, public information. An efficient market would incorporate that information into the prices of the firms' shares such that abnormal returns could not be reaped. Indeed, in an efficient market you should not expect these firms to earn above-average returns.

13.12 By the time the Wall Street Journal comes out, the stock price reaction would have already taken place. Since semi-strong form of market efficiency holds, nobody can systematically profit from this publicly available information.

13.13 Technical analysis is not consistent with EMH. Technical analysts can't systematically profit from trading rules based on historical stock prices. If technical analysts can systematically profit from trading rules based on patterns in the historical stock price, then weak form of market efficiency is violated.

13.14 One explanation given to the 1987 market crash and the high price to earnings ratio of Japanese market is the bubble theory. It tries to interpret the deviation from EMH by the fluctuation of investor sentiments and psychology. Namely, the fluctuation in investor sentiments and psychology lead to abnormal prices.

13.15 a.   In an efficient market, the CAR for Prospectors would rise substantially at the announcement of a new discovery. Then it should remain constant until the next discovery.

   b.   As long as there is no relationship between the discovery of one vein and another, the CAR is a random walk.

   c.   The behavior of Prospectors' CAR is consistent with market efficiency. Although the market knows the miners will eventually find another vein, it does not incorporate the increase in value into the stock price until the announcement is made.

13.16 Abnormal Return ($R_i - R_m$):

Days from announcement	Delta	United	Pan Am	Sum	Average abnormal return	Cumulative average residual
-4	-0.2	-0.2	-0.2	-0.6	-0.2	-0.2
-3	0.2	-0.1	0.2	0.3	0.1	-0.1
-2	0.2	-0.2	0.0	0.0	0.0	-0.1
-1	0.2	0.2	-0.4	0.0	0.0	-0.1
0	3.3	0.2	1.9	5.4	1.8	1.7
1	0.2	0.1	0.0	0.3	0.1	1.8
2	-0.1	0.0	0.1	0.0	0.0	1.8
3	-0.2	0.1	-0.2	-0.3	-0.1	1.7
4	-0.1	-0.1	-0.1	-0.3	-0.1	1.6

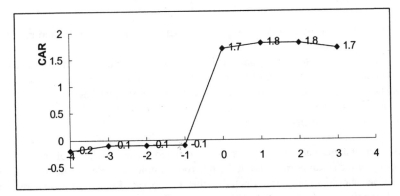

Days from announcement

The market reacts favorably to the announcements of acquisition of new planes. Moreover, it reacts only on the day of the announcement. Before and after the event, the CARs are relatively flat and they jump only on the day of the event. This CAR behavior demonstrates market efficiency.

13.17 This diagram does not support the efficient markets hypothesis. After the announcement of a discovery, the CAR should remain relatively flat at the level it attained on the event day.

13.18 The diagram is not consistent with the efficient markets hypothesis (EMH). The diagram is consistent with the EMH through the event day. After the announcement of the court decision, the CAR declines which would allow investors to earn undue returns. As facts about the case are released during the litigation, returns may fluctuate. Once the case is resolved, such price behavior should stop. Thus, the CAR should remain constant even if an appeal is in progress.

13.19 Figure A: Supports - Until day zero, the CAR was falling due to the release of negative information. After the event the CAR is constant.

Figure B: Supports - Again returns are not moving up or down after the event.

Figure C: Rejects - Because returns increase after the event date, it is possible to formulate advantageous trades. Such possibilities are inconsistent with the efficient markets hypothesis.

Figure D: Supports - the diagram indicates that the information was of no value.

13.20 The scenario depicts a case in which the knowledge that the marketable securities were worth more than the market value of Kennecott Copper was not public. It was not until Arco purchased Kennecott that the information became public. (Kennecott managers may even have been unaware of the situation.) Since no public information was available about the securities' values, semi-strong form efficiency is not in doubt. Also, it is possible that other Kennecott assets had negative NPVs that outweighed the positive value of the marketable securities.

13.21 a. No. Earnings information is in the public domain and therefore, reflected in the current stock price.

b. Possibly. If the rumors were publicly disseminated, the prices would have already accounted for the probability of a merger. If the rumor is information that you got from an insider, you could earn excess returns, but clearly, trading on that information is illegal.

c. No. Again, the information is already public.

13.22 Your stock price changes should not be serially correlated. If the market is efficient, the information about the serial correlation in the macroeconomic variable and its relationship to the stock price should already be reflected in the stock price. Remember, correlation of pieces of information is information itself !

13.23   The statement is false because every investor has different risk preference. Although the expected return from every well-diversified portfolio is the same after adjusting for the risk, investors still need to choose funds that are consistent with their particular risk level to invest.

13.24 a.   There are mixed empirical findings concerning price pressure of block trading. On the one hand, Scholes found that there is no price pressure effect. On the other hand, Kraus and Stoll found clear evidence of price pressure effects although the effects were very small. Practitioners generally believe that the sale of large blocks of shares can temporarily depress the price of a company's stock.

     b.   It might be a good idea for the block seller to break a very large block into several lots to reduce a potentially large price pressure effect.

     c.   If the EMH holds, the expected price effect will be zero.

13.25   c

Chapter 14: Long-Term Financing: An Introduction

14.1 a. $\dfrac{\text{Common Stock Account}}{\text{Par Value}} = \dfrac{\$135,430}{\$2} = 67,715$ shares

   b.   Net capital from the sale of shares = Common Stock + Capital Surplus
   Net capital = $135,430 + $203,145 = $338,575
   Therefore, the average price is $338,575 / 67,715 = $5 per share

   Alternate solution:
   Average price = Par value + Average capital surplus
   $\qquad\qquad$ = $2 + $203,145 / 67,715
   $\qquad\qquad$ = $5 per share

   c.   Book value = Assets - Liabilities = Equity
   $\qquad\qquad$ = Common stock + Capital surplus + Retained earnings
   $\qquad\qquad$ = $2,708,600

   Therefore, book value per share is $2,708,600 / 67,715= $40.

14.2 a.   Common stock = (Shares outstanding) x (Par value)
   $\qquad\qquad$ = 500 x $1
   $\qquad\qquad$ = $500
   Total = $150,500

   b.

Common stock (1500 shares outstanding, $1 par)	$1,500
Capital surplus*	79,000
Retained earnings	100,000
Total	$180,500

   * Capital Surplus = Old surplus + Surplus on sale
   $\qquad\qquad$ = $50,000 + ($30 - $1) x 1,000
   $\qquad\qquad$ =$79,000

14.3 a.

Shareholders' equity	
Common stock ($5 par value; authorized 500,000 shares; issued and outstanding 325,000 shares)	$1,625,000
Capital in excess of par*	195,000
Retained earnings**	3,794,600
Total	$5,614,600

   *Capital surplus = 12% of Common Stock
   $\qquad\qquad$ = (0.12) ($1,625,000)
   $\qquad\qquad$ = $195,000
   **Retained earnings = Old retained earnings + Net income - Dividends
   $\qquad\qquad$ = $3,545,000 + $260,000 - ($260,000)(0.04)
   $\qquad\qquad$ = 3,794,600

b.

Shareholders' equity

Common stock ($5 par value; authorized 500,000 shares; issued and outstanding 350,000 shares)	$1,750,000
Capital in excess of par*	170,000
Retained earnings	3,794,600
Total	$5,714,600

*Capital surplus is reduced by the below par sale, i.e. $195,000 - ($1)(25,000) = $170,000

14.4 a.   Under straight voting, one share equals one vote. Thus, to ensure the election of one director you must hold a majority of the shares. Since two million shares are outstanding, you must hold more than 1,000,000 shares to have a majority of votes.

b.   Cumulative voting is often more easily understood through a story. Remember that your goal is to elect one board member of the seven who will be chosen today. Suppose the firm has 28 shares outstanding. You own 4 of the shares and one other person owns the remaining 24 shares. Under cumulative voting, the total number of votes equals the number of shares times the number of directors being elected, $(28)(7) = 196$. Therefore, you have 28 votes and the other stockholder has 168 votes.

Also, suppose the other shareholder does not wish to have your favorite candidate on the board. If that is true, the best you can do to try to ensure electing one member is to place all of your votes on your favorite candidate. To keep your candidate off the board, the other shareholder must have enough votes to elect all seven members who will be chosen. If the other shareholder splits her votes evenly across her seven favorite candidates, then eight people, your one favorite and her seven favorites, will all have the same number of votes. There will be a tie! If she does not split her votes evenly (for example 29 28 28 28 28 28 27) then your candidate will win a seat. To avoid a tie and assure your candidate of victory, you must have 29 votes which means you must own more than 4 shares.

Notice what happened. If seven board members will be elected and you want to be certain that one of your favorite candidates will win, you must have more than one-eighth of the shares. That is, the percentage of the shares you must have to win is more than

$$\frac{1}{(\text{The number of members being elected} + \text{The number you want to select})}.$$

Also notice that the number of shares you need does not change if more than one person owns the remaining shares. If several people owned the remaining 168 shares they could form a coalition and vote together.

Thus, in the Unicorn election, you will need more than $1/(7+1) = 12.5\%$ of the shares to elect one board member. You will need more than $(2,000,000)(0.125) = 250,000$ shares.

Cumulative voting can be viewed more rigorously. Use the facts from the Unicorn election. Under cumulative voting, the total number of votes equals the number of shares times the number of directors being elected, 2,000,000 x 7 = 14,000,000. Let x be the number of shares you need. The number of shares necessary is

$$7x > \frac{14,000,000 - 7x}{7} ==> x > 250,000.$$ You will need more than 250,000 shares.

14.5   She can be certain to have one of her candidate friends be elected under the cumulative voting rule. The lowest percentage of shares she needs to own to elect at least one out of 6 candidates is higher than $1/7 = 14.3\%$. Her current ownership of 17.3% is more than enough to ensure one seat. If the voting rule is staggered as described in the question, she would need to own more than $1/4 = 25\%$ of the shares to elect one out of the three candidates for certain. In this case, she will not have enough shares.

14.6   a.   You currently own 120 shares or 28.57% of the outstanding shares. You need to control 1/3 of the votes, which requires 140 shares. You need just over 20 additional shares to elect yourself to the board.

   b.   You need just over 25% of the shares, which is 250,000 shares. At $5 a share it will cost you $2,500,000 to guarantee yourself a seat on the board.

14.7   The differences between preferred stock and debt are:

   a.   The dividends of preferred stock cannot be deducted as interest expenses when determining taxable corporate income. From the individual investor's point of view, preferred dividends are ordinary income for tax purposes. From corporate investors, 80% of the amount they receive as dividends from preferred stock are exempt from income taxes.

   b.   In liquidation, the seniority of preferred stock follows that of the debt and leads that of the common stock.

   c.   There is no legal obligation for firms to pay out preferred dividends as opposed to the obligated payment of interest on bonds. Therefore, firms cannot be forced into default if a preferred stock dividend is not paid in a given year. Preferred dividends can be cumulative or non-cumulative, and they can also be deferred indefinitely.

14.8   Some firms can benefit from issuing preferred stock. The reasons can be:

   a.   Public utilities can pass the tax disadvantage of issuing preferred stock on to their customers, so there is substantial amount of straight preferred stock issued by utilities.

   b.   Firms reporting losses to the IRS already don't have positive income for tax deduction, so they are not affected by the tax disadvantage of dividend vs. interest payment. They may be willing to issue preferred stock.

   c.   Firms that issue preferred stock can avoid the threat of bankruptcy that exists with debt financing because preferred dividends are not legal obligation as interest payment on corporate debt.

14.9 a.   The return on non-convertible preferred stock is lower than the return on corporate bond for two reasons:

   i. Corporate investors receive 80% tax deductibility on dividends if they hold the stock. Therefore, they are willing to pay more for the stock; that lowers its return.

   ii. Issuing corporations are willing and able to offer higher returns on debt since the interest on the debt reduces their tax liabilities. Preferred dividends are paid out of net income, hence they provide no tax shield.

   b.   Corporate investors are the primary holders of preferred stock since, unlike individual investors, they can deduct 80% of the dividend when computing their tax liability. Therefore, they are willing to accept the lower return which the stock generates.

14.10 The following table summarizes the main difference between debt and equity.

	Debt	Equity
Repayment is an obligation of the firm	Yes	No
Grants ownership of the firm	No	Yes
Provides a tax shield	Yes	No
Liquidation will result if not paid	Yes	No

Companies often issue hybrid securities because of the potential tax shield and the bankruptcy advantage. If the IRS accepts the security as debt, the firm can use it as a tax shield. If the security maintains the bankruptcy and ownership advantages of equity, the firm has the best of both worlds.

14.11 The trends in long-term financing in the United States were presented in the text. If Cable Company follows the trends, it will probably use 80% internal financing, net income of the project plus depreciation less dividends, and 20% external financing, long term debt and equity.

Chapter 15: Capital Structure: Basic Concepts

15.1 a. The value of Nadus' stock is ($20)(5,000) = $100,000. Since Nadus is an all-equity firm, $100,000 is also the value of the firm.

b. The value of any firm is the sum of the market value of its bonds and the market value of its stocks, i.e. V=B+S, For Logis, the value of the stock is not yet known, nor is the value of the firm. The market value of Logis' bonds is $25,000. Thus, the value of Logis' stock is
S=V - $25,000.

c. Costs:
    Nadus: 0.20 ($100,000) = $20,000
    Logis: 0.20 (V - $25,000)
Returns: You are entitled to 20% of the net income of each firm.
    Nadus: 0.20 ($350,000) = $70,000
    Logis: 0.20 [$350,000-0.12($25,000)] = $69,400

d. From the standpoint of the stockholders, Logis is riskier. If you hold Logis stock, you can receive returns only after the bondholders have been paid.

e. In this problem, positive signs denote negative signs denote all cash inflows and all outflows. You should expect the immediate flows to be on net negative (an outflow). The future flows should be on net positive (an inflow).

Immediate flows:	
Borrow from the bank an amount equal to 20% of Logis' debt	$5,000
Buy 20% of Nadus' stock	-20,000
Total Immediate Flows	-$15,000

Future flows:	
Pay the interest on the loan 0.12 ($5,000)	-$600
Receive 20% of Nadus' net income	70,000
Total Future Flows	$69,400

f. Since the returns from the purchase of the Logis stock are the same as the returns in the strategy you constructed in part e, the two investments must cost the same.
Cost of the strategy = Cost of Logis stock
$15,000 = 0.20 (V-$25,000)
Therefore, V=$100,000
Note: This is an application of MM-Proposition I, In this MM world with no taxes and no financial distress costs, the value of an levered firm will equal the value of an un-levered firm. Thus, capital structure does not matter.

g. If the value of the Logis firm is $135,000 then the value of Logis stock is $110,000 (= $135,000 - $25,000). If that is true, purchasing 20% of Logis' stock would cost you $22,000 (= 0.20 x $110,000). You will receive the same return as before ($69,400). You can receive the same return for only $15,000 by following the strategy in part e. Thus, if Logis is worth $135,000, you should borrow on your own account an amount equal to 20% of Logis' debt and purchase 20% of Nadus' stock.

15.2 a.   B=$10 million   S=$20 million
            Therefore, B/S=$10 / $20 = 1/2
      b.   The required return is the firm's after-tax overall cost of capital. In this no tax
            world, that is simply

$$r_0 = \frac{B}{V} r_B + \frac{S}{V} r_S$$

Use CAPM to find the required return on equity.

$$r_S = 8\% + (0.9)(10\%) = 17\%$$

The cost of debt is 14%.
Therefore,

$$r_0 = \frac{\$10 \text{ million}}{\$30 \text{ million}} 0.14 + \frac{\$20 \text{ million}}{\$30 \text{ million}} 0.17 = 16\%$$

15.3 You expect to earn a 20% return on your investment of $25,000. Thus, you are earning
      $5,000 (=$25,000 x 0.20) per year. Since you borrowed $75,000, you will be making
      interest payments of $7,500 (=$75,000 x 0.10) per annum. Your share of the stock must
      earn $12,500 (= $5,000 + $7,500). The return without leverage is 0.125 (=$12,500 /
      $100,000).

15.4 The firms are identical except for their capital structures. Thus, under MM-Proposition I
      their market values must be the same regardless of their capital structures. If they are not
      equal, the lower valued stock is a better purchase.
      Market values:
      Levered: V=$275 million + $100 x 4.5 million = $725 million
      Unlevered: V= $80 x 10 million = $800 million

      Since Levered's market value is less than Unlevered's market value, you should buy
      Levered's stock. To understand why, construct the strategies that were presented in the
      text. Suppose you want to own 5% of the equity of each firm.

      Strategy One: Buy 5% of Unlevered's equity
      Strategy Two: Buy 5% of Levered's equity
      Strategy Three: Create the dollar returns of Levered through borrowing an amount equal to
                      5% of Levered's debt and purchasing 5% of Unlevered's stock. If you
                      follow this strategy you will own what amounts to 5% of the equity of
                      Levered. The reason why is that the dollar returns will be identical to
                      purchasing 5% of Levered outright.

	Dollar Investment	Dollar Return
Strategy One:	-(0.05)($800)	(0.05)($96)
Strategy Two:	-(0.05)($450)	(0.05)[$96 - (0.08)($275)]
Strategy Three:		
Borrow	(0.05)($275)	-[(0.05) ($275)] (0.08)
Buy Unlevered	-(0.05)($800)	(0.05)($96)
Net $ Flows	-(0.05)($525)	(0.05)[$96 - (0.08)($275)]

Note: Dollar amounts are in millions.
Note: Negative signs denote outflows and positive denotes inflows.

Since the payoffs to strategies Two and Three are identical, their costs should be the same. Yet, strategy three is more expensive than strategy two ($26.25 million versus $22.5 million). Thus, Levered's stock is underpriced relative to Unlevered's stock. You should purchase Levered's stock.

15.5 a. In this MM world, the market value of Veblen must be the same as the market value of Knight. If they are not equal, an investor can improve his net returns through borrowing and buying Veblen stock. To understand the improvement, construct the strategies discussed in the text. The investor already owns 0.0058343 (=$10,000 / $1,714,000) of the equity of Knight. Suppose he is willing to purchase the same amount of Veblen's equity.

Strategy One (SI):   Buy 0.58343% of Veblen's equity.
Strategy Two (SII): Continue to hold the 0.58343% of Knight's equity.
Strategy Three (SIII): Create the dollar returns of Knight through borrowing an amount equal to 0.58343% of Knight's debt and purchasing 0.58343% of Veblen's stock. If you follow this strategy you will own what amounts to 0.58343% of the equity of Knight. The reason why is that the dollar returns will be identical to purchasing 0.58343% of Knight outright.

	Dollar Investment	Dollar Return
SI:	-(0.0058343)($2.4)	(0.0058343)($0.3)
SII:	-(0.0058343)($1.714)	(0.0058343)($0.24)
SIII:		
Borrow	(0.0058343)($1)	-[(0.0058343) ($1)] (0.06)
Buy Veblen	-(0.0058343)($2.4)	(0.0058343)($0.3)
Net $ Flows	-(0.0058343)($1.4)	(0.0058343)($0.24)

Note: Dollar amounts are in millions.
Note: Negative signs denote outflows and positive denotes inflows.

Since strategies Two and Three have the same payoffs, they should cost the same. Strategy three is cheaper, thus, Knight stock is overpriced relative to Veblen stock. An investor can benefit by selling the Knight stock, borrowing an amount equal to 0.0058343 of Knights debt and buying the same portion of Veblen stock. The investor's dollar returns will be identical to holding the Knight stock, but the cost will be less.

b. Modigliani and Miller argue that everyone would attempt to construct the strategy. Investors would attempt to follow the strategy and the act of them doing so will lower the market value of Knight and raise the market value of Veblen until they are equal.

15.6 Each lady has purchased shares of the all-equity NLAW and borrowed or lent to create the net dollar returns she desires. Once NLAW becomes levered, the return that the ladies receive for owning stock will be decreased by the interest payments. Thus, to continue to receive the same net dollar returns, each lady must rebalance her portfolio. The easiest approach to this problem is to consider each lady individually. Determine the dollar returns that the investor would receive from an all-equity NLAW. Determine what she will receive from the firm if it is levered. Then adjust her borrowing or lending position to create the returns she received from the all-equity firm.

Before looking at the women's positions, look at the firm value.
All-equity: V=100,000 x $50 = $5,000,000
Levered: V=$1,000,000 + 80,000 x $50 = $5,000,000
Remember, the firm repurchased 20,000 shares.

The income of the firm is unknown. Since we need it to compute the investor's returns, we will denote it as Y. Assume that the income of the firm does not change due to the capital restructuring and that it is constant for the foreseeable future.

Ms. A before rebalancing: Ms. A owns $10,000 worth of NLAW stock. That ownership represents ownership of 0.002 (=$10,000/$5,000,000) of the all-equity firm. That ownership entitles her to receive 0.002 of the firm's income; i.e. her dollar return is 0.002Y. Also, Ms. A has borrowed $2,000. That loan will require her to make an interest payment of $400 ($2,000 x 0.20). Thus, the dollar investment and dollar return positions of Ms. A are:

	Dollar Investment	Dollar Return
NLAW Stock	-$10,000	0.002Y
Borrowing	2,000	-$400
Net	-$8,000	0.002Y-$400

Note: Negative signs denote outflows and positive denotes inflows.

Ms. A after rebalancing: After rebalancing, Ms. A will want to receive net dollar returns of 0.002Y-$400. The only way to receive the 0.002Y is to own 0.002 of NLAW's stock. Examine the returns she will receive from the levered NLAW if she owns 0.002 of the firm's equity. She will receive $(0.002) [Y - (\$1,000,000)(0.20)] = 0.002Y - \$400$. This is exactly the dollar return she desires! Therefore, Ms. A should own 0.002 of the levered firm's equity and neither lends nor borrow. Owning 0.002 of the firm's equity means she has $8,000 (= 0.0002 x $4,000,000) invested in NLAW stock.

	Dollar Investment	Dollar Return
NLAW stock	-$8,000	0.002Y - $400

Ms. B before rebalancing: Ms. B owns $50,000 worth of NLAW stock. That ownership represents ownership of 0.01 (=$50,000/$5,000,000) of the all-equity firm. That ownership entitles her to receive 0.01 of the firm's income; i.e. her dollar return is 0.01Y. Also, Ms. B has lent $6,000. That loan will generate interest income for her of the amount $1,200 (=$6,000 x 0.20). Thus, the dollar investment and dollar return positions of Ms. B are:

	Dollar Investment	Dollar Return
NLAW Stock	-$50,000	0.01Y
Lending	-6,000	$1,200
Net	-$56,000	0.01Y + $1,200

Ms. B after rebalancing: After rebalancing, Ms. B will want to receive net dollar returns of 0.01Y + $1,200. The only way to receive the 0.01Y is to own 0.01 of NLAW's stock. Examine the returns she will receive from the levered NLAW if she owns 0.01 of the firm's equity. She will receive $(0.01) [Y - (\$1,000,000) (0.20)] = 0.01Y - \$2,000$. This is not the return which Ms. B desires, so she must lend enough money to generate interest income of $3,200 (=$2,000 + $1,200). Since the interest rate is 20% she must lend

$16,000 (= $3,200 / 0.20). The 0.01 equity interest of Ms. B means she will have $40,000 (=0.01 x $4,000,000) invested in NLAW.

	Dollar Investment	Dollar Return
NLAW Stock	-$40,000	0.01Y - $2,000
Lending	-16,000	$3,200
Net	-$56,000	0.01Y + $1,200

Ms. C before rebalancing: Ms. C owns $20,000 worth of NLAW stock. That ownership represents ownership of 0.004 (=$20,000 / $5,000,000) of the all-equity firm. That ownership entitles her to receive 0.004 of the firm's income; i.e. her dollar return is 0.004Y. The dollar investment and dollar return positions of Ms. A are:

	Dollar Investment	Dollar Return
NLAW Stock	-$20,000	0.004Y

Ms. C after rebalancing: After rebalancing, Ms. C will want to receive net dollar returns of 0.004Y. The only way to receive the 0.004Y is to own 0.004 of NLAW's stock. Examine the returns she will receive from the levered NLAW if she owns 0.004 of the firm's equity. She will receive (0.004) [Y - ($1,000,000) (0.20)] = 0.004Y - $800. This is not the dollar return she desires. Therefore, Ms. C must lend enough money to offset the $800 she loses once the firm becomes levered. Since the interest rate is 20% she must lend $4,000 (=$800 / 0.20). The 0.004 equity interest of Ms. C means she will have $16,000 (0.004 x $4,000,000) invested in NLAW.

	Dollar Investment	Dollar Return
NLAW Stock	-$16,000	0.004Y - $800
Lending	-4,000	$800
Net	-$20,000	0.004Y

15.7 a. Since Rayburn is currently an all-equity firm, the value of the firm's assets equals the value of its equity. Under MM-Proposition One, the value of a firm will not change due to a capital structure change, and the overall cost of capital will remain unchanged. Therefore, Rayburn's overall cost of capital is 18%.

b. MM-Proposition Two states $r_S = r_0 + (B/S)(r_0 - r_B)$.

Applying this formula you can find the cost of equity.

r_S = 18% + ($400,000 / $1,600,000) (18% - 10%) = 20%

c. In accordance with Proposition Two, the expected return on Rayburn's equity will rise with the amount of leverage. This rise occurs because of the risk which the debt adds.

15.8 a.

Strom, Inc.	
Old Assets = $750,000/0.15 = 5,000,000	Debt = 0
	Equity = $20 (250,000) = $5,000,000

b.
   i. According to efficient markets, Strom's stock price will rise immediately to reflect the NPV of the project.

  ii. The NPV of the facilities that Strom is buying is
NPV= -$300,000 + ($120,000 / 0.15) = $500,000
The sum of the old assets and the NPV of the new facilities is the new value of the firm ($5.5 million). Since new shares have not yet been sold, the price of the outstanding shares must rise. The new price is $5,500,000 / 250,000 = $22.

	Strom, Inc.
Old Assets = $750,000/0.15 = $5,000,000	Debt = 0
NPV of the new facilities = $500,000	Equity = $22 (250,000) = $5,500,000

  iii. Strom needed to raise $300,000 through the sale of stock that sells for $22. Thus, Strom sold 13,636.364 (=$300,000 / $22) shares.

  iv.

	Strom, Inc.
Old Assets = $750,000/0.15 = $5,000,000	Debt =0
NPV = $500,000	Equity =$22 (263,636.364) = $5,800,000
Cash from sale of stock = $300,000	

  v.

	Strom, Inc.
Old Assets = $750,000/0.15 = $5,000,000	Debt = 0
PV of the new facilities = $120,000 / 0.15 = $800,000	Equity = $22 (263,636.364) = $5,800,000

  vi. The returns available to the shareholders are the sum of the returns from each portion of the firm.
Total earnings = $750,000 + $120,000 = $870,000
Return = ($870,000 / $5,800,000) = 15%

Note: The returns to the shareholder had to be the same since r_0 was unchanged and the firm added no debt.

c.
   i.

	Strom, Inc.
Old Assets = $5,000,000	Debt = 0
NPV of the new facilities = 500,000	Equity = $22 (250,000) = $5,500,000

Under efficient markets the price of the shares must rise to reflect the NPV of the new facilities. The value will be the same as with all-equity financing because
1. Strom purchased the same competitor and
2. In this MM world debt is no better or no worse than equity.

11.

Strom, Inc.

Old Assets	= $5,000,000	Debt	= $300,000
PV of the new facilities =	500,000	Equity = $22 (250,000) = $5,500,000
Cash from sale of bonds =	300,000		

    iii. The cost of equity will be the earnings after interest and taxes divided by the market value of common. Since Strom pays no taxes, the cost of equity is simply the earnings after interest (EAI) divided by the market value of common.
      EAI = $750,000 + $120,000 - $300,000 (0.10) = $840,000
      Cost of equity = $840,000 / $5,500,000 = 15.27%
    iv. The debt causes the equity of the firm to be riskier. Remember, stockholders are residual owners of the firm.
    v. MM-Proposition Two states,
      $r_S = r_0 + (B / S)(r_0 - r_B) = 15\% + (\$300,000 / \$5,500,000)(15\% - 10\%) = 15.27\%$

    d.   Examine the final balance sheet for the firm and you will see that the price is $22 under each plan.

15.9 a.   The market value of the firm will be the present value of Gulf's earnings after the new plant is built. Since the firm is an all-equity firm, the overall required return is the required return on equity.
        Annual earnings = Original plant + New Plant
                   = $27 million + $3 million = $30 million
        Value = $30 million / 0.1 = $300 million

    b.   Gulf Power is in an MM world (no taxes, no costs of financial distress). Therefore, the value of the firm is unchanged by a change in the capital structure.

    c.   The overall required rate of return is also unchanged by the capital structure change. Thus, according to MM-Proposition Two, $r_S = r_0 + (B / S)(r_0 - r_B)$. The firm is valued at $300 million of which $20 million is debt. The remaining $280 million is the value of the stock.
      r_S = 10% + ($20 million / $280 million) (10% - 8%) = 10.14%

15.10 a.   False. Leverage increases both the risks of the stock and its expected return. MM point out that these two effects exactly cancel out each other and leave the price of the stock and the value of the firm invariant to leverage. Since leverage is being reduced in this firm, the risk of the shares is lower; however, the price of the stock remains the same in accordance with MM.

    b.   False. If moderate borrowing does not affect the probability of financial distress, then the required return on equity is proportional to the debt-equity ratio [i.e. $r_S = r_0 + (B / S)(r_0 - r_B)$]. Increasing the amount of debt will increase the return on equity.

15.11 a.

    i.   Individuals can borrow at the same interest rate at which firms borrow.
    ii. There are no taxes.
    iii. There are no costs of financial distress.

b.

i. If firms are able to borrow at a rate that is lower than that at which individuals borrow, then it is possible to increase the firm's value through borrowing. As the text discussed, since investors can purchase securities on margin, the individuals' effective rate is probably no higher than that of the firms.

ii. In the presence of corporate taxes, the value of the firm is positively related to the level of debt. Since interest payments are deductible, increasing debt minimizes tax expenditure and thus maximizes the value of the firm for the stockholders. As will be shown in the next chapter, personal taxes offset the positive effect of debt.

iii. Because these costs are substantial and stockholders eventually bear them, they are incentives to lower the amount of debt. This implies that the capital structure may matter. This topic will also be discussed more fully in the next chapter.

15.12 a and b.

Total investment in the firm's assets = $10 x 1million x 1% = $0.1 million

3 choices of financing	20% debt	40% debt	60% debt
Total asset investment	0.1	0.1	0.1
x ROA (15%)	0.015	0.015	0.015
- Interest	0.2 x 0.1 x0.1	0.4 x 0.1 x 0.1	0.6 x 0.1 x 0.1
Profit after interest	0.013	0.011	0.009
/ Investment in equity	0.1 x 0.8	0.1 x 0.6	0.1 x 0.4
ROE	16.25%	18.33%	22.5%

Susan can expect to earn $0.013 million, $0.011 million, and $0.009 million, respectively, from the correspondent three scenarios of financing choices, i.e. borrowing 20%, 40%, or 60% of the total investment. The respective returns on equity are 16.25%, 18.33% and 22.5%.

c. From part a and b, we can see that in an MM with no tax world, higher leverage brings about higher return on equity. The high ROE is due to the increased risk of equity while the WACC remains unchanged. See below.

WACC for 20% debt = 16.25% x 0.8 + 10% x 0.2 = 15%
WACC for 40% debt = 18.33% x 0.6 + 10% x 0.4 = 15%
WACC for 60% debt = 22.5% x 0.4 + 10% x 0.6 = 15%

This example is a case of homemade leverage, so the results are parallel to that of a leveraged firm.

15.13 Suppose individuals can borrow at the same rate as the corporation, there is no need for the firm to change its capital structure because of the different forecasts of earnings growth rates, as investors can always duplicate the leverage by creating homemade leverage. Different expectation of earnings growth rates can affect the expected return on assets. But this change is the result of the change in expected operating performance of the corporation and/or other macroeconomic factors. The leverage ratio is irrelevant here since we are in an MM without tax world.

Answers to End-of-Chapter Problems

15.14 a.   current debt = 0.75 / 10% = \$7.5 million
         current equity = 7.5 / 40% = \$18.75 million
         Total firm value = 7.5 + 18.75 = \$26.25 million

    b. r_s = earnings after interest/total equity value = \$(3.75 - .75)/\$18.75 = 16%
         r_B = 10%
         r_0 = (.4/1.4)(10%) + (1/1.4)(16%) = 14.29%
         r_s after repurchase = 14.29% + (50%)(14.29% - 10%) = 16.44%
         So, the return on equity would increase from 16% to 16.44% with the completion of
         the planned stock repurchase.

    c.   The stock price wouldn't change because in an MM world, there's no added value to
         a change in firm leverage. In other words, it's a zero NPV transaction.

15.15 a.   Since $V_L = V_U + T_C B$, $V_U = V_L - T_C B$. V_L = \$1,700,000, B = \$500,000 and T_C =
         0.34. Therefore, the value of the unlevered firm is
         V_U = \$1,700,000 - (0.34)(\$500,000) = \$1,530,000

    b.   Equity holders earn 20% after-tax in an all-equity firm. That amount is \$306,000
         (=\$1,530,000 x 0.20). The yearly, after-tax interest expense in the levered firm is
         \$33,000 [=\$500,000 x 0.10 (1-0.34)]. Thus, the after-tax earnings of the equity
         holders in a levered firm are \$273,000 (=\$306,000 - \$33,000). This amount is the
         firm's net income.

15.16 The initial market value of the equity is given as \$3,500,000. On a per share basis this is
       \$20 (=\$3,500,000 / 175,000). The firm buys back \$1,000,000 worth of shares, or 50,000 (=
       \$1,000,000 / \$20) shares.
       In this MM world with taxes,
       $V_L = V_U + T_C B$ = \$3,500,000 + (0.3) (\$1,000,000) = \$3,800,000
       Since V = B + S, the market value of the equity is \$2,800,000 (= \$3,800,000 - \$1,000,000).

15.17 a.   Since Streiber is an all-equity firm,
         V = EBIT (1 - T_C) / r_0 = \$2,500,000 (1 - 0.34) / 0.20 = \$8,250,000

    b. $V_L = V_U + T_C B$ = \$8,250,000 + (0.34)(\$600,000) = \$8,454,000

    c.   The presence of debt creates a tax shield for the firm. That tax shield has value and
         accounts for the increase in the value of the firm.

    d.   You are making the MM assumptions:
         i. No personal taxes
         ii. No costs of financial distress
         iii. Debt level of the firm is constant through time

15.18 a.   In this MM world with no financial distress costs, the value of the levered firm is
         given by $V_L = V_U + T_C B$. The value of the unlevered firm is V = EBIT (1 - T_C) / r_0.
         The market value of the debt of Olbet is B = \$200,000 / 0.08 = \$2,500,000.
         Therefore, V = \$1,200,000 (1 - 0.35) / 0.12 + (\$2,500,000) (0.35) = \$7,375,000

    b.   Since debt adds to the value of the firm, it implies that the firm should be financed
         entirely with debt if it wishes to maximize its value.

    c.   This conclusion is incorrect because it does not consider the costs of financial
         distress or other agency costs that might offset the positive contribution of the debt.
         These costs will be discussed in further detail in the next chapter.

15.19 a. Since Green is currently an all-equity firm, the value of the firm is the value of its outstanding equity, $10 million. The value of the firm must also equal the PV of the after-tax earnings, discounted at the overall required return. The after-tax earnings are simply ($1,500,000) (1 - 0.4) = $900,000. Thus, $10,000,000 = $900,000 / r_0

$r_0 = 0.09$

b. With 500,000 shares outstanding, the current price of a share is $20 (=$10,000,000 / 500,000). Green's market value balance sheet is

Green Manufacturing, Inc.	
Assets = PV of earnings = $10,000,000	Debt = 0
	Equity = $20 (500,000) = $10,000,000

c. Recall that the value to the firm of issuing debt is the tax shield the debt provides. Therefore, at the announcement, the value of the firm will rise by the PV of the tax shield (PVTS). The PVTS is ($2,000,000) (0.4) = $800,000. Since the value of the firm has risen $800,000 and the debt has not yet been issued, the price of Green stock must rise to reflect the increase in firm value. Since the firm is worth $10,800,000 (=$10,000,000 + 800,000) and there are 500,000 shares outstanding, the price of a share rises to $21.60 (= $10,800,000 / 500,000).

Green Manufacturing, Inc.	
Assets = PV of earnings = $10,000,000	Debt = 0
PVTS = $800,000	Equity = $21.60 (500,000) = $10,800,000

d. Green intends to issue $2,000,000 of debt. Once the announcement is made the price of the stock rises to $21.60. Thus, Green will retire $2,000,000 / $21.60 = $92,592.59 shares.

e. After the restructuring, the value of the firm will still be $10,800,000. Debt will be $2,000,000 and the 407,407.41 (=500,000 - 92,592.59) outstanding shares of stock will sell for $21.60.

Green Manufacturing, Inc.	
Assets = PV of earnings = $10,000,000	Debt = 2,000,000
PVTS = $800,000	Equity = $21.60 (407,407.41) = $8,800,000

f. $r_S = r_0 + (B/S)(r_0 - r_B)(1 - T_C)$

   $= 0.09 + (\$2,000,000 / \$8,800,000) (0.09 - 0.06) (1 - 0.4) = 9.41\%$

15.20 a.

$$V_L = V_U + T_C B$$

$$= \frac{EBIT(1-T_C)}{r_0} + T_C B$$

$$= \frac{\$4(0.65)}{0.15} + 0.35 \times \$10$$

$$= \$20.83 \text{ million}$$

b.

$$r_{WACC} = \frac{B}{V_L} r_B (1-T_C) + \frac{S}{V_L} r_S$$

$$= \frac{EBIT(1-T_C)}{V_L} = 12.48\%$$

c. $r_S = r_0 + (B/S)(r_0 - r_B)(1-T_C)$
$= 0.15 + [10/(20.83 - 10)](0.65)(0.15 - 0.10) = 18.01\%$

15.21 a. $r_S = r_0 + (B/S)(r_0 - r_B)(1-T_C)$
$= 15\% + (2.5)(15\% - 11\%)(1 - 35\%)$
$= 21.50\%$

b. If there is no debt, $r_{WACC} = r_S = 15\%$

c. $r_S = 15\% + 0.75(15\% - 11\%)(1 - 35\%)$
$= 16.95\%$
B/S = 0.75, B = 0.75S
B/(B+S) = 0.75S/(0.75S +S)
$= 0.75/1.75$
S/(B+S) = 1 - (0.75/1.75) = (1/1.75)
r_{WACC} = (0.75/1.75)(0.11)(1 - 0.35) + (1/1.75)(16.95%)
$= 12.75\%$

$r_S = 15\% + 1.5(15\% - 11\%)(1 - 35\%)$
$= 18.90\%$
B/S = 1.5, B = 1.5S
B/(B+S) = 1.5S/(1.5S +S)
$= 1.5/2.5$
S/(B+S) = 1 - (1.5/2.5)
r_{WACC} = (1.5/2.5)(0.11)(1 - 0.35) + (1/2.5)(0.1890)
$= 11.85\%$

15.22   Since this is an all-equity firm, the WACC = r_S.

$$V_U = \frac{EBIT(1-T_C)}{r_S}$$

$$= \frac{\$100{,}000(1-0.4)}{0.25}$$

$$= \$240{,}000$$

If the firm borrows to repurchase its own shares, then the value of GT will be:

$$V_L = V_U + T_C B$$

$$= \frac{\$100{,}000(0.6)}{0.25} + (0.4 \times \$500{,}000)$$

$$= \$440{,}000$$

Answers to End-of-Chapter Problems

Chapter 16: Capital Structure: Limits to the Use of Debt

16.1   a. $V = (\$250 \times 60\% + \$100 \times 40\%) / (1+12\%) = \$169.64$ million under risk neutrality.
             $S = (\$100 \times 60\% + \$0 \times 40\%) / (1+12\%) = \$53.57$ million
             The total stock value of the firm is $53.57 million.

     b.   Assume the expected debt payment in case of recession is $X million.
             $B = (\$150 \times 60\% + \$X \times 40\%) / (1+12\%) = \$108.93$ million $\Rightarrow X = \$80$ million
             Therefore, the bankruptcy cost is expected to be $20 (=100 - 80) million with a
             probability of 40% in recession.

     c.   Firm value, $V = S + B = \$53.57 + \$108.93 = \$162.50$ million

     d.   Promised return on bond $= (\$150 / \$108.93) - 1 = 37.70\%$

16.2   a.   Duane is not correct. This risk of bankruptcy *per se* does not affect firm's value. It
             is the costs of bankruptcy, which lower firm value.

	VanSant		Matta	
	Expansion	Recession	Expansion	Recession
EBIT	$2.0	$0.8	$2.0	$0.8
Interest	0.75	0.75	1.0	0.8
Earnings after Interest*	$1.25	$0.05	$1.0	$0

(Amounts in millions)
*Since there are no taxes in this world, an earnings after interest (EAI) is the same
as earnings after interest and taxes. Thus, EAI is the income available to the
common equity holders.

The value of each firm is the sum of the value of its stocks and the value of its
bonds. Under the assumption of risk-neutrality, the value of the stock is the PV of
the expected earnings available to common stockholders. The value of the bonds is
the PV of the expected interest payments.
VanSant:

$$\text{Stock: } \frac{\$1,250,000(0.8) + \$50,000(0.2)}{1.15} = \$878,260.870$$

$$\text{Bonds: } \frac{\$750,000(0.8) + \$750,000(0.2)}{1.15} = \$652,173.913$$

Firm: $878,260.870 + $652,173.913 = $1,530,434.783

Matta:

$$\text{Stock: } \frac{\$1,000,000(0.8) + \$0(0.2)}{1..15} = \$695,652.174$$

$$\text{Bonds: } \frac{\$1,000,000(0.8) + \$800,000(0.2)}{1.15} = \$834,782.609$$

Firm: $695,652.174 + $834,782.609 = $1,530,434.783

     c.   If there are significant costs associated with Matta's insolvency, then the firms'
             values will differ.

16.3 Direct:
Legal and administrative costs: Costs associated with the litigation arising from a liquidation or bankruptcy. These costs include lawyers' fees, courtroom costs and expert witness fees.

Indirect:
Impaired ability to conduct business: Loss of sales due to a decrease in consumer confidence and loss of reliable supplies due to lack of confidence by suppliers.

Incentive to take large risks: when faced with projects of different risk levels, managers (who often are major stockholders) have an incentive to undertake high risk projects. If the projects pay off, the firm is solvent and the stockholders benefit. If the project does not perform well, then the firm still ends up in bankruptcy, but the bondholders bear the burden.

Incentive to under-invest: investments benefit bondholders through their increased cash flows to the firm. This benefit is at the cost of stockholders who usually must finance the investment. Thus, the stockholders may have an incentive to encourage under-investment.

Milking the property: In a bankruptcy the bondholders have first claim to the assets of the firm. When faced with a possible bankruptcy, the stockholders have strong incentives to vote themselves increased dividends or other distributions. This will ensure them of getting some of the assets of the firm before the bondholders can lay claim to them.

16.4 The tax carry forwards will make Chrysler's effective tax rate zero. Therefore, the company does not need any tax deductions such as those provided by debt. Moreover, although the firm faces no taxes, it does face the very real threat of bankruptcy. Additional debt would only increase the likelihood of insolvency. Since the firm does not need the tax shield of debt and because additional debt will increase the probability of bankruptcy, Chrysler should issue equity.

16.5 Look at the expected values of Fountain's prospective projects.
Firm = Stock + Bonds
Low-risk $600 = $100 + $500
High-risk $450 = $150 + $300

Stockholders would prefer the high-risk project. Although the expected value of the firm is less, the expected value of the equity is greater. If the bad economy arises, the shareholders receive no benefit irrespective of which project Fountain chooses. If the economy is good, they will receive $100 more with the high-risk project. Notice that there is a significant (50%) probability that the firm will be barely solvent or be pushed into bankruptcy. In such a situation, stockholders have strong incentives to take large risks. If the gamble pays off, they profit highly; if it fails, they are no worse off than if they had played it safe.

16.6 Disagree. If a firm has debt, it might be advantageous to the stockholders for the firm to undertake risky projects, even those with negative NPVs. This incentive comes from the fact that the risk is borne by the bondholders. Therefore, value is transferred from the bondholders to the shareholders by undertaking risky (including negative NPV) projects. This incentive is even stronger when the probability and costs of bankruptcy are high.

16.7   Bondholders need to raise the debt payment to $140 in case of a high risk project being taken, so that the expected payoff to stockholders in either case would be 50% x 0 + 50% x 100 = 50. This example implies that rational bondholders can price to protect themselves ex ante and stockholders ultimately are to bear the cost of selfish investment strategy by paying a higher interest demanded by the creditors.

16.8   i.   Protective covenants: Agreements in the bond indenture which are designed to decrease the cost of debt.
              1. Negative covenants: Prohibit company actions which would cause bondholders to require higher returns.
              2. Positive covenants: Require actions which are designed to ensure bondholders of company solvency.

       ii.   Repurchase Debt: Eliminate the costs of bankruptcy by eliminating the debt.
       iii.   Consolidation of debt: Decrease the number of debt holders, thereby decreasing the direct costs should bankruptcy occur.

16.9   The MM Proposition with corporate tax suggests that there is positive tax advantage of debt financing. However, in reality, it cannot be optimal for a firm to adopt an all-debt financing strategy. Due to the direct and the indirect financial distress costs and the agency costs of debt, there can exist an optimal level of debt-equity ratio, i.e. optimal capital structure. At the optimal point, there is no marginal benefit to the increase/decrease of debt anymore.

16.10 There can be two major sources of the agency costs of equity. One, shirking of the management due to the fact that management doesn't own all of the stocks of the firm. Two, more on the job perquisites for the management. These two elements constitute the agency cost of equity and will reduce the firm value accordingly.

16.11 a.

	Equity Plan	Debt Plan
Stockholders:		
Dividends	$1,800,000	$990,000
Taxes (0.30)	540,000	297,000
	$1,260,000	$693,000
Bondholders:		
Interest income	0	$1,350,000
Taxes (0.30)	0	405,000
	0	945,000

Total cash flows to stakeholders:
Equity Plan: $1,260,000 + 0 = $1,260,000
Debt Plan: $693,000 + $945,000 = $1,638,000
Under MM without personal taxes, we know that debt increased the cash flows to all stakeholders. Since interest and dividends are taxed at the same personal rate, personal taxes only reduce the final cash flows to the stakeholders. Personal taxes do not alter the conclusion that debt increases the value of the firm.

b. The IRS prefers the plan with the higher total amount of taxes paid. That is the equity plan. The total tax bill includes the amounts paid by firms, stockholders and bondholders.

Debt:

Total taxes = $660,000 + $297,000 + $405,000
= $1,362,000

Equity:

Total taxes = $1,200,000 + $540,000 + 0
= $1,740,000

c. All-equity plan:

$$V_U = \frac{EBIT(1-T_C)(1-T_S)}{r_0}$$

$$= \$3,000,000(1-0.4)(1-0.3)/0.2$$

$$= \$6,300,000$$

Debt Plan:

$$V_L = V_U + \left[1 - \frac{(1-T_C)(1-T_S)}{(1-T_B)}\right]B$$

$$= \$6,300,000 + [1 - (0.6)(0.7)/(0.7)]\$13,500,000$$

$$= \$11,700,000$$

d.

	Equity Plan	Debt Plan
Stockholders:		
Dividends	$1,800,000	$990,000
Taxes (0.20)	360,000	198,000
	$1,440,000	$792,000
Bondholders:		
Interest income	0	$1,350,000
Taxes (0.55)	0	742,500
	0	$607,500

Total cash flows to stakeholders:
Equity plan: $1,440,000 + 0 = $1,440,000
Debt Plan: $792,000 + $607,500 = $1,399,500

16.12 a. MM assume the T_C, T_B and C(B) are all zero. Under these assumptions, the capital structure is irrelevant. Thus, the debt-equity ratio can be anything.

b. For the model with corporate taxes $T_C>0$, but both T_S and C(B) are still zero. Therefore the higher the amount of debt, the higher the value of the firm. In this model the debt-equity ratio should be infinite.

c. In general, if $T_C>T_B$ the value of the firm rises with additional debt, so the firm should be all-debt. If $T_C<T_B$ the value of the firm falls with additional debt, so the firm should be all-equity. If $T_C=T_B$ the value of the firm is unchanged by changes in debt, so the firm's capital structure is irrelevant.

Answers to End-of-Chapter Problems

For IBM: $\Delta V_L = \Delta V_U + \left[1 - \dfrac{(1-T_C)}{(1-T_B)}\right]\Delta B - \Delta C(B)$

Since ΔV_U and $\Delta C(B)$ are zero,

$\Delta V_L = \left[1 - \dfrac{(1-0.35)}{(1-0.20)}\right]($1\text{billion})$

$\quad = \$187.5 \quad \text{million}$

d. The effective corporate tax rate for USX is zero.

$\Delta V_L = \left[1 - \dfrac{(1-0.0)}{(1-0.20)}\right]($1)$

$\quad = -\$0.25$

The value of USX will fall by $0.25 for every dollar of debt the firm adds to its financial structure.

e. For a firm, which may or may not be able to use the interest deduction, the value of the firm will change according to the expected value of an additional dollar of debt.

$\Delta V_L = 0.65[1 - \dfrac{(1-0.35)}{(1-0.20)}] + 0.35 \quad [1 - \dfrac{(1-0)}{(1-0.20)}]($1)$

$\quad = .03438$

The value of a firm in this situation will rise $.03438, for every dollar of debt the firm adds to its capital structure.

16.13 The market value of the firm will change by the difference in the value of the firm with or without leverage.

The Miller Model is

$V_L = V_U + [1 - \dfrac{(1-T_C)(1-T_S)}{(1-T_B)}]B$

The difference in the value of the firm is $V_L - V_U$, which is simply the second term of the Miller Model.

For OPC that difference is [1 - (1 - 0.35) / (1 - 0.10)] $2 million = $555,555.56

16.14 a. Currently EXES is unlevered, so the value of the firm is the PV of the expected EBIT
Expected EBIT = (0.1)($1,000) + (0.4)($2,000) + (0.5)($4,200) = $3,000
Value = $3,000 / 0.2 = $15,000

b. In this MM world, changes in the capital structure do not change the value of the firm.
i. V=$15,000
ii. B=$7,500
iii. S=$7,500

c. $r_s = r_0 + (B/S)(r_0 - r_s)$

    i. $r_0 = 0.20$. Remember the overall return on an all-equity firm is the return on equity.

$$r_s = 0.20 + (\$7,500 / \$7,500) (0.20 - 0.10)$$
$$= 0.30$$
$$= 30\%$$

    ii. r_0 is unchanged at 20%. This can be verified with the formula:

$$r_0 = (B/V)r_B + (S/V)r_S$$

$$= (1/2)(0.10) + (1/2)(0.30)$$

$$= 0.20$$

d.

    i. $$V_U = \frac{E(EBIT)(1 - T_c)}{r_0}$$

$$= \$3,000(1 - 0.4)/0.2 = \$9,000$$

$$V_L = V_U + T_C B$$

$$= \$9,000 + (0.4)(\$7,500) = \$12,000$$

    ii. Taxes decrease the value of the firm because the government becomes a claimant on the firm's assets. Recall that the size of the pie does not change, but now less is available to the stakeholders.

    iii. The presence of bankruptcy costs will further lower the value of the firm.

e.

$$V_L = V_U + \left[1 - \frac{(1 - T_C)(1 - T_S)}{(1 - T_B)} \right] B$$

$$= \$9,000 + \left[1 - \frac{(1 - 0.4)}{(1 - 0.4)} \right] (\$7,500)$$

$$= \$9,000$$

The debt no longer adds value to the firm.

    ii. As T_B increases, additional debt lowers the value of the firm. For example, if $T_B = 0.55$,

$$V_L = \$9,000 + \left[1 - \frac{(1 - 0.4)}{(1 - 0.55)} \right] (\$7,500)$$

$$= \$6,500$$

16.15 a.   9.5% is not the lowest after-tax rate that Mueller can obtain. The lowest is 6.5% from the pollution control bonds. Therefore, the president is incorrect when he claims the common stock is the cheapest source of financing. If there are bonds that appeal to high bracket investors, personal taxes should be considered when issuing bonds. The increase in firm value would be:

$$\Delta V_L = V_U + \left[1 - \frac{(1 - T_C)(1 - T_S)}{(1 - T_B)} \right] \Delta B$$

In the case of the pollution control bonds, $T_B = 0$, so $\Delta V_L = T_C \Delta B$. With the corporate bonds though, value will decrease as T_B increases. Any increase in firm value is less with the corporate bonds. Thus, Mr. Daniels is incorrect in his belief that debt always adds to the value of the firm. It depends upon the differential tax rates, T_C vs. T_B. Finally, because it does matter which type of bond is issued, Ms. Harris' claim that the debt choice does not matter is also incorrect.

       b.   Mueller should not be indifferent since the bonds add different amounts to the value of the firm.
             Ranking the alternatives:

	After-tax cost	Value added
1. Pollution control bonds	6.5%	$35 million
2. Corporate bonds	13%	Less than $35 million
3. Common stock	9.5%	

             Notes:
             1. If $T_c < T_B$ then the ranking of the corporate bonds and the common stock may be reversed. Bankruptcy costs and agency costs also favor stock issues.
             2. Our analysis implies that bonds add value relative to equity. Actually, the value of the firm is likely to fall with any financing alternative since pollution control equipment represents a cash outflow.

16.16   Added value of debt = [1 - (1-35%) / (1-15%)] x 1.2 - 5% x 1.2 = $0.22 million
             Firm Value = V_U + Added value of debt
                = $0.8 million x (1-35%) / 10% + 0.22 = $5.42 million

16.17 a. $V_U = \dfrac{EBIT}{r_S} = \dfrac{(27 + 3)}{0.1}$ = $300 Million

       b.   Given there's no taxes, no bankruptcy costs, perfect capital market, capital structure does not matter. Thus, the total value of the firm remains the same at $300 million.

       c. $r_S = r_0 + B/S (r_0 - r_B)(1 - T_C)$
                = 10% + 20/280 (10% – 8%) = 10.1429%

16.18 a.   Cost of capital:

             $r_S = r_f + \beta_i [E(R_M) - r_f]$,   where $\beta_i = \dfrac{\sigma_{im}}{\sigma_m^2} = \dfrac{0.048}{0.04} = 1.2$

                = 0.1 + 1.2 [0.2 – 0.1]
                = 0.22 = 22%

b. Neither of the two models should NETC purchase.

$$NPV_{HD} = -1,000 + 340\,A^4_{0.22}$$
$$= -\$152.16$$

$$NPV_{LW} = (-500 + 316\,A^2_{0.22}) + \frac{\left(-500 + 316A^2_{0.22}\right)}{\left(1 + 22\%\right)^2}$$
$$= (-\$28.6751) + \frac{-\$28.6751}{\left(1.22\right)^2}$$
$$= -\$47.94$$

c. Heavy-Duty Model:

$$\$1,000 = C\,A^4_{0.22}$$
$$C = \$401.02$$

d. i) $V_L = V_U + T_C B = 10 + 2(0.34) = 10.68$ Million

ii) $S = V_L - B = 10.68 - 2 = 8.68$ Million

iii) $r_S = r_0 + B/S\,(r_0 - r_B)\,(1 - T_C)$

$$= 22\% + \left(\frac{2}{8.68}\right)(22\% - 10\%)(1 - 34\%)$$
$$= 23.82\%$$

$$WACC = (B/V)\,r_B\left(1 - T_C\right) + (S/V)r_S$$
$$= 2/10.68\,(10\%)(1 - 34\%) + 8.68/10.68\,(23.82\%)$$
$$= 20.60\%$$

e. Mr. Wool is correct.
Mr. Orlon is incorrect since the tax shield associated with the interest expense does add value to the firm.
Mr. Nylon is incorrect since there's a tax shield associated with the interest expense. This subsequently lower the overall cost of capital to the firm since the cost of equity is 22%, which is still higher than the cost of debt.
Mr. Rayon is incorrect since the present value of the tax shield ultimately depends on the tax rate and the debt level.

f. $V_L = \$10.68$ million $(1 - 2\%) = \$10.47$ million
No, it does not change the analysis.

g. The market risk (beta) of NETC is greater than 1, which means it's more volatile than the market as a whole. Conceivably, NETC's earnings are more cyclical than that of the Cotton Mather Electric Utility Company. Mr. Buck may want to consider NETC's potential bankruptcy risk.

Appendix 16B

16.19 a. In equilibrium, $r_B \times (1-T_C) = r_s$
$r_B = 11\% / (1-35\%) = 16.92\%$

b. Investors with marginal tax rate of 10% and 20% would invest in debt and those with marginal tax rate of 40% would invest in equity.

c. Firm value for Quantex Corp. would not vary with its capital structure in equilibrium. So the firm value would equal to an all-equity-financed firm with EBIT of $1 million in perpetuity.
$V = EBIT \times (1-T_c) / r_s = 1 \times (1-35\%) / 11\% = \$5.91$ million

16.20 a. The equilibrium return on corporate bonds is the return that makes aggregate corporations indifferent between stocks and bonds.
$(1 - 0.35) r_B = 0.081$
$r_B = 12.46\%$

b. First we must determine the bond rate which makes the investors indifferent. The groups will invest in bonds if their after-tax return on the bonds is greater than the return on stocks; i.e. if $(1-T_B) r_B > 8.1\%$.
Group A: $(1-0.5) r_B > 8.1\% ==> r_B > 16.2\%$
Group B: $(1-0.325) r_B > 8.1\% ==> r_B > 12\%$
Group C: $(1-0.1) r_B > 8.1\% ==> r_B > 9\%$
Since corporations are paying 12.46% on bonds, groups B and C will place all of their investable funds in bonds. Group A investors will place their money in stocks.

c. The total amount of bonds outstanding is $325 million (= $220 million + $105 million). The value of stocks is the PV of the earnings available to common.

$$S = \frac{(EBIT - r_B B)(1 - T_C)}{r_S}$$
$$= \frac{[\$85,000,000 - .1246(\$325,000,000)](1 - 0.35)}{0.081}$$

$= \$357,138,888.89$

Therefore, the market value of all companies is
$V = \$325,000,000 + \$357,138,888.89$
$= \$682,138,888.89$

d. The total tax bill is the sum of the taxes paid by corporations and individuals.
Corporate taxes:
[85 million - (12.46%)(325 million)] x 35% = $15,576,750
Interest income:
Group B: $[(\$220,000,000)(.1246)](0.325) = 8,908,900$
Group C: $[(\$105,000,000)(.1246)](0.10) = \$1,308,300$
Dividend income: $[(357,138,888.89)(.081)](0.5) = \$14,464,125$
Total taxes = $24,681,325 + $15,576,750 = $40,258,075.

16.21 a.   The equilibrium interest rate paid by corporations is 10% [=6% / (1 - 0.4)]. Given the tax rates for the various groups, the investors will invest in bonds for interest rates that exceed:

L: 12%

M: 10%

N: 7.5%

O: 6%

The indifference interest rate = 6% / (1- T_B).

The N and O groups will invest in bonds. The M group is indifferent between bonds and stocks. If the Ms put all of their wealth into stocks, the amount of bonds will be $700 million (= $200 million + $500 million). If the Ms put all of their wealth in bonds, the amount of bonds will be $1,000 million (= $200 million + $500 million + $300 million).

The amount of equity is given by

$$S = \frac{(EBIT - r_B B)(1 - T_C)}{r_S}$$

If Ms buy no bonds, the value of equity is

$$S = \frac{[\$150\,\text{million} - (0.1)(\$700\text{million})](0.6)}{0.06}$$

= $800 million

If Ms buy bonds, the value of equity is

$$S = \frac{[\$150\,\text{million} - (0.1)(\$1,000\text{million})](0.6)}{0.06}$$

= $500 million

Thus, the debt-equity ratio can range from $700 million / $800 million = 7/8 to $1,000 million / $500 million = 2.

b.   If the corporate tax rate is 30%, the equilibrium interest rate will be 8.57%. At this equilibrium, only the N and the O groups will purchase bonds. The amount of equity in the economy is

$$S = \frac{[\$150\,\text{million} - (0.0857)(\$700\text{million})](0.7)}{0.06}$$

= $1,050 million

The debt-equity ratio is $700 million / $1,050 million = 0.667.

Chapter 17: Valuation and Capital Budgeting for the Levered Firm

17.1 a. The maximum price that Hertz should be willing to pay for a fleet of cars with all equity funding is the price that makes the NPV of the fleet zero. Let I be the cost of the fleet. Then the NPV is simply the outflows (-I) plus the PV of the after-tax earnings plus the PV of the depreciation tax shield.

$$NPV = 0 = -I + (1 - 0.34)(\$100,000)\left[\frac{1 - \frac{1}{(1.10)^5}}{0.10}\right] + (0.34)(I/5)\left[\frac{1 - \frac{1}{(1.06)^5}}{0.06}\right]$$

I = \$350,625.29

b. APV = Base-case (B/C) NPV + NPV of the Loan
Base-case NPV:
There are two ways to determine the B/C NPV. One way is to compute it directly using the formula in part a and substituting \$325,000 for I.

Alternatively,
$$NPV = -I[1 - (0.34/5)A_{0.06}^5] + \$66,000A_{0.1}^5$$
Since, I = \$325,000, NPV = \$18,285.17

NPV of the Loan:
There are two ways to compute the NPV of the loan. You can compute the actual NPV of the loan, or you can compute the PV of the interest tax shield.

Method One:
NPV(Loan) = Amount borrowed - PV of the after-tax interest payment - PV of the principal

$$= \$200,000 - (1 - 0.34)(0.08)(\$200,000)\left[\frac{1 - \frac{1}{(1.08)^5}}{0.08}\right] - \frac{\$200,000}{1.08^5}$$

$$= \$21,720.34$$

Method Two:

$$PV(\text{Tax Shield}) = (0.34)(0.08)(\$200,000)\left[\frac{1 - \frac{1}{(1.08)^5}}{0.08}\right] = \$21,720.34$$

Therefore, the APV is:
APV = \$18,285.17 + \$21,720.34 = \$40,005.51

c. Use of the subsidized loan will increase the NPV of the loan. Thus, it will allow Honda to charge more for the fleet of cars. To compute the maximum price Hertz will pay, set the APV equal to zero.

$$APV = 0 = -I + (1-0.34)(\$100,000)\left[\frac{1-\frac{1}{1.10^5}}{0.10}\right] + (0.34)(I/5)\left[\frac{1-\frac{1}{1.06^5}}{0.06}\right] + \$200,000$$

$$- (1-0.34)(0.05)(\$200,000)\left[\frac{1-\frac{1}{(1.08)^5}}{0.08}\right] - \frac{\$200,000}{(1.08)^5}$$

$$I = \$403,222.85$$

Note: When a subsidy exists on a loan, you cannot use the PV (Tax Shield) method to compute the NPV of the loan. This is true because even with an interest rate subsidy, the appropriate rate by which to discount the after-tax interest payments is the market rate of interest. The PV (Tax Shield) method presumes the interest rate and the discount rate are the same.

17.2 a. APV= Base-case (B/C) NPV - Floatation costs + NPV of the Loan
Base-case NPV:
Base-case NPV= Outflows + Present value of the depreciation tax shield + Present value of the after-tax cash revenues less expenses

$$= -\$2,100,000 + (0.3)(\$700,000)\left[\frac{1-\frac{1}{1.06^3}}{0.06}\right] + (1-0.3)(\$9,000,000)\left[\frac{1-\frac{1}{1.18^3}}{0.18}\right]$$

$$= -\$168,875.54$$

Flotation Costs:
Net proceeds are $2.1 million and flotation costs are 1% of gross.
Gross proceeds = $2,100,000/(1-0.01)=$2,121,212.12
Flotation costs = $21,212.12
Annual tax deduction = $21,212.12/3 = $7,070.71
Annual tax shield = $7,070.71 x 0.30 = $2,121.21
Net cost = Flotation cost - NPV (tax shield)
        = $21,212.12 - ($2,121.21)(2.6730)
        = $15,542.12

NPV of the Loan:
There are two ways to compute the NPV of the loan. You can compute the actual NPV of the loan, or you can compute the PV of the interest tax shield.

Method One:

NPV (Loan) = Amount Borrowed - PV of the after-tax interest payments - PV of the principal

$$NPV(\text{Loan}) = \$2,121,212.12 - (1-0.3)(0.125)(\$2,121,212.12)\left[\frac{1-\dfrac{1}{(1.125)^3}}{0.125}\right] - \frac{\$2,121,212.12}{(1.125)^3}$$

$$= \$189,425.11$$

Method Two:

$$PV\ (\text{Tax shield}) = (0.3)(0.125)(\$2,121,212.12)\left[\frac{1-\dfrac{1}{(1.125)^3}}{0.125}\right]$$

$$= \$189,425.11$$

Therefore, the APV is:
APV = -$168,875.54 - $15,542.12 + $189,425.11
    = $5,007.45

Peatco should undertake the project!

b.   Using the City Council's loan, the only numbers that will change are those in the NPV of the loan. Now the interest payments are $212,121.21 (=0.10 x $2,121,212.12) rather than $265,151.51 (= 0.125 x $2,121,212.12).

$$NPV(\text{Loan}) = \$2,121,212.12 - (1-0.3)(0.10)(\$2,121,212.12)\left[\frac{1-\dfrac{1}{(1.125)^3}}{0.125}\right] - \frac{\$2,121,212.12}{(1.125)^3}$$

$$= \$227,823.50$$

Therefore, the APV is:
APV = -$168,875.54 - $15,542.12 + $277,823.50
    = $93,405.84

Peatco should accept the City Council's offer and begin the project.

Note: When a subsidy exists on a loan, you cannot use the PV (Tax Shield) method to compute the NPV of the loan. This is true because even with an interest rate subsidy, the appropriate rate by which to discount the after-tax interest payments is the market rate of interest. The PV (Tax Shield) method presumes the interest rate and the discount rate are the same.

17.3 The calculation of the APV allows us to judge the attractiveness of the new project. The first step is to calculate the all-equity (base-case) NPV. The unlevered cash flows are given, but we must infer the required return on assets from:

$$r_S = r_0 + \frac{B}{S}(1 - T_C)(r_0 - r_B), \text{ or}$$

$$0.18 = r_0 + 0.25(1 - 0.4)(r_0 - 0.10)$$

This relation implies that r_0 is approximately equal to 17.0%. Using the asset cash flows, the all-equity NPV is:

$$NPV(\text{all - equity}) = -15 + \frac{5}{(1.170)} + \frac{8}{(1.170)^2} + \frac{10}{(1.170)^3} = 1.37$$

The additional value provided by the debt issue can be computed as:

$$NPV(\text{debt issue}) = PVTS = \frac{T_C r_B B_0}{(1 + r_B)} + \frac{T_C r_B B_1}{(1 + r_B)^2} + \frac{T_C r_B B_2}{(1 + r_B)^3}$$

$$= \frac{.4(.1)6}{(1.1)} + \frac{.4(.1)4}{(1.1)^2} + \frac{.4(.1)2}{(1.1)^3} = 0.41$$

The APV of the expansion is therefore $1.37 + 0.41 = 1.78$. Since this is positive, MEO should go through with the capacity increase.

17.4

Base Case $NPV = -20 - 10(1 - .25)A^2_{0.12} + 6(1 - .25)A^{20}_{0.12} / (1.12)^2 + (20/5).25A^5_{0.09}$

$= -20 - 10(.75) \times 1.6901 + 6(.75) \times 7.4694 \times .7972 + 4(.25) \times 3.8897$

$= \$-1.99$ million

NPV of subsidized government $loan = 10 - 10(1 - .25)(.05)A^{15}_{0.09} - 10/(1.09)^{15}$

$= [1 - (0.75)(0.05)(8.0607) - 0.27457](10)$

$= \$4.232$ million

Total NPV of the project $= 4.232 - 1.99 = \$2.242$ million

17.5

Annual cash flow from each store:

Sales	1,000,000
-Cost of goods sold	-400,000
-General administrative costs	-300,000
-Interest	-900,000 (30%) (9.5%)
Income before tax	274,350
-Tax	-274,350 (40%)
Net income	164,610 (annual cash flow)

$$r_S = r_0 + \frac{B}{S}(1 - T_C)(r_0 - r_B)$$

$$= 15\% + 30\%(1 - 40\%)(15\% - 9.5\%)$$

$$= 15.99\%$$

$V_{\text{equity value of each store}} = 164{,}610 / 15.99\% = \$1{,}029{,}455.91$
$V_{\text{each store}} = \$1{,}029{,}455.91 + \$270{,}000 = \$1{,}299{,}455.91$
$V_{\text{milano pizza club}} = 3\ V_{\text{each store}} = \$3{,}898{,}367.73$

17.6 a. You must apply the CAPM to determine the cost of equity for Wild Widgets. To apply the CAPM to equity, you need the equity beta.
$$\beta_S = \beta_0\,[1 + (1\text{-}T_C)(B/S)]$$
where, β_S = Equity beta
β_0 = Overall firm beta

Therefore, $\beta_S = .9\,[\,1 + (0.66)\,(0.5)] = 1.197$
Applying CAPM you get
$r_S = 0.08 + 1.197\,(0.16 - 0.08) = 0.17576 = 17.576\%$

b. $r_B = \$1070 / \$972.72 -1 = 10\%$
Therefore, the after-tax cost of debt is 6.6% (=10% x 0.66)

c. To compute the WACC you need the debt-to-value and equity-to-value ratios. Since the debt-to-equity ratio is 1/2 (=D/E) and the value of the firm is the sum of the debt and equity (=D+E), the debt-to-value ratio D/(D+E) is 1 / (1+2) = 1/3. The equity-to-value ratio is 2/3.
WACC = (1/3)(6.6%) + (2/3)(17.576%) = 13.917%

17.7 This firm has a capital structure which has three parts. As a capital structure becomes more complex, the WACC simply adds additional terms.
a. Book value:
WACC = ($5/$20)(0.08)(1-0.34) + ($5/$20)(0.10)(1-0.34) + ($10/$20)(0.15)
= 0.1047
Market value:
WACC = ($5/$20)(0.08)(1-0.34) + ($2/$20)(0.10)(1-0.34) + ($13/$20)(0.15)
= 0.1173
Target value: The firm wants the market values of long and short term debt to be equal. Let x be the amount of long-term debt. Then total debt equals 2x. Since the firm also wants its debt-equity ratio to be 100% (or 1), the amount of equity must also be 2x. The value of the firm will be the sum of these terms which is 4x. Thus, the long-term-debt-value ratio is x/4x = 1/4. The short-term-debt-value ratio is the same, and the equity-value ratio is 1/2 (=2x / 4x). These weights should be used to compute the target WACC.

WACC = (1/4)(0.08)(1-0.34) + (1/4)(0.10)(1-0.34) + (1/2)(0.15) = 0.1047

b. The differences in the WACCs are due to the weights. The WACC using market weights is the firm's current WACC. The WACC computed using the target weights is the WACC used for project evaluation. It should be used when the project is financed in such a way that the debt-to-equity ratio of the firm is unchanged by the project. Since we assume firms fund projects at their company's WACC, target weights are the correct weights to use in the WACC.

17.8 The capital budgeting decision requires the calculation of the NPV of the equipment. The NPV calculation requires the WACC.

Cost of Equity: $\beta_S = 0.031/0.16^2 = 1.21$
$$r_S = 7\% + 1.21 (8.5\%) = 17.293\%$$
After-tax cost of debt: $11\% (1-0.34) = 7.26\%$
Value of the firm: $V = B + S$
$$= \$24,000,000 + (\$15)(4,000,000)$$
$$= \$84,000,000$$
WACC $= (\$24,000,000 / \$84,000,000) (7.26\%) + (\$60,000,000 / \$84,000,000) (17.293\%)$
$$= 14.426\%$$

The new machinery provides earnings that are an annuity for five years. The net present value of the additional equipment is

$$NPV = -\$27.5 + \$9 \left[\frac{1 - \dfrac{1}{(1.14426)^5}}{0.14426} \right] = \$3.084 \text{million}$$

Yes, Baber should purchase the additional equipment.

17.9 a. NEC's debt-equity ratio is 2. That means that for every dollar of equity the firm has, it has two dollars in debt. The debt-to-value ratio of the firm is $B / (B + S)$, so it is equal to $2/(2+1) = 2/3$. The equity-to-value ratio is $1/3$. Thus, the WACC is
$$WACC = (2/3)(0.10)(1-0.34) + (1/3)(0.20) = 0.1107$$
Thus,
$$NPV = -\$20,000,000 + \$8,000,000 / 0.1107 = \$52,267,389.34$$
Yes, NEC should accept the project.

b. Mr. Edison's conclusion is incorrect. Even though the issuing costs of debt are far lower than those of equity, the firm must try to maintain its optimal capital structure. Recall, if a firm's objective is to maximize shareholder wealth, it should maintain its optimal capital structure. Thus, anytime all-debt financing is used, the firm will have to issue more equity in the future to bring the capital structure back to the optimal.

17.10 Baber's WACC does not change if the firm chooses to fund the project entirely with debt. Thus, the WACC for Baber is still 14.426%. The use of target weights is based upon the assumption that the current capital structure is optimal. Indeed, if the firm's objective is to maximize shareholder wealth, it should always use its target weights in the computation of WACC. All debt funding for this project simply implies that the firm will have to use more equity in the future to bring the capital structure back to optimal.

17.11 The all-equity value of the firm is given by:
$$V_U = 30 (1-0.34) / 0.18 = \$110 \text{ million}$$
The share price before the recap is therefore $110 / share. Because there are no personal taxes or costs of financial distress, the value of the leverage per se is $T_C B = 0.34 (50) = \$17$ million. The value of the firm after the recap is therefore $110 + 17 = \$127$ million, which implies a share price of $127. At this price, the $50 million proceeds from the debt issue enables the firm to repurchase $50,000,000 / 127 = 393,700$ shares. Thus, about 606,300 shares will remain outstanding. Earning per share will be:
$$EPS = [30 \text{ million} - 0.10 (50 \text{ million})] (1-0.34) / 606,300 = \$27.21 / \text{share}$$

Answers to End-of-Chapter Problems

The required return on equity will be:

$$r_S^L = r_0 + \frac{B}{S}(1 - T_C)(r_0 - r_B)$$

$$= 18\% + 50/77(1 - 34\%)(18\% - 10\%)$$

$$= 21.43\%$$

These values together verify the stock price by the FTE approach, since $27.21 / 0.2143 = \$127$.

17.12 a. The unlevered free cash flows for the Kinedyne division can be calculated as

Sales	$19,740
Variable costs	11,844
Depreciation	1,800
Taxable income	$6,096
Taxes	2,438
After-tax income	$3,658
Depreciation	1,800
Investment	1,800
UCF	$3,658

In all-equity form, the division is therefore worth $3,658 / 0.16 = \$22.86$ MM.

b. If the division were leveraged as the parent, its weighted average cost of capital would be:

$$r_{WACC} = r_0 \times (1 - T_C)\frac{B}{V}$$

$$= 0.16[1 - 0.4(0.4)]$$

$$= 0.1344$$

Using this rate to discount the unlevered free cash flows, the levered division value would be $3,658 / 1.344 = \$27.21$ MM.

c. At this capital structure, the shareholders would require the return:

$$r_S = r_0 + \frac{B}{S}(1 - T_C)(r_0 - r_B)$$

$$= 16\% + (4/6)(1 - 40\%)(16\% - 10\%)$$

$$= 18.4\%$$

d. We need to show that the cash flow to the shareholders, discounted at the 18.4% required return, implies the value of the equity outstanding, which is .60 x $V_L = 0.60$ ($27.21 MM) = $16.33 MM. To see this, note that the shareholders have a claim on the unlevered cash flow less the after-tax interest payment. This amount is $(1 - T_C)r_B B = .6 (.1) 10.89$ MM $= 0.65$ MM, where the debt level is 40% of V_L above. Deducting this after-tax interest payment from the unlevered cash flow implies a flow to equity (FTE) of (3.66 - 0.65) = 3.01 MM, which, when divided by the equity return of 18.4%, yields the value for shares outstanding of $16.33 MM.

17.13 APV:
$$V_U = UCF / r_0 = \$151.52(1-34\%)/\ 0.2 = \$500.016$$
$$APV = V_U + T_C B = \$500 + (34\%)\ (\$500) = \$670$$

WACC:
$$r_S = r_0 + B/S\ (1-T_C)(r_0 - r_B),\quad \text{where}\quad S = V_L - B = \$670 - \$500 = \$170$$
$$= 0.2 + 500/170\ (0.66)(0.2-0.1)$$
$$= 0.3941 = 39.41\%$$
$$r_{wacc} = \frac{S}{S+B}\ r_S + \frac{B}{S+B}\ r_B\ (1-T_C)$$
$$= 170/670\ (39.41\%) + 500/670\ (10\%)(1-34\%)$$
$$= 14.92\%$$
$$V_L = \frac{UCF}{r_{WACC}} = \frac{151.52\ (1-34\%)}{14.92\%} = \$670$$

FTE:
$$LCF = (EBIT - r_B B)(1 - T_C)$$
$$= (\$151.52 - \$50)(1-34\%) = \$67.0032$$
$$V_L = PV = (\$67.0032\ /\ 39.41\%) - (-\$500)$$
$$= \$170 + \$500 = \$670$$

17.14 For the benchmark:
$$r_S = r_f + \beta\ (R_M - r_f) = 9\% + 1.5\ (\ 17\% - 9\%) = 21\%$$
$$r_{wacc\ benchmark} = r_{wacc\ project}$$
$$21\%\ \underline{(1/1.3)} + 10\%\ (0.3/1/3)\ (1-40\%) = r_{S\ project}\ (1/1.35) + 10\%\ (0.35/1.35)\ (1-40\%)$$
$$r_{S\ project} = 21.58\%$$

$$\text{PV of the project} = \frac{55,000}{1+21.58\%} + \frac{55,000(1+5\%)}{(1+21.58\%)^2} + ... + \frac{55,000(1+5\%)^4}{(1+21.58\%)^5} + \sum\nolimits_{t=6}^{\infty} \frac{55,000(1+5\%)^4}{(1+21.58\%)^t}$$
$$= 172,352.26 + 116,615.90 = \$288,968.16$$

As PV of the project is less than the initial investment of $325,000, Schwartz & Brothers Inc. should give up the project.

17.15 Flotation Cost $= 4,250,000\ /\ (1-1.25\%) - 4,250,000 = \$53,797$

NPV of the loan = (Proceeds net of flotation cost) – (After tax present value of interest and principal payment) +(flotation costs tax shield)

$$= 4,250,000 - [4,303,797(9\%)(1-40\%)A_{9.4\%}^{10} + 4,303,797\ /(1.094)^{10}] + \frac{53,797(40\%)}{10}\ A_{9.4\%}^{10}$$
$$= 4,250,000 - [232,405 \times 6.3062 + 4,303,797 \times 0.4072] + 2,152 \times 6.3062$$
$$= \$1,045,472.39$$

17.16 a. $\beta_n = [1+(1-35\%) \times 1,000,000 / 1,500,000] \times 1.2 = 1.72$
           $\beta_s = [1+(1-35\%) \times 1,500,000 / 1,000,000] \times 1.2 = 2.37$

b. $R_{sn} = r_f + \beta_n (R_M - r_f) = 4.25\% + 1.72(12.75\% - 4.25\%) = 18.87\%$
     $R_{ss} = r_f + \beta_n (R_M - r_f) = 4.25\% + 2.37 (12.75\% - 4.25\%) = 24.40\%$

c.   Although the two firms have the same risk level in case of all equity financing, the levered β for South Pole Fishing Equipment Corp. is higher as a result of its higher leverage. Consequently, the required rate of return on the levered equity is higher for South Pole Fishing Equipment too.

Chapter 18: Dividend Policy: Why Does It Matter?

18.1   February 16: Declaration date - the board of directors declares a dividend payment that will be made on March 14.

       February 24: Ex-dividend date - the shares trade ex dividend on and after this date. Sellers before this date receive the dividend. Purchasers on or after this date do not receive the dividend.

       February 26: Record date - the declared dividends are distributable to shareholders of record on this date.

       March 14:   Payable date - the checks are mailed.

18.2   Based on Miller and Modigliani reasoning, the stock will sell for $8.75. This is the same price you purchased the stock. When the stock goes ex-dividend the stock is expected to fall $0.75 a share.

18.3 a.   If the dividend is declared, the price of the stock will drop on the ex-dividend date by the value of the dividend, $5. It will then trade for $95.

     b.   If it is not declared, the price will remain at $100.

     c.   Mann's outflows for investments are $2,000,000. These outflows occur immediately. One year from now, the firm will realize $1,000,000 in net income and it will pay $500,000 in dividends. Since the only immediate financing need is for the investments, Mann must finance $2,000,000 through the sale of shares worth $100. It must sell $2,000,000 / $100 = 20,000 shares.

     d.   The MM model is not realistic since it does not account for taxes, brokerage fees, uncertainty over future cash flows, investors' preferences, signaling effects, and agency costs.

18.4 a.   The ex-dividend date is Feb. 27, which is two business days before the record date.

     b.   The stock price should drop by $1.25 on the ex-dividend date.

18.5   Knowing that share price can be expressed as the present value of expected future dividends does not make dividend policy relevant. Under the growing perpetuity model, if overall corporate cash flows are unchanged, then a change in dividend policy only changes the timing of the dividends. The PV of those dividends is the same. This is true because, given that future earnings are held constant, dividend policy simply represents a transfer between current and future stockholders.

    In a more realistic context and assuming a finite holding period, the value of the shares should represent the future stock price as well as the dividends. Any cash flow not paid as a dividend will be reflected in the future stock price. As such the PV of the flows will not change with shifts in dividend policy; dividend policy is still irrelevant.

18.6 a.   The price is the PV of the dividends,

$$\frac{\$2}{1.15} + \frac{\$17.5375}{1.15^2} = \$15$$

b. The current value of your shares is ($15)(500) = $7,500. The annuity you receive must solve

$$\$7,500 = \frac{X}{1.15} + \frac{X}{1.15^2} ;$$

You desire $4,613.3721 each year. You will receive $1,000 in dividends in the first year, so you must sell enough shares to generate $3,613.3721. The end-of-year price at which you will sell your shares is the PV of the liquidating dividend, $17.5375 / 1.15 = $15.25, so you must sell 236.942 shares. The remaining shares will each earn the liquidating dividend. At the end of the second year, you will receive $4,613.38 [= (500 - 236.942) x $17.5375]. (Rounding causes the discrepancies).

18.7 a. The value is the PV of the cash flows.
Value = $32,000 + $1,545,600 / 1.12 = $1,412,000

b. The current price of $141.20 per share will fall by the value of the dividend to $138.

c. i. According to MM, it cannot be true that the low dividend is depressing the price. Since dividend policy is irrelevant, the level of the dividend should not matter. Any funds not distributed as dividends add to the value of the firm hence the stock price. These directors merely want to change the timing of the dividends (more now, less in the future). As the calculations below indicate, the value of the firm is unchanged by their proposal. Therefore, share price will be unchanged.

To pay the $4.25 dividend, new shares, which total $10,500 (-$42,500 - $32,000) in value, must be sold. Those shares must also earn 12% so the value of the old shareholders' interest one year hence will fall $11,760 (=10,500 x 1.12). Under this scenario, the current value of the firm is Value = $42,500 + $1,533,840 / 1.12 = $1,412,000

ii. The new shareholders are not entitled to receive the current dividend. They will receive only the value of the equity one year hence. The PV of those flows is $1,533,840 / 1.12 = $1,369,500, so the share price will be $136.95 and 76.67 shares will be sold.

18.8 a. (1.2 + 15) / 1 = $16.2
Expected share price is $16.2.

b. He can invest the dividends into the Gibson stock.
Dividends that he gets = $1.2 million x 50% x 1,000 / 1,000,000 = $600
Expected share price after dividend = (0.6 + 15) / 1 =$15.6
Number of shares that Jeff needs to buy = 600 / 15.6 = 38

18.9 Alternative 1: Dividends are paid out to the shareholders now.
2 (1-31%) (1+7% (1-31%))³ = $1.59 million

Alternative 2: NBM invests cash in the financial assets:

i. T-bill
2 (1+7% (1-35%))³ (1-31%) = $1.58 million

ii. Preferred stock
$$2 \{1+11\% [1-(1-30\%) \times 35\%]^3\} (1-31\%) = \$1.75 \text{ million}$$

The after-tax cash flow for the shareholders is maximized when the firm invests the cash in the preferred stocks.

18.10 You should not expect to find either low dividend, high growth stocks or tax-free municipal bonds in the University of Pennsylvania's portfolio. Since the university does not pay taxes on investment income, it will want to invest in securities, which provide the highest pre-tax return. Since tax-free municipal bonds generally provide lower returns than taxable securities, there is no reason for the university to hold municipal bonds.
The Litzenberger-Ramaswamy research (discussed in the section on empirical evidence) found that high dividend stocks pay higher pre-tax returns than risk comparable low dividend stocks because of the taxes on dividend income. Since the University of Pennsylvania does not pay taxes, it would be wise to invest in high dividend stocks rather than low dividend stocks in the same risk class.

18.11 a.   If $T_C = T_0$ then $(P_e - P_b) / D = 1$. The stock price will fall by the amount of the dividend.

b.   If $T_C = 0$ and $T_0 \neq 0$ then $(P_e - P_b) / D = 1 - T_0$. The stock price will fall by the after-tax proceeds from the dividend.

c.   In a, there was no tax disadvantage to dividends. Thus, investors are indifferent between buying the stock at P_b and receiving the dividend or waiting, buying the stock at P_e and receiving a subsequent capital gain. When only the dividend is taxed, after-tax proceeds must be equated for investors to be indifferent. Since the after-tax proceeds from the dividend are $D (1 - T_0)$, the price will fall by that amount.

d.   No, Elton and Gruber's paper is not a prescription for dividend policy. In a world with taxes, a firm should never issue stock to pay a dividend, but the presence of taxes does not imply that firms should not pay dividends from excess cash. The prudent firm, when faced with other financial considerations and legal constraints may choose to pay dividends.

18.12 a.   Let x be the ordinary income tax rate. The individual receives an after-tax dividend of $1,000(1-x) which she invests in Treasury bonds. The T-bond will generate after-tax cash flows to the investor of $1,000 (1 - x)[1+0.08(1-x)].

If the firm invests the money, its proceeds are $1,000 [1 + 0.08 (1-0.35)]

To be indifferent, the investor's proceeds must be the same whether she invests the after-tax dividend or receives the proceeds from the firm's investment and pays taxes on that amount.
$$1,000 (1 - x) [1 + 0.08 (1 - x)] = (1 - x) \{1,000 [1 + 0.08 (1 - 0.35)]\}$$
$$x = 0.35$$
Note: This argument does not depend upon the length of time the investment is held.

b.   Yes, this is a reasonable answer. She is only indifferent if the after-tax proceeds from the $1,000 investment in identical securities are identical; that occurs only when the tax rates are identical.

c.   Since both investors will receive the same pre-tax return, you would expect the same answer as in part a. Yet, because Carlson enjoys a tax benefit from investing in stock, the tax rate on ordinary income, which induces indifference, is much lower.
$$1{,}000\,(1-x)\,[1+0.12(1-x)] = (1-x)\,\{1{,}000\,[1+0.12\,(1-0.3)\,(0.35)]\}$$
$$x = 24.5\%$$

d.   It is a compelling argument, but there are legal constraints, which deter firms from investing large sums in stock of other companies.

18.13 The fallacy behind both groups' arguments is that they are considering dividends the only return on a stock. They ignored capital gains. If dividends are controlled, firms are likely to decrease their dividends. When dividends are reduced, the companies retain more income, which causes share price to increase. That increase in share price will add to the investors' capital gains. Since dividends and capital gains are both ways of compensating investors, if transaction costs are negligible and there are no taxes, investors will be indifferent between the two forms of compensation.

18.14 a.   The after-tax expected return on Grebe stock is $4/20 = 0.2$. Since Deaton stock is in the same risk class, it will be priced to yield the same after-tax expected return.
$$0.2 = \frac{(20 - P_0)(1 - T_g) + 4(0.75)}{P_0}; T_g = 0$$

$$P_0 = \$19.17$$

b.   If $T_g = 25\%$, the after-tax expected return on Grebe stock is $(4)\,(1\text{-}0.25)/20 = 0.15$. Deaton's price will be
$$0.15 = \frac{(20 - P_0)(0.75) + 4(0.75)}{P_0}$$

$$P_0 = \$20$$

c.   In this MM world, when the tax rates are identical, there is no tax disadvantage to the dividend. Investors are indifferent between $1 in capital gains and $1 in dividends. Hence, Deaton's price will also be $20.

18.15 P (Payall) = $[100 + 25\,(1\text{-}25\%)]/(1+25\%) = \$95$
P (Payless) = $[100 + 25\,(50\%) + 25\,(50\%)\,(1-25\%)]/(1+25\%) = \$97.5$
P (Paynone) = $\$100$

18.16 a.   Dividend yield: $4.5/50.50 = 0.0891$
b.   The pricing of bonds was discussed in an earlier chapter. Whenever a bond is selling at par, the yield to maturity is the coupon rate. So, the yield on the DuPont bonds is 11%.
c.   After-tax shield = (Pre-tax yield) (1 - T)

	Preferred stock	Debt
i. GM's pension fund; T=0	8.91%	11.00%
ii. GM; T=.34	8.00%	7.26%
iii Roger Smith; T = 0.28	6.42%	7.92%

*GM is exempt from 70% of taxes on dividend income, therefore, its effective tax rate is $(0.3)\,(0.34) = 0.102$.

d.   Corporations, which are exempt from 70% of taxes on dividend income, would hold the preferred stock.

18.17 The bird-in-the-hand argument is based upon the erroneous assumption that increased dividends make a firm less risky. If capital spending and investment spending are unchanged, the firm's overall cash flows are not affected by the dividend policy.

18.18 This argument is theoretically correct. In the real world with transaction costs of security trading, home-made dividends can be more expensive than dividends directly paid out by the firms. However, the existence of financial intermediaries such as mutual funds reduces the transaction costs for individuals greatly. Thus, as a whole, the desire for current income shouldn't be a major factor favoring high-current-dividend policy.

18.19 To minimize her tax burden, your aunt should divest herself of high dividend yield stocks and invest in low dividend yield stock. Or, if possible, she should keep her high dividend stocks, borrow an equivalent amount of money and invest that money in a tax deferred account.

18.20 This is not evidence on investor preferences. A rise in stock price when the current dividend is increased may reflect expectations that future earnings, cash flows, etc. will rise. The better performance of the 115 companies, which raised their payouts, may also reflect a signal by management through the dividends that the firms were expected to do well in the future.

18.21 Virginia Power's investors probably were not aware of the cash flow crunch. Thus, the price drop was due to the negative information about the cost overruns. Even if they were suspicious that there were overruns, the announcement would still cause a drop in price because it removed all uncertainty about overruns and indicated their magnitude.

18.22 As the firm has been paying out regular dividends for more than 10 years, the current severe cut in dividends can cause the shareholders to lower their expectations on current and future cash flows of the firm. It then results in the drop in the stock price.

18.23 a.   Cap's past behavior suggests a preference for capital gains while Widow Jones exhibits a preference for current income.
       b.   Cap could show the widow how to construct homemade dividends through the sale of stock. Of course, Cap will also have to convince her that she lives in an MM world. Remember that homemade dividends can only be constructed under the MM assumptions.
       c.   Widow Jones may still not invest in Neotech because of the transaction costs involved in constructing homemade dividends. Also the Widow may desire the uncertainty resolution which comes with high dividend stocks.

18.24 The capital investment needs of small, growing companies are very high. Therefore, payment of dividends could curtail their investment opportunities. Their other option is to issue stock to pay the dividend thereby incurring issuance costs. In either case, the companies and thus their investors are better off with a zero dividend policy during the firms' rapid growth phases. This fact makes these firms attractive only to low dividend clienteles.

This example demonstrates that dividend policy is relevant when there are issuance costs. Indeed, it may be relevant whenever the assumptions behind the MM model are not met.

18.25 Unless there is an unsatisfied high dividend clientele, a firm cannot improve its share price by switching policies. If the market is in equilibrium, the number of people who desire high dividend payout stocks should exactly equal the number of such stocks available. The supplies and demands of each clientele will be exactly met in equilibrium. If the market is not in equilibrium, the supply of high dividend payout stocks may be less than the demand. Only in such a situation could a firm benefit from a policy shift.

18.26 a. $Div_1 = Div_0 + s\,(t\,EPS_1 - Div_0)$
  $= 1.25 + 0.3\,(0.4 \times 4.5 - 1.25)$
  $= 1.415$

   b. $Div_1 = Div_0 + s\,(t\,EPS_1 - Div_0)$
  $= 1.25 + 0.6\,(0.4 \times 4.5 - 1.25)$
  $= 1.58$

   Note: Part "a" is more conservative since the adjustment rate is lower.

18.27   This finding implies that firms use initial dividends to "signal" their potential growth and positive NPV prospects to the stock market. The initiation of regular cash dividends also serves to convince the market that their high current earnings are not temporary.

Answers to End-of-Chapter Problems

Chapter 19: Issuing Equity Securities to the Public

19.1 a. A general cash offer is a public issue of a security that is sold to all interested investors. A general cash offer is not restricted to current stockholders.

b. A rights offer is an issuance that gives the current stockholders the opportunity to maintain a proportionate ownership of the company. The shares are offered to the current shareholders before they are offered to the general public.

c. A registration statement is the filing with the SEC, which discloses all pertinent information concerning the corporation that wants to make a public offering.

d. A prospectus is the legal document that must be given to every investor who contemplates purchasing registered securities in a public offering. The prospectus describes the details of the company and the particular issue.

e. An initial public offering (IPO) is the original sale of a company's securities to the public. An IPO is also called an unseasoned issue.

f. A seasoned new issue is a new issue of stock after the company's securities have previously been publicly traded.

g. Shelf registration is an SEC procedure, which allows a firm to file a master registration statement summarizing the planned financing for a two year period. The firm files short forms whenever it wishes to sell any of the approved master registration securities during the two year period.

19.2 a. The Securities Exchange Act of 1933 regulates the trading of new, unseasoned securities.

b. The Securities Exchange Act of 1934 regulates the trading of seasoned securities. This act regulates trading in what is called the secondary market.

19.3 Competitive offer and negotiated offer are two methods to select investment bankers for underwriting. Under the competitive offers, the issuing firm can award its securities to the underwriter with the highest bid, which in turn implies the lowest cost. On the other hand, in negotiated deals, underwriter gains much information about the issuing firm through negotiation, which helps increase the possibility of a successful offering.

19.4 a. Firm commitment underwriting is an underwriting in which an investment banking firm commits to buy the entire issue. It will then sell the shares to the public. The investment banking firm assumes all financial responsibility for any unsold shares.

b. A syndicate is a group of investment banking companies that agree to cooperate in a joint venture to underwrite an offering of securities.

c. The spread is the difference between the underwriter's buying price and the offering price. The spread is a fee for the services of the underwriting syndicate.

d. Best efforts underwriting is an offering in which the underwriter agrees to distribute as much of the offering as possible. Any unsold portions of the offering are returned to the issuing firm.

19.5 a. The risk in a firm commitment underwriting is borne by the underwriter(s). The syndicate agrees to purchase all of an offering. Then they sell as much of it as possible. Any unsold shares remain the responsibility of the underwriter(s). The risk that the security's price may become unfavorable also lies with the underwriter(s).

b. The issuing firm bears the risk in a best efforts underwriting. The underwriter(s) agrees to make its best effort to sell the securities for the firm. Any unsold securities are the responsibility of the firm.

19.6 In general, the new price per share after the offering is:
      P = (market value + proceeds from offering) / total number of shares
      i.   At $40 P = ($400,000 + ($40 x 5,000)) / 15,000 =$40
      ii.   At $20 P = ($400,000 + ($20 x 5,000)) / 15,000 = $33.33
      iii. At $10 P = ($400,000 + ($10 x 5,000)) / 15,000 = $30

19.7 The poor performance result should not surprise the professor. Since he subscribed to every initial public offering, he was bound to get fewer superior performers and more poor performers. Financial analysts studied the companies and separated the bad prospects from the good ones. The analysts invested in only the good prospects. These issues became oversubscribed. Since these good prospects were oversubscribed, the professor received a limited amount of stock from them. The poor prospects were probably under-subscribed, so he received as much of their stock as he desired. The result was that his performance was below average because the weight on the poor performers in his portfolio was greater than the weight on the superior performers. This result is called the winner's curse. The professor "won" the shares, but his bane was that the shares he "won" were poor performers.

19.8 There are two possible reasons for stock price drops on the announcement of a new equity issue:
      i.   Management may attempt to issue new shares of stock when the stock is over-valued, that is, the intrinsic value is lower than the market price. The price drop is the result of the downward adjustment of the overvaluation.
      ii.   With the increase of financial distress possibility, the firm is more likely to raise capital through equity than debt. The market price drops because it interprets the equity issue announcement as bad news.

19.9 The costs of new issues include underwriter's spread, direct and indirect expenses, negative abnormal returns associated with the equity offer announcement, under-pricing, and green-shoe option.

19.10 a. $12,000,000/$15 = 800,000
      b.   2,400,000/800,000 = 3
      c.   The shareholders must remit $15 and three rights for each share of new stock they wish to purchase.

19.11 a.   In general, the ex-rights price is
           P = (Market value + Proceeds from offering) / Total number of shares
           P = ($25 x 100,000 + $20 x 10,000) / (100,000 + 10,000) = $24.55
      b.   The value of a right is the difference between the rights-on price of the stock and the ex-rights price of the stock. The value of a right is $0.45 (=$25 - $24.55).
           Alternative solution:
           The value of a right can also be computed as:
           (Ex-rights price - Subscription price) / Number of rights required to buy a share of stock
           Value of a right = ($24.55 - $20) / 10 = $0.45
      c.   The market value of the firm after the issue is the number of shares times the ex-rights price.
           Value = 110,000 x $24.55 ≈ $2,700,000 (Note that the exact ex-rights price is $24.5454.)

Answers to End-of-Chapter Problems

d.   The most important reason to offer rights is to reduce issuance costs. Also, rights offerings do not dilute ownership and they provide shareholders with more flexibility. Shareholders can either exercise or sell their rights.

19.12 The value of a right = $50 - $45 = $5
The number of new shares = $5,000,000 / $25 = 200,000
The number of rights / share = ($45 - $25) / $5 = 4
The number of old shares = 200,000 x 4 = 800,000

19.13 a.   Assume you hold three shares of the company's stock. The value of your holdings before you exercise your rights is 3 x $45 = $135. When you exercise, you must remit the three rights you receive for owning three shares, and ten dollars. You have increased your equity investment by $10. The value of your holdings is $135 + $10 = $145. After exercise, you own four shares of stock. Thus, the price per share of your stock is $145 / 4 = $36.25.

b.   The value of a right is the difference between the rights-on price of the stock and the ex-rights price of the stock. The value of a right is $8.75 (=$45 - $36.25).

c.   The price drop will occur on the ex-rights date. Although the ex-rights date is neither the expiration date nor the date on which the rights are first exercisable, it is the day that the price will drop. If you purchase the stock before the ex-rights date, you will receive the rights. If you purchase the stock on or after the ex-rights date, you will not receive the rights. Since rights have value, the stockholder receiving the rights must pay for them. The stock price drop on the ex-rights day is similar to the stock price drop on an ex-dividend day.

19.14 a.   Stock price (ex-right) = (13+2) / (1+0.5) = $10
Subscription price = 2 / 0.5 = $4
Right's price = 13-10 = $3
$\qquad$ = (10-4) / 2 = $3

b.   Stock price (ex-right) = (13+2) / (1+0.25) = $12
Subscription price = 2 / 0.25 = $8
Right's price = 13-12 = $1
$\qquad$ = (12-8) / 4 = $1

c.   The stockholders' wealth is the same between the two arrangements.

19.15 If the interest of management is to increase the wealth of the current shareholders, a rights offering may be preferable because issuing costs as a percentage of capital raised is lower for rights offerings. Management does not have to worry about underpricing because shareholders get the rights, which are worth something. Rights offerings also prevent existing shareholders from losing proportionate ownership control. Finally, whether the shareholders exercise or sell their rights, they are the only beneficiaries.

19.16 Reasons for shelf registration include:
i.   Flexibility in raising money only when necessary without incurring additional issuance costs.
ii. As Bhagat, Marr and Thompson showed, shelf registration is less costly than conventional underwritten issues.
iii. Issuance of securities is greatly simplified.

19.17 Suppliers of venture capital can include:
   i.   Wealthy families / individuals.
   ii. Investment funds provided by a number of private partnerships and corporations.
   iii. Venture capital subsidiaries established by large industrial or financial corporations.
   iv. "Angels" in an informal venture capital market.

19.18 The proceeds from IPO are used to:
   i. exchange inside equity ownership for outside equity ownership
   ii. finance the present and future operations of the IPO firms.

19.19 Basic empirical regularities in IPOs include:
   i.   underpricing of the offer price,
   ii. best-efforts offerings are generally used for small IPOs and firm-commitment offerings are generally used for large IPOs,
   iii. the underwriter price stabilization of the after market and,
   iv. that issuing costs are higher in negotiated deals than in competitive ones.

Answers to End-of-Chapter Problems

Chapter 20: Long-Term Debt

20.1 a.   If you purchase the bond on March 1, you owe the seller two months of interest. The seller owned the bond for two months since the last interest payment date (January 1). She is entitled to the interest earned during those two months. Since Raeo Corp.'s interest payment will not go to her, you must pay it to her now.

The interest rate on the bond is 10%. The interest per month is 0.8333% (=10% / 12). 1.6667% (= 0.8333% x 2) is the interest for two months. The bonds are selling at 100, 100% of face value. If today is March 1, you will pay 100% of the face plus 1.6667% for the bond. If the face value of the bonds is $1,000, then you will pay $1,000 + $1,000 (0.016667) = $1,016.67.

   b.   If you purchase the bond on October 1, you owe the seller three months of interest. The seller owned the bond for three months since the last interest payment date (July 1). She is entitled to the interest earned during those three months. Since Raeo Corp.'s interest payment will not go to her, you must pay it to her now.
The interest rate on the bond is 10%. The interest per month is 0.8333% (= 10% / 12). 2.5% (0.8333% x 3) is the interest for three months. The bonds are selling at 100, 100% of face value. If today is October 1, you will pay 100% of the face value plus 2.5% for the bond. If the face value of the bonds is $1,000, then you will pay $1,000 + $1,000 (0.025) = $1,025.

   c.   Since July 1 is an interest payment date, there is no accrued interest on the Raeo bonds. If today is July 1, you will pay 100% of the face value for the bond. If the face value of the bonds is $1,000, then you will pay $1,000.

   d.   If you purchase the bond on August 15, you owe the seller six weeks of interest. The seller owned the bond for six weeks since the last interest payment date (July 1). She is entitled to the interest earned during those six weeks (a month and a half). Since Raeo Corp.'s interest payment will not go to her, you must pay it to her now.

The interest rate on the bond is 10%. The interest per two week period is 0.41667% (10% / 24). 1.25% (=0.41667% x 3) is the interest for one and a half months. The bonds are selling at 100, 100% of face value. If today is August 15, you will pay 100% of the face plus 1.25% for the bond. If the face value of the bonds is $1,000, then you will pay $1,000 + $1,000 (0.0125) = $1,012.50.

20.2 a.   A protective covenant is the part of an indenture or loan agreement that limits the actions of the borrowing company.
   b.   A negative covenant prohibits actions that the company may want to take. Examples include limits on dividends, inability to pledge assets, prohibition of mergers and prohibitions on additional issue of long-term debt.
   c.   A positive covenant specifies actions that the firm is obliged to take. Examples include maintaining a minimum level of working capital and furnishing additional financial statements to the lender.
   d.   A sinking fund is an account managed by a bond trustee for the purpose of repaying bonds.

20.3 Sinking funds provide additional security to bonds. If a firm is experiencing financial difficulty, it is likely to have trouble making its sinking fund payments. Thus, the sinking fund provides an early warning system to the bondholders about the quality of the bonds. A drawback to sinking funds is that they give the firm an option that the bondholders may find distasteful. If bond prices are low, the firm may satisfy its sinking fund by buying bonds in the open market. If bond prices are high though, the firm may satisfy its sinking fund by purchasing bonds at face value. Those bonds being repurchased are chosen through a lottery.

20.4 Open-end mortgage is riskier because the firm can issue additional bonds on its property, making the existing bonds riskier.

20.5 The difference between the call price and the face value is the call premium. The first few years during which a company is prohibited from calling its bonds is the call-protected period (or the grace period).

20.6 a. If KIC's bonds are non-callable, the price today is the PV of the coupon, which will be received at the end of the next year plus the expected value of the bond one year hence. The price of the bond one year from now will depend upon the interest rate which prevails in the market. If the interest rate is 14%, the price of the KIC bond will be $857.14 (= $120 / 0.14). If the interest rate is 7%, the price of the KIC bond will be $1,714.29 (=$120 / 0.07). The coupon which the KIC bond will pay is 12% of the face, or $120 (=0.12 x $1,000). The expected price of the bond is 0.5x($857.14) + 0.5x($1,714.29) = $1,285.71. Discounting by the prevailing market interest rate yields the current price of the KIC bond.

P = ($120 + $1,285.71) / 1.11 = $1,266.41

[Note for students who have studied term structure: the assumption of risk-neutrality implies that the forward rate is equal to the expected future spot rate.]

b. If the KIC bond is callable, then the bond value will be less than the amount computed in part a. If the bond price rises above $1,450, KIC will call it. The call will effectively transfer wealth from the bondholders to the stockholders.

20.7 If interest rates rise to 15%, the price of the Bowdeen bonds will fall. If the price of the firm's bonds is low, Bowdeen will not call them. The firm would be foolish to pay the call price for something worth less than the call price. In this case, the bondholders will receive the coupon payment, C. They will still be holding a bond worth C/0.15. Their total holding will be C + C / 0.15.

If interest rates fall to 8%, it is highly likely that the price of the bonds will rise above the call price. If this happens, Bowdeen will call the bonds. In this case, the bondholders will receive the call price, $1,250, plus the coupon payment, C.

The selling price today of the bonds is the PV of the expected payoffs to the bondholders. The expected payoff is 0.6 (C + C / 0.15) + 0.4 (C + $1,250). Since Bowdeen wants today's price of the bonds to be $1,000, discount the expected payoffs at the current rate of interest and solve for C.

$1,000 = [0.6 (C + C/0.15) + 0.4 (C + $1,250)] / 1.12
C = $124.00

The coupon payment for the year must be $124.00. Thus, the coupon rate which ensures that the bonds will sell at par is 0.124 (=$124.00 / $1,000).

Answers to End-of-Chapter Problems

20.8 a. The value of the non-callable bond is given by:
$V_{NC} = [\$80 + 0.65 (\$80 / 0.06) + 0.35 (\$80 / 0.09)] / 1.08 = \$1,164.61$

b. Let C = Call Premium. The value of the callable bond is:
$V_C = [C + 0.65 (\$1,000 + C) + 0.35 (C / 0.09)] / 1.08$
Set $V_C = \$1,000$ and solve for C. C = \$77.63.

c. To the company, the value of the call provision will be given by the difference between the value of an outstanding, non-callable bond and the call provision.

Non-callable bond value = \$77.63 / 0.06 = \$1,293.83
Value to the company of the call provision = [0.65 (\$1,293.83 - \$1,077.63)] / 1.08
= \$130.12

20.9 Next year's bond price if it is non-callable:
40% chance: (1,000 x 9%) /12% = \$750
60% chance: (1,000 x 9%) / 6% = \$1,500 > \$1,150
So if the interest rate falls to 6%, New Business Venture Inc. would call back its bond at \$1,150. So current bond price = [90 + (40% x 750 + 60% x 1,150)] / (1 + 10%) = \$981.82

20.10 The NPV of the refunding is the difference between the gain from refunding and the refunding costs.
Gain = B $(r_1 - r_2) / r_2$
Cost = (CB) / F + K
Where C = the call premium
F = the face value
B = the par value of the old bonds
K = the issuing costs
r_1 = the coupon rate of the old bonds and
r_2 = the coupon rate of the new bonds.
Gain = \$500 million (0.09 - 0.07) / 0.07 = \$142,857,143
Cost = 90 (\$500 million) / \$1,000 + \$80 million = \$125 million
NPV = \$142,857,143 - \$125,000,000 = \$17,857,143

20.11 NPV = 250 x (0.08 - r_2) / r_2 - 0.12 x 250 x 0.65 = 0
r_2 = 7.42%
Refinancing is a wise option if borrowing costs are below 7.42%.

20.12 8% perpetual bond:
NPV = 75 x (8% - 7%) / 7% - 75 x 8.5% -10 = -\$5.66 million < 0
9% perpetual bond:
NPV = 87.5 x (9% - 7.25%) - 87.5 x 9.5% - 12 = \$0.8082 million

So Ms. Kimberly should recommend the re-financing of the 9% perpetual bond, since the NPV of the refunding is \$0.8082 million.

20.13 Bonds with an S&P's rating of BB and below or a Moody's rating of Ba and below are called junk bonds (or below-investment grade bonds). The recent controversies of junk bonds are:
i. Junk bonds increase the firm's interest deduction.
ii. Junk bonds increase the possibility of high leverage, which may lead to wholesale default in economic downturns.
iii. The recent wave of mergers financed by junk bonds has frequently resulted in dislocations and loss of jobs.

20.14 a. For a floating rate bond, the coupon payments are adjustable. The adjustments are usually tied to an interest rate index.

b. Deep discount bonds are also called pure discount bonds or zero coupon bonds. As the latter name implies, these bonds do not pay a coupon. To generate a return, these bonds are sold at prices well below par.

c. Income bonds are similar to conventional bonds, except their coupon payments are tied to the firm's income. The bondholders are paid only if the firm generates enough income to do so. These bonds are attractive for firms to issue because if the firm cannot make an interest payment, it is not in default.

20.15

Characteristic	Public issues	Direct financing
a. Require SEC registration	Yes	No
b. Higher interest cost	No	Yes
c. Higher fixed cost	Yes	No
d. Quicker access to funds	No	Yes
e. Active secondary market	Yes	No
f. Easily renegotiated	No	Yes
g. Lower floatation costs	No	Yes
h. Require regular amortization	Yes	No
i Ease of repurchase at favorable prices	Yes	No
j. High total cost to small borrowers	Yes	No
k. Flexible terms	No	Yes
l. Require less intensive investigation	Yes	No

20.16 a. Yes. The statement is true. In an efficient market, the callable bonds will be sold at a lower price than that of the non-callable bonds, other things being equal. This is because the holder of callable bonds effectively sold a call option to the bond issuer. Since the issuer holds the right to call the bonds, the price of the bonds will reflect the disadvantage to the bondholders and the advantage to the bond issuer (i.e., the bondholder has the obligation to surrender their bonds when the call option is exercised by the bond issuer.)

b. As interest rate falls, the call option of the callable bonds are more likely to be exercised by the bond issuer. Since the non-callable bonds do not have such a drawback, the value of the bond will go up to reflect the decrease in the market rate of interest. Thus, the price of non-callable bonds will move higher than that of the callable bonds.

Chapter 21: Leasing

21.1   a.   Leasing can reduce uncertainty regarding the resale value of the asset that is leased.

      b.   Leasing does not provide 100% financing although it may look as though it does. Since firms must try to maintain their optimal debt ratio, the use of lease simply displaces debt. Thus, leasing does not provide 100% financing.

      c.   Although it is true that leasing displaces debt, empirical studies show that the companies that do a large amount of leasing also have a high debt-to-equity ratios.

      d.   If the tax advantages of leasing were eliminated, leasing would probably disappear. The main reason for the existence of long-term leasing is the differential in the tax rates paid by the lessee and the lessor.

21.2   a.   NPV (lease) $= \$250{,}000 - L\,A_{0.08}^{5}$

$$= \$250{,}000 - 3.9927\,L$$
$$= \$0$$

$L = \$62{,}614.11$

The lease payment is Quartz'a reservation price.

      b.   Depreciation $= \$250{,}000 / 5$
$$= \$50{,}000 \text{ per annum}$$

Depreciation tax shield
$$= \$50{,}000 \times 0.35$$
$$= \$17{,}500$$

After-tax discount rate
$$= 0.08\,(1 - 0.35)$$
$$= 0.052$$

NPV (lease) $= -\$250{,}000 + L\,(1 - 0.35)\,A_{0.052}^{5} + \$17{,}500\,A_{0.052}^{5}$

$$= \$0$$

$L = \$62{,}405.09$

This lease payment is New Leasing Co's reservation price.

      c.   If the lease price is greater than Quartz's reservation price, the lease is a negative NPV proposal for Quartz. Quartz would rather purchase the equipment than lease at a payment above its reservation price. Thus, the lessee's reservation price is the maximum of the negotiation range.

21.3 Incremental cash flows from leasing instead of purchasing:

Lease minus Buy	Year 0	Year 1 - 5
Lease		
Lease payment		-$94,200
Tax benefit of lease payment		$32,970
Buy (minus)		
Cost of machine	-(-$350,000)	
Lost depreciation tax benefit		-$350,000/5 × 0.35
		= -$24,500
Total	$350,000	-$85,730

$$\text{NPV} = \$350,000 - \$85,730 \ A^{5}_{0.11(0.65)}$$
$$= -\$102.66 < \$0$$
The firm should buy the machine.

24.4 Maxwell's reservation price:
$$\text{NPV (lease)} = \$200,000 - L \ A^{5}_{0.10}$$
$$= \$200,000 - 3.7908 \ L$$
$$= \$0$$
$$L = \$52,759.50$$
Mercer's reservation price:
$$\text{Depreciation} = \$200,000 \ / \ 5$$
$$= \$40,000 \text{ per annum}$$
Depreciation tax shield
$$= \$40,000 \times 0.35$$
$$= \$14,000$$
After-tax discount rate
$$= 0.10 \ (1 - 0.35)$$
$$= 0.065$$
$$\text{NPV (lease)} = -\$200,000 + L \ (1 - 0.35) \ A^{5}_{0.065} + \$14,000 \ A^{5}_{0.065}$$
$$= \$0$$
$$L = \$52,502.94$$
Therefore, the negotiation range is from $52,502.94 to $52,759.50.

21.5 Reservation payment of Raymond:
$$\text{Value of lease} = \$100,000 - 0.75 \ L \ A^{5}_{0.08(0.75)} = \$0$$
$$L = \$31,652.85$$
Reservation payment of Liberty:
$$\text{Value of lease} = -\$100,000 + \left(\frac{100,000}{5}\right) \times 0.35 A^{5}_{0.08(0.65)}$$
$$L = \$24,962.04$$
Therefore, the negotiation range is from $24,962.04 to $31,652.85. For lease payments higher than $31,652.85, Raymond will not enter into the arrangement. For lease payments lower than $24,962.04, Liberty will not enter into the arrangement.

21.6 a.   The lease payment, which makes both parties equally well off, is the payment, which equates the NPVs for the firms. Since the tax rates of the two firms are equal, the perspective of the lessor is the opposite of the perspective of the lessee. This condition ensures that the NPV is zero.

After-tax cash flows to the lessor
= L (1 - 0.34) + Depreciation (0.34)

Depreciation = $86.87 / 2 = $43.435

The NPV is zero when the NPV of the lessor's after-tax cash flows equals the cost of the asset. The appropriate discount rate is the after-tax rate. That rate is 6.6% [= 10% × 0.66].

$$\$86.87 = [0.66\, L + \$43.435\,(0.34)]\; A^2_{0.066}$$

$$\$86.87 = [0.66\, L + \$43.435\,(0.34)]\,(1.8181)$$

$$L = \$50.02$$

b.   Generalize the result from part a.

Let T_1 denote the lessor's tax rate.

Let T_2 denote the lessee's tax rate.

Let P denote the purchase price of the asset.

Let Dep equal the annual depreciation expense.

Let N denote the length of the lease in years.

$$\text{Value to the lessor} = -P + \sum_{t=1}^{N} \frac{L(1-T_1)+\text{Dep}(T_1)}{[1+r(1-T_1)]^t}$$

$$\text{Value to the lessee} = P - \sum_{t=1}^{N} \frac{L(1-T_2)+\text{Dep}(T_2)}{[1+r(1-T_2)]^t}$$

The values of the lease to its two parties will be opposite in sign only if $T_1 = T_2$.

c.   Since the lessor's tax bracket is unchanged, the lease has a zero NPV to the lessor when the lease payment is $50.02.

If the lessee pays no taxes, the pre-tax and after-tax lease payment are the same. Also, one of the lessee's cash flows is the depreciation that is foregone when leasing is chosen over purchasing. If the lessee's tax rate is zero, it will not benefit from depreciation. Thus, if the lessee chooses leasing, the lost depreciation is no longer a cash flow. The lease has a zero NPV to the lessee when L = $50.05.

$$L\; A^2_{0.10} = \$86.87$$

$$L = \$86.87 / 1.7355$$

$$= \$50.05$$

If L > $50.05 the NPV to the lessee is < $0.
If L < $50.05 the NPV to the lessee is > $0.
If L > $50.05 the NPV to the lessor is > $0.
If L < $50.05 the NPV to the lessor is < $0.

Both parties have positive NPV for $50.02 < L < $50.05.

21.7 a.   Assume that 10% is the market-wide interest rate. The decision to buy or lease is made by looking at the incremental cash flows.

Cash flows from leasing:

Year	0	1	2	3	4	5
A/T savings*		$3,960	$3,960	$3,960	$3,960	$3,960
Lease payment		-2,100	-2,100	-2,100	-2,100	-2,100
Tax benefit**		714	714	714	714	714
Net cash flows		2,574	2,574	2,574	2,574	2,574

* After tax savings on operations
   = $6,000 × 0.66
   = $3,960
** Tax benefit
   = $2,100 × 0.34
   = $714

Cash flows from purchasing:

Year	0	1	2	3	4	5
A/T savings*		$5,940	$5,940	$5,940	$5,940	$5,940
Purchase	-15,000					
Dep tax shield**		1,020	1,020	1,020	1,020	1,020
Net cash flows	-15,000	6,960	6,960	6,960	6,960	6,960

* After tax savings on operations
   = $9,000 × 0.66
   = $5,940
** Depreciation = $15,000 / 5 = $3,000 per annum
   Depreciation tax shield
   = $3,000 × 0.34
   = $1,020

Incremental cash flows from leasing vs. purchasing:

Year	0	1	2	3	4	5
Lease		$2,574	$2,574	$2,574	$2,574	$2,574
Purchase	-15,000	6,960	6,960	6,960	6,960	6,960
L – P	15,000	-4,386	-4,386	-4,386	-4,386	-4,386

NPV of the incremental cash flows:

The cash flows must be discounted at the after tax rate which is 6.6% [= 10% × 0.66].

$$NPV = \$15,000 - \$4,386 \ A^5_{0.066}$$
$$= \$15,000 - \$4,386 \ (4.1445)$$
$$= -\$3,177.78$$

Since the NPV of the lease-vs.-buy incremental cash flows is negative, Farmer should buy, not lease the equipment.

b.   As long as the company maintains its target debt-equity ratio, the answer does not depend upon the form of financing used for the direct purchase. A financial lease will displace debt regardless of the form of financing.

c.   The amount of displaced debt is the PV of the incremental cash flows from year one through five.
   $$PV = \$4,386 \ (4.1445) = \$18,177.78$$

21.8 Redwood:

	Year 0	Year 1 - 6	Year 7
Cost of machine	$420,000	$0	$0
Lease payment	-L	-L	$0

$420,000 - L = A^6_{0.06} L$

L = $70,978.03

American:

	Year 0	Year 1 - 6	Year 7
Cost of machine	-$420,000	$0	$0
Dep tax shield		$21,000	$21,000
A/T lease payment	0.65 L	0.65 L	$0

Value of lease

$= -\$420,000 + \$21,000 \ A^7_{0.06(0.65)} + 0.65 \ L + 0.65 \ L \ A^6_{0.06(0.65)}$

$= -\$420,000 + \$21,000 \ (6.0243) + 4.0685 \ L = \$0$

L = $72,137

The negotiating range is from $72,137 to $70,978.03.

21.9 The decision to buy or lease is made by looking at the incremental cash flows.

a. Cash flow from leasing:

Year	0	1	2	3
Lease payment		-$1,200,000	-$1,200,000	-$1,200,000
Tax benefit*		420,000	420,000	420,000
Net cash flow		-$780,000	-$780,000	-$780,000

*Tax benefit = $1,200,000 x .35 = $420,000

Cash flow from purchasing:

Year	0	1	2	3
Purchase cost	-$3,000,000			
Dep tax shield*		$350,000	$350,000	$350,000
Net cash flow	-3,000,000	350,000	350,000	350,000

*Depreciation tax shield = [$3,000,000 / 3] x 35% = $350,000

Incremental cash flows from leasing vs. purchasing:

Year	0	1	2	3
Lease		-$780,000	-$780,000	-$780,000
Purchase (minus)	$3,000,000	-350,000	-350,000	-350,000
Net cash flow	$3,000,000	-1,130,000	-1,130,000	-1,130,000

After-tax discount rate

$= 0.12 \times 0.65$

$= 0.078$

NPV of incremental cash flows

$= \$3,000,000 - \$1,130,000 \ A^3_{0.078}$

$= \$3,000,000 - \$1,130,000 \ (2.5864)$

$= \$77,339.09$

Therefore, Wolfson should lease the machine.

b.   Wolfson is indifferent at the lease payment which makes the NPV of the incremental cash flows zero.

$$NPV = \$0$$
$$= \$3,000,000 - (0.65\ L + \$350,000)\ A^3_{0.078}$$
$$= \$3,000,000 - (0.65\ L + \$350,000)\ (2.5864)$$
$$L = \$1,246,002.96$$

Chapter 22: Options and Corporate Finance

22.1   a.   An option is a contract which gives its owner the right to buy or sell an underlying asset at a fixed price on or before a given date.

       b.   Exercise is the act of buying or selling the underlying asset under the terms of the option contract.

       c.   The strike price is the fixed price at which the option holder can buy or sell the underlying asset. The strike price is also called the exercise price.

       d.   The expiration date is the maturity date of the option. It is the last date on which an American option can be exercised. It is the only date on which a European option can be exercised.

       e.   A call is an option contract, which gives its owner the right to buy an underlying asset at a fixed price on or before a given date.

       f.   A put is an option contract, which gives its owner the right to sell an underlying asset at a fixed price on or before a given date.

22.2   American options can be exercised on any date up to and including the exercise date. A European option can be exercised only on the expiration date.

22.3   The lower bound of the value of the put is Max $\{E - S, 0\} = \$40 - \$35 = \$5$. Since the option is selling for $4.5, the best strategy is (1) buy more put options at $4.5 and (2) exercise them to get arbitrage.

22.4   a.   It can be exercised on any date up to and including the expiration date.

       b.   It can be exercised only on February 18 of next year.

       c.   The option is not worthless.

22.5   Payoff

	$S < \$80$	$S = \$80$	$S > \$80$
Short 10 puts	$-10 (\$80 - S)$	$0	0
Long 5 calls	$0	$0	$5 (S - \$80)$
Total payoff	$-10 (\$80 - S)$	$0	$5 (S - \$80)$

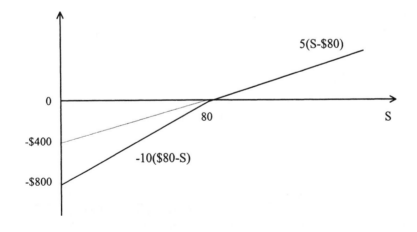

22.6   a.   Payoff = $55 - $50 = $5
        b.   Payoff = max {$45 - $50, $0} = $0
        c.

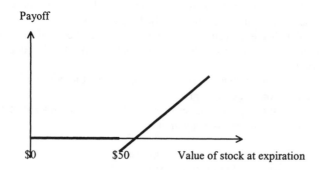

Payoff

$0 $50   Value of stock at expiration

22.7   a.   Payoff = $0
        b.   Payoff = $50 - $45 = $5
        c

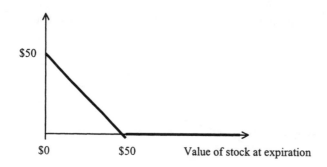

$50

$0 $50   Value of stock at expiration

22.8   a.

	S = $65	S = $72	S = $80
Long 2 calls	$0	200($72-$70)=$400	200($80-$70)=$2,000
Long 1 put	100($75-$65)=$1,000	100($75-$72)=$300	$0
Total payoff	$1,000	$700	$2,000

Answers to End-of-Chapter Problems

b.

	S < $70	$70 < S < $75	S ≥ $75
Long 2 calls	$0	200(S-$70)	200(S-$70)
Long 1 put	100($75-S)	100($75-S)	$0
Total payoff	100($75-S)	100(S-$65)	200(S-$70)

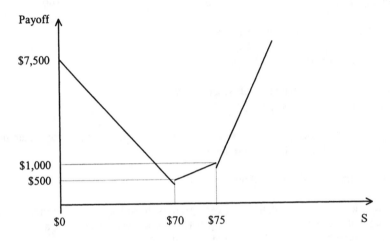

22.9   a.   You would exercise the call option contract by paying the strike price of $100/share and receiving stock worth $130 / share. The total profit from the contract is ($130 - 100) x 100 = $3,000.

      b.   If the stock price is lower than the strike price, the option will be expired unexercised.

22.10 Assume the options will expire in one year, apply the put-call parity formula.
$$S + P - C = PV(E)$$
$$S = -\$2 + \$8 + \$40 / 1.1$$
$$= \$42.36$$

22.11 a.   To eliminate the risk of the put, sell a call and buy stock. Buying stock makes stock available to you in the event that its price falls. If the price falls below the exercise price, the put will be exercised against you. The call provides additional income if the price of the stock rises above the exercise price. The combination, buy stock, buy a put and sell a call, ensures that the net payoff is the same whether the stock price rises to $172 or falls to $138.

b.	Payoffs at expiration

	S = $172	S = $138
Buy stock	$172	$138
Buy put	expires	give up stock worth $138, receive $160
Sell call	give up stock worth $172, receive $160	
Net payoff	$160	$160

22.12	a.	You should buy the call and exercise it immediately.

b.	Profit = ($60 - $50) - $8 = $2

c.	The lower bound on the price of American calls is
[Stock price - Exercise price].

d.	Upper bound = stock price because no one would be willing to pay more than the stock price for the right to receive the stock.

21.13	Factors determining the value of an American call:

1.	Strike price: The value of an American call must be at least the difference between the stock price and the exercise price [S - E]. For a given stock price, a higher exercise price will reduce the value of the call.

2.	Expiration date: The time to expiration of a call affects the price of the option. Compare two calls, which are identical except for the time to expiration. The longer-term option has all the rights and benefits of the shorter-term option, plus more. It has all of those benefits and rights for a longer period of time. Thus, as the time to expiration increases, the value of the call increases.

3.	Stock price: The value of an American call must be at least the difference between the stock price and the exercise price [S - E]. For a given exercise price, a higher stock price will increase the value of the call.

4.	Variability of the price of the underlying asset: The higher the variability of the price of the underlying asset is, the higher is the probability that the call will be in the money at the expiration date. Thus, higher variability of the asset's price will enhance the option's value.

5.	Interest rate: If you buy a call, you do not have to pay the strike price until the expiration date. The delay in the payment has value. As interest rates rise, the delayed payment has more value. To convince yourself, consider what else you can do with the strike price until the expiration date (your opportunity cost). You can put that money in an account and earn interest on the amount until the expiration date. If the interest rate increases, you will earn more interest.

21.14 Factors determining the value of an American put:

1.   Strike price: The value of an American put must be at least the difference between the exercise price and the stock price [E - S]. For a given stock price, a higher exercise price will increase the value of the put.

2.   Expiration date: The time to expiration of a put affects the price of the option. Compare two puts which are identical except for the time to expiration. The longer-term option has all the rights and benefits of the shorter-term option, plus more. It has all of those benefits and rights for a longer period of time. Thus, as the time to expiration increases, the value of the put increases.

3.   Stock price: The value of an American put must be at least the difference between the exercise price and the stock price [E - S]. For a given exercise price, a higher stock price will reduce the value of the put.

4.   Variability of the price of the underlying asset: The higher the variability of the price of the underlying asset is, the higher is the probability that the put will be in the money at the expiration date. Thus, higher variability of the asset's price will enhance the option's value.

5.   Interest rate: If you buy a put, you have the right to sell the stock for a fixed price in the future. The present value of the delayed receipt decreases as the interest rate rises. Thus, if the interest rate rises, the value of the put will fall.

22.15 a.   An increase in the risk of the stock implies an increase in the volatility of the stock price. As the volatility of the stock price rises, the value of a call increases. Call holders gain only if the stock price is greater than the exercise price. Call holders do not lose if the stock price is less than the exercise price. The volatility increases the probability that the call will be in the money.

b.   An increase in the risk of the stock implies an increase in the volatility of the stock price. As the volatility of the stock price rises, the value of a put increases. Put holders gain only if the stock price is less than the exercise price. Put holders do not lose if the stock price is greater than the exercise price. The volatility increases the probability that the put will be in the money.

22.16 Value the call by examining the value of the investment combination, which duplicates the payoffs of the call. The investment strategy, which duplicates the payoffs of the call, is buy stock and borrow money.

Payoffs of buying a call:	$S_T = \$120$	$S_T = \$95$
Call (A contract covers 100 shares) Payoff	100 ($120 - $112) = $800	Expires = $0

Payoffs of the strategy:		
Buy 32 shares of the stock	32 × $120 = $3,840	32 × $95 = $3,040
Borrow $3,012.26*	-$3,040	-$3,040
Net payoff	$800	$0

* The net payoffs of the duplicating strategy must be the same as the payoffs of the call. To have the payoff be $800 when the stock price is $120, the repayment of the loan and its interest must be $3,040. If the annual interest rate is 10%, then the interest rate applicable for the five week life of the call is $(1.10)^{5/52} - 1 = 0.00921$. Thus, the amount which you must borrow to be sure you repay $3,040 is $3,012.26 [= $3,040 / 1.00921].

To prevent arbitrage, the value of the call must be equal to the value of setting up this strategy. The cost today of purchasing 32 shares of stock is 32 × $96 = $3,072. In addition you will borrow $3,012.26. The borrowing generates a cash inflow. The cost of establishing this strategy is $3,072 - $3,012.26 = $59.74. $59.74 is the cost of setting up a strategy, which duplicates the contract. Since the contract covers 100 shares, each call is worth $0.5974 [= $59.74 / 100].

22.17

Payoff at expiration	$S = \$25$	$S = \$35$
1. Call	$0	$3 × 100 = $300

2. Stock (N shares)	25 N	$35N
Borrow ($25N/1.05)	-25 N	-$25N
Net payoff	$0	$10N

Duplicating amount = $25 N / 1.05
     where $10 N = $300
     N = 30 shares
Borrow $25 × 30 shares / 1.05 = $714.29.
Thus, buying one call contract
     = (1) buy 30 shares of stock $900
        (2) borrow $714.29   -$714.29
                       $185.71

Call option value = $185.71
Call price per share = $1.857
From put-call parity,
     $P = C + PV(E) - S$
       = $1.857 + $32 / 1.05 - $30 = $2.333

22.18

Payoff at expiration	$S_T = \$40$	$S_T = \$60$
1. Call	$0	100 ($60 - $50) = $1,000
2. Buy N shares	$40N	$60N
Borrow	-$40N	-$40N
Net payoff	$0	$20N

To equate, $20N = $1,000

N = 50 shares

Thus, borrowing amount = $40 × 50 / 1.09 = $1,834.86

Call value = Value of 50 shares + Borrowing $1,834.86

= 50 × $55 - $1,834.86

= $915.14

Each call is worth $9.1514.

22.19 d_1 $= [\ln (\$62 / \$70) + (0.05 + 0.35 / 2) \times (4 / 52)] / [0.35 \times (4 / 52)]^{0.5}$

             $= -0.6342$

     d_2 $= -0.6342 - [0.35 \times (4 / 52)]^{0.5}$

             $= -0.7982$

   $N(d_1)$ $= 0.2643$

   $N(d_2)$ $= 0.2119$

     C $= [\$62 \times N(d_1)] - [\$70 \, e^{-(0.05)(4/52)} \times N(d_2)]$

             $= [\$62 (0.2643)] - [\$70 \, e^{-(0.05)(4/52)} (0.2119)]$

             $= \$1.61$

22.20 d_1 $= [\ln (\$52 / \$48) + (0.05 + 0.02) \times (1 / 3)] / [0.04 \times (1 / 3)]^{0.5}$

             $= 0.8953$

     d_2 $= 0.8953 - [0.04 \times (1 / 3)]^{0.5}$

             $= 0.7798$

   $N(d_1)$ $= 0.8147$

   $N(d_2)$ $= 0.7822$

     C $= [\$52 \times 0.8147] - [\$48 \, e^{-(0.05)(1/3)} \times 0.7822] = \$5.4394$

22.21   a. d_1 $= [\ln (\$45 / \$52) + (0.065 + 0.4 / 2) \times 0.5] / [0.4 \times 0.5]^{0.5}$

                 $= -0.0270$

        d_2 $= -0.0270 - [0.4 \times 0.5]^{0.5}$

                 $= -0.4742$

     $N(d_1)$ $= 0.4880$

     $N(d_2)$ $= 0.3192$

        C $= \$45 \times 0.4880 - \$52 \, e^{-(0.065)(0.5)} \times 0.3192$

                 $= \$5.89$

    b.   Since the time period is only six months, the exponent used in the calculation of the PV of the exercise price is 0.5.

        P $= C + PV(E) - S$

             $= \$5.89 + \$52 / (1 + 0.065)^{0.5} - \$45$

             $= \$11.28$

22.22 a. d_1 $= [\ln (\$70 / \$90) + (0.06 + 0.25 / 2) \times 0.5] / [0.25 \times 0.5]^{0.5}$
                      $= -0.4492$
              d_2 $= -0.4492 - [0.25 \times 0.5]^{0.5}$
                      $= -0.8028$
              $N(d_1)$ $= 0.3267$
              $N(d_2)$ $= 0.2111$
              C $= \$70 \times 0.3267 - \$90\ e^{-(0.06)(0.5)} \times 0.2111$
                      $= \$4.4315$
       b.   P $= C + PV(E) - S$
                      $= \$4.4315 + \$90 / (1 + 0.06)^{0.5} - \$70$
                      $= \$21.8472$

22.23 a. d_1 $= [\ln (\$37 / \$35) + (0.07 + 0.004 / 2)] / 0.0632$
                      $= 2.0185$
              d_2 $= 2.0185 - 0.0632$
                      $= 1.9553$
              $N(d_1)$ $= 0.9782$
              $N(d_2)$ $= 0.9747$
              C $= \$37 \times 0.9782 - \$35\ e^{-0.07} \times 0.9747$
                      $= \$4.3853$
       b. d_1 $= [\ln (\$37 / \$35) + (0.07 + 0.0064 / 2)] / 0.08$
                      $= 1.6096$
              d_2 $= 1.6096 - 0.08$
                      $= 1.5296$
              $N(d_1)$ $= 0.9463$
              $N(d_2)$ $= 0.9369$
              C $= \$37 \times 0.9463 - \$35\ e^{-0.07} \times 0.9369$
                      $= \$4.4385$
       c. d_1 $= [\$0 + (0.07 + 0.0064 / 2)] / 0.08$
                      $= 0.915$
              d_2 $= 0.915 - 0.08$
                      $= 0.835$
              $N(d_1)$ $= 0.8199$
              $N(d_2)$ $= 0.7981$
              C $= \$35 \times 0.8199 - \$35\ e^{-0.07} \times 0.7981$
                      $= \$2.6515$

22.24   S $= \$27$
        E $= \$25$
        t $= 120 / 365$
        σ^2 $= 0.0576$
        r_f $= 0.07$
        d_1 $= [\ln (\$27 / \$25) + (0.07 + 0.0576 / 2) \times (120 / 365)] / [0.0576 \times (120 / 365)]^{0.5}$
                $= 0.7953$
        d_2 $= 0.7953 - [0.0576 \times (120 / 365)]]^{0.5}$
                $= 0.6577$
        $N(d_1)$ $= 0.7867$
        $N(d_2)$ $= 0.7447$
        C $= \$27 \times 0.7867 - \$25\ e^{-(0.07)(120/365)} \times 0.7447$
                $= \$3.0470$

22.25 For a firm with debt, shares of stock can be thought of as call options on the assets of the firm due to the limited liability of stock. If the value of the assets exceeds the value of the debt, the stockholders will pay the debt-holders and enjoy the benefits of ownership of the remaining assets. The stockholders have the property rights over the assets in excess of the debt.

If the value of the assets of the firm is less than the value of the debt, the stockholders will simply give the bondholders the assets of the firm. The shareholders will walk away owning nothing.

Thus, the return to the shareholders at the end of a period is the maximum between zero and the excess of assets over debt, [V - B] where V is the value of the assets of the firm and B is the value of the debt. This payoff is exactly the payoffs of a call where V is analogous to the stock price and B is analogous to the exercise price.

22.26 The equity of the firm is regarded as a call option.

Payoff at expiration (million)	$250	$650
1. Call	$0	$350
2. Buy N shares	$250N	$650N
Borrow	-$250N	-$250N
Net payoff	$0	$400N

To equate, $400N = $350
        N = 0.875 shares of assets.
Thus, borrowing amount = $250 × 0.875 / 1.07 = $204.44 million
Call value = Value of 0.875 shares of the asset + Borrowing $204.44 million
        = $350 million - $204.44 million
        = $145.56 million
The value of the equity
        = $145.56 million
The value of the debt
        = $400 - $145.56
        = $254.44 million

22.27

Payoff at expiration (million)	$100	$800
1. Call	$0	$500
2. Buy N shares	$100N	$800N
Borrow	-$100N	-$100N
Net payoff	$0	$700N

To equate, $700N = $550
        N = (5 / 7) shares of assets.
Thus, borrowing amount = $100 × (5 / 7) / 1.07 = $66.76 million
Call value = Value of (5 / 7) shares of the asset + Borrowing $66.76 million
        = $285.71 million - $66.76 million

= $218.95 million
The value of the equity
= $218.95 million
The value of the debt
= $400 - $218.95
= $181.05 million
Thus, bondholders prefer the less risky project.

23.1 $d_1 = [(r + \frac{1}{2}\sigma^2)\,t]/\sqrt{\sigma^2\,t}$

$= [(0.06 + \frac{1}{2}(0.25)^2)\,4]/\sqrt{(0.25)^2\,(4)} = 0.73$

$N(d_1) = 0.7673$

$d_2 = d_1 - \sqrt{\sigma^2\,t} = 0.73 - \sqrt{(0.25)^2\,(4)} = 0.23$

$N(0.23) = 0.5910$

$C = 50(0.7673) - 50e^{-0.06 \times 4}(0.5910)$

$= \$38.365 - \$23.245 = \$15.12$

Total Value:

$\$15.12 \times \dfrac{\$1\ million}{\$50} = \$302,400$

23.2 Option A: use discount rate of 6%

Total pay value $= \$1\mathrm{mil}\ A^4_{0.06} + 1.2096$ million

Option B:

Total pay value $= \$1.25$ mil $A^4_{0.06}$

The question is whether the incremental $1.25 mil straight pay value is greater or lower than the options value of $1.2096 mil. If we use the riskless rate of 6%, the cost of additional $0.25 mil is $0.8663 mil (As opposed to $1.2096 mil). Holding everything else constant, Mr. Hurt is right and the Board is wrong. It's cheaper for the firm to pay Mr. Hurt a $1.25 mil straight pay without opitons. However, diversification may make the $1.25 mil straignt pay better off for Mr. Hurt. From the bounding effect, the firm will be better off to offer Mr. Hurt the options.

23.3 Fixed plant: $r = 12\%$

$NPV = -1\mathrm{million} + \dfrac{150,000(\$20)}{(1+0.12)^1} + \dfrac{\{0.5\,(150,000)\,(\$20) + 0.5\,(150,000/2)(\$20)\}A^9_{0.12}}{(1+0.12)^1}$

$= -1\mathrm{million} + \$2,678,571.43 + \$10,704,073.24$

$= \$12,382,644.67$

Flexible plant:

$NPV = -1.5\mathrm{million} + \dfrac{150,000(\$10)}{(1+0.12)^1} + \dfrac{\{0.5\,(150,000)\,(\$10)A^9_{0.12} + 0.5\,(150,000)(\$15)\}A^9_{0.12}}{(1+0.12)^1}$

$= -1.5\mathrm{million} + \$1,339,285.71 + \$8,920,061.03$

$= \$8,759,346.74$

TGC should choose the fixed plant since it has a larger NPV.

23.4   If rate = 11%;

$$NPV = \left(-\$50 + \frac{\$55}{1.11} \right) = -\$0.4505 \text{ million} < 0$$

If rate = 9%;

$$NPV = \left(-\$50 + \frac{\$55}{1.09} \right) = \$0.4588 \text{ million}$$

NPV = 0.5 (0) + 0.5 (0.4588 million) = \$229,400 > \$500
He should not take the offer to sell his option.

23.5 a. $NPV = -7 \text{ million} + (10,000 \times \$200)\ A_{0.15}^{5}$
          $= -\$295,689.80$

     b. $\$100,000 = CA_{0.15}^{4}$
          $C = \$35,026.54$
          (level of sales) × (\$200) = \$35,026.54
                        =175.13 units
                        ≈ 176 units

23.6 $NPV = -7 \text{ mil} + (10,000 \times \$200 / 1.15) + [(0.5 \times 15,000 \times \$200 \times A_{0.15}^{9}) + (0.5 \times 100,000)]/1.15$
          $= -7 \text{ mil} + \$1,739,130.43 + \$6,267,283.37$
          $= \$1,006,413.80$

Chapter 24: Warrants and Convertibles

24.1 a. Warrant is a security which gives its holder the right, though not the obligation, to buy common stock from the issuing firm at a fixed price for a given period of time. (Note that some warrants are perpetual.)

b. A convertible is a security, usually a bond, which gives its holder the right, though not the obligation, to exchange the security for common stock at a fixed ratio for a specific period.

24.2 a. If the stock price is below the exercise price, it would be foolish to exercise the warrant. Exercise would require payment of the high exercise price. For that price you would receive a share of stock worth less than what you paid. If you want to own the stock it is cheaper to buy the shares in the market. Thus, the warrant is worthless at expiration; its value is zero. Prior to expiration, the warrant will have value as long as there is some probability that the stock price will rise above the exercise price in the time remaining until expiration.

b. If the stock price is above the exercise price, the warrant has a value. That value is the difference between the stock price and the exercise price. If the warrant were priced below [stock price - exercise price], an investor could earn arbitrage profit by acquiring the warrant for less than [stock price - exercise price], exercising it for exercise price, and immediately selling the stock for stock price.

c. Even when the exercise price is zero, if the warrant is priced above the stock price, it would be cheaper to purchase the stock than to exercise the warrant.

24.3 a. The primary difference between warrants and calls is that the firm issues warrants while calls are issued between individuals.

b. The implication of the difference is that when a call is exercised, the number of shares outstanding does not change. There is simply a transfer of the shares between different parties. Also, when the call is exercised, the firm receives no additional funds. Neither of these facts is true about warrants. When a warrant is exercised, the number of outstanding shares increases by one. This effect is called dilution. The firm also receives the exercise price of the warrant.

24.4 a. Before the warrant is sold, the price of GR stock is the value of its assets, seven ounces of platinum, divided by the two shares outstanding.
$(7 \times \$500) / 2 = \$1,750$

b. Mrs. Fiske will exercise when the price of a share of GR Company reaches the exercise price of the warrant, $1,800. Solve for the price of platinum.
$(7 \times \text{Price of platinum}) / 2 = \$1,800$
Price of platinum = $514.29

c. i. $7 \times \$520 = \$3,640$
ii. Mrs. Fiske will exercise her warrant.

iii. The new price of GR stock will be the new value of the firm divided by the number of shares outstanding. The number of shares outstanding rose to three when Mrs. Fiske exercised her warrant. There are two ways to compute the value of the firm.

Method one: The new value of the firm is the old value plus the exercise price that Mrs. Fiske paid to receive her share of stock.

Value of GR = $(7 \times \$520) + \$1,800$

= $5,440

Thus, the price per share is $1,813.33 [= $5,440 / 3].

Method two: With the $1,800 from Mrs. Fiske, GR Company will buy 3.46154 [= $1,800 / $520] ounces of platinum. The total holdings of platinum by GR Company are $7 + 3.46154 = 10.46154$ ounces. After the purchase the value of the firm is $10.46154 \times \$520 = \$5,440$. Again, the price per share is $1,813.33 [= $5,440 / 3].

iv.   Mrs. Fiske's gain is the value of the share she now owns less the exercise price that she paid.

Gain   = $1,813.33 - $1,800

= $13.33

d.   If Mrs. Fiske had bought a call from Mr. Gould, she would have exercised it when the price of platinum jumped to $520 per ounce. Mrs. Fiske would have received Mr. Gould's share of stock, so the number of shares outstanding would remain unchanged. When platinum is $520 per ounce, the price of GR stock is $(7 \times \$520) / 2 = \$1,820$. Upon exercise of her call, Mrs. Fiske would receive stock worth $1,820 for which she paid $1,800. Thus, her gain would have been $20.

e.   The reason the gains are different is that the warrant dilutes the value of the stock. After exercise of a warrant, there are more shareholders making claims against the assets of the firm. Dilution does not occur with the exercise of a call.

24.5 a.   Lower limit = $0
Upper limit = $0.25 \times \$8 = \$2$

b.   Lower limit = $0.25 \times (\$12 - \$10) = \$0.5$
Upper limit = $0.25 \times \$12 = \$3$

24.6 Total value of equity before the exercise
= 10 million × $17 = $170 million
Number of shares being increased
= 5 × 200,000 = 1 million
Total value of equity after the exercise
= $170 million + 200,000 × $15 x 5
= $185 million
Thus, stock price after the exercise
= $185 million / (10 + 1) million
= $16.82

24.7 No, the market price of the warrant will not be zero. Unless the warrant will expire momentarily, the remaining period to expiration has value. If there is a positive probability that the market price of the stock will rise above $21 during the remaining period to expiration, the warrant is still valuable. Thus, the market price of the warrant would be greater than zero.

24.8 Warrant price = [4 million / (4 + 0.5) million] × call price
               = 0.8889 call price
       $d_1 = [\ln(\$22 / \$20) + (0.05 + 0.005 / 2)] / 0.005^{0.5}$
           = 2.0904
       $d_2 = 2.0904 - 0.005^{0.5}$
           = 2.0197
       $N(d_1)$ = 0.9817
       $N(d_2)$ = 0.9783
       $C = \$22 \times 0.9817 - \$20\, e^{-0.05} \times 0.9783$
           = \$2.9856
       Thus, warrant price = 0.8889 × \$2.9856
                       = \$2.654

24.9   #sh = 1.5 million
       $\#_w$ = 100,000 × 5 = 0.5 million
       #sh / (#sh + $\#_w$) = 1.5 / (1.5 + 0.5) = 0.75
       Therefore, warrant price = \$4.70 × 0.75
                       = \$3.525

24.10 a.   Minimum value of warrant X
                    = 3 × (\$30 - \$20) = \$30
       b.   Minimum value of warrant Y
                    = 2 × (\$40 - \$30) = \$20

24.11 B is more likely.
       Convertible bond price is the maximum of straight bond value and the conversion value.
       Bond A's conversion value = \$1,000 > Bond A's offering price. This is not feasible.

24.12 a.   Conversion value:
               Conversion ratio = \$1,000 / \$25 = 40
               Conversion value = 40 × \$24 = \$960
               Straight bond value < \$950.
               Therefore, minimum value = conversion value = \$960
       b.   Since the bond is not callable, the option of being able to wait to convert the bond
               has value. Bondholders can wait until it is most advantageous to convert their
               bonds without the fear that the firm will call the bonds. That feature has value and
               will account for the premium of the market value of the convertible debenture
               over its conversion value.

24.13 Ownership before the call = 500,000 / 4,000,000 = 0.125
                       = 12.5%
       Total number of shares outstanding after the call:
               4 million + (\$1,000 / \$20) × (\$20 million / \$1,000) = 5 million
       Therefore, ownership after the call
               = 500,000 / 5,000,000 = 0.10
               = 10%
       Her ownership dropped from 12.5% to 10%.

24.14 a. i. The conversion ratio is the number of shares a bondholder receives if he converts. For the Ryan bonds, that is 28.

ii. The conversion price is the face value, $1,000, divided by the conversion ratio. It is $35.71.

iii. The conversion premium is the conversion price divided by the stock price minus one. For Ryan it is $35.71 / $31.25 - 1 = 0.1427 = 14.27\%$.

b. i. The conversion ratio is unchanged when the bond price changes. It is still 28.

ii. The conversion price is only meaningful if the bond is selling at par. Since this bond no longer is selling at par, this price is meaningless.

iii. The conversion premium is only meaningful if the bond is selling at par. Since this bond no longer is selling at par, this price is meaningless.

c. The conversion value is the conversion ratio times the current stock price.

$$28 \times \$31.25 = \$875.$$

d. There are two ways to find the new conversion value.

Method one: Multiply the new price by the conversion ratio.

$$28 \times \$33.25 = \$931.$$

Method two: The conversion ratio tells you how much the conversion value will increase for every $1 increase in the price of the stock. Since the price increased two dollars, the conversion value should rise by $56 [= $2 \times 28]. The new price is then $931 [= $875 + $56].

24.15 a. Straight bond value $= \$1,000 / 1.1^{10} = \$385.54$

b. Conversion value $= 25 \times \$12 = \$300$

c. Option value $= \$400 - \$385.54$
   $= \$14.46$

24.16 The conversion value is $(\$1,000 / \$180) \times \$60 = \$333.33$

24.17 a. Straight Bond value $= \$60\, A_{0.10}^{30} + \dfrac{\$1,000}{\left(1+0.10\right)^{30}} = \$622.92$

b. Conversion value $= \left(\dfrac{\$1,000}{\$125}\right) \times \$35 = \$280$

c. $35\,(1 + 15\%)^{t} = \$1,100$
   $t = 24.67$ years, other things being equal, it's about 25 years.
   If the conversion value exceeds 1,100 then, it will be called.

Answers to End-of-Chapter Problems

Chapter 25: Derivatives and Hedging Risk

25.1   a.   A forward contract is an agreement to either purchase or sell a specific amount of a specific good on a specific date at a specific price. It represents an obligation on both parties—the party agreeing to buy in the future at a specified price and the party agreeing to sell in the future at a specified price.

      b.   A futures contract is identical to a forward contract in that it is an agreement to either purchase or sell a specific amount of a specific good on a specific date at a specific price. It represents an obligation on both parties—the party agreeing to buy in the future at a specified price and the party agreeing to sell in the future at a specified price. The difference between futures and forwards is that futures are standardized contracts trading on exchanges with daily resettlement while forwards are agreements tailored to the needs of the counterparties.

25.2   1.   Futures contracts have standard features and are traded on exchanges, while forward contracts are less standard and are not traded on exchanges.

      2.   Risk positions in futures are generally reversed prior to delivery, while forward contracts usually involve delivery.

      3.   The futures market is largely insulated from default risk by features such as mark-to-market and margin call provisions.

25.3   a.   i) $5.10
           ii) $5.00
           iii) $0.03 + $0.05 + $0.04 - $0.02 - $5.10 = -$5.00

      b.   i) $4.98
           ii) $5.00
           iii) $0.03 + $0.05 + $0.04 - $0.02 - $0.12 - $4.98 = -$5.00

25.4 $P_{Forw.Cont}$ = Face value $(1 + r_1) / (1 + r_{11})^{11}$

Both r_1 and r_{11} decreased, but r_{11} has 11th power. Thus, $(1 + r_{11})^{11}$ has more effect of downward shift. Therefore, the price of the forward contract will increase.

25.5   a.   Sell a futures contract.

      b.   A short hedge is a wise strategy if you must hold inventory, the price of which may change before you can sell it.

      c.   Buy a futures contract.

      d.   A long hedge is a wise strategy if you are locked into a future selling price for a good.

25.6   Mary Johnson is investing on wheat futures not on commodity wheat. Since she believes that wheat futures price will fall in the future, she will take a short position on the wheat futures contract.

25.7   Your friend is a little naive about the capabilities of hedging. Hedging will reduce risk, but it cannot eliminate it. There can be a difference in basis between the prices in two different locales. The random nature of the basis adds risk to hedging. A party to a futures contract is also subject to mark-to-mark risk. Finally, very few contracts ever make delivery. Without assured delivery, the basis risk may be magnified. For example, a farmers contracts for wheat on the Chicago exchange, but is unable to deliver to Chicago. He must sell his wheat on the local market. The local prices may be very different from the Chicago prices. The text discusses these differences more fully.

25.8   a. $P = 50 \, (1.048) / (1.050)^2 + 50 \, (1.048) / (1.052)^3 + 50 \, (1.048) / (1.055)^4$
            $+ \, 1050 \, (1.048) / (1.057)^5$
            $= \$968.84$

      b.   i).   The value of the forward contract should fall.
           ii) $P = 50 \, (1.048) / (1.053)^2 + 50 \, (1.048) / (1.055)^3 + 50 \, (1.048) / (1.058)^4$
               $+ \, 1050 \, (1.048) / (1.060)^5$
               $= \$918.32$

25.9

Strategy	Today's cash flow	Cash flow at maturity
1. Buy silver	$-S_0$	S_1
2. Long on futures	0	$S_1 - F$
Lend $\$F / (1 + r_f)$	$-F / (1 + r_f)$	F

Payoff for the two strategies are the same in one month at the maturity of the futures contract.
Therefore, $S_0 = F / (1 + r_f)$
      or $F = S_0 \, (1 + r_f)$

25.10 Since she needs US dollars one year later, she should buy US dollar futures to hedge against exchange rate risk.

25.11 a. $\$300,000 = C \, A_{0.10}^{20} = 8.51356 \, C$
            $C = \$35,237.89$
      b.   Interest rate changes.
      c.   Hedge by writing a futures contract on Treasury bonds.

25.12 a.   i) $\$35,237.89 \, A_{0.12}^{20} = \$263,207.43$
          ii)   Interest rate $\uparrow \Rightarrow$ T bond $\downarrow$ and Short position in T bond $\uparrow$
                $\Rightarrow$ Mortgage $\downarrow$
          iii)   The loss on the mortgage is entirely offset by the gain in the futures market. The net gain or loss is zero.
      b.   i) $\$35,237.89 \, A_{0.09}^{20} = \$321,670.69$
          ii)   The opposite to ii) in a.
          iii)   The net gain or loss is zero.

25.13 a.   A: $\$1,000 / 1.11 = \$900.90$
          B: $\$1,000 / 1.11^5 = \$593.45$
          C: $\$1,000 / 1.11^{10} = \$352.18$
      b.   A: $\$1,000 / 1.14 = \$877.19$
          B: $\$1,000 / 1.14^5 = \$519.37$
          C: $\$1,000 / 1.14^{10} = \$269.74$

    c.   A: $-(\$900.90 - \$877.19) / \$900.90 = -0.0263 = -2.63\%$

B: -($593.45 - $519.37) / $593.45 = -0.1248 = -12.48%

C: -($352.18 - $269.74) / $352.18 = -0.2341 = -23.41%

25.14

Year	Payment	Present value	Relative value
1	$100	$100 / (1 + r)	{$100/(1+r)}/($100/r) = r/(1+r)
2	$100	$100 / (1 + r)^2	{$100/(1+r)^2}/($100/r) = r/(1+r)^2
3	$100	$100 / (1 + r)^3	{$100/(1+r)^3}/($100/r) = r/(1+r)^3
4	$100	$100 / (1 + r)^4	{$100/(1+r)^4}/($100/r) = r/(1+r)^4
.	.	.	.
.	.	.	.
.	.	.	.
		100 / r	1.0

Duration $= 1 \times r / (1 + r) + 2 \times r / (1 + r)^2 + 3 \times r / (1 + r)^3 + 4 \times r / (1 + r)^4 + ...$
                $= r [1 / (1 + r) + 2 / (1 + r)^2 + 3 / (1 + r)^3 + 4 / (1 + r)^4 + ...]$

Duration $/ (1 + r)$
                $= r [1 / (1 + r)^2 + 2 / (1 + r)^3 + 3 / (1 + r)^4 + ...]$

Duration - Duration $/ (1 + r)$
             $= \{1 - 1 / (1 + r)\}$ Duration
             $= r [1 / (1 + r) + 1 / (1 + r)^2 + 1 / (1 + r)^3 + 1 / (1 + r)^4 + ...]$
             $= r (1 / r)$
             $= 1$

Therefore, $\{r / (1 + r)\}$ Duration $= 1$
or Duration $= (1 + r) / r$

$r = 12\%$
    Duration $= (1 + 0.12) / 0.12$
              $= 9.333$ years
$r = 10\%$
    Duration $= (1 + 0.10) / 0.10$
              $= 11.0$ years

25.15 a.   A: $\$70 / 1.1 + \$70 / 1.1^2 + \$70 / 1.1^3 + \$1,070 / 1.1^4$
            $= \$904.90$
      B: $\$110 / 1.1 + \$110 / 1.1^2 + \$110 / 1.1^3 + \$1,110 / 1.1^4$
            $= \$1,031.70$

    b.   A: This bond is selling at par. Its price is $1,000.
      B: $\$110 / 1.07 + \$110 / 1.07^2 + \$110 / 1.07^3 + \$1,110 / 1.07^4$
            $= \$1,135.49$

    c.   A: ($1,000 - $904.90) / $904.90 = 0.1051 = 10.51%
      B: ($1,135.49 - $1,031.70) / $1,031.70 = 0.1006 = 10.06%

    d.   The 7% bond has a higher duration since more of its total repayments occur in the later years. Bond with higher duration have greater percentage changes in their prices than do low duration bonds for a given percentage change in the interest rate.

25.16

Payment	PV	Relative value	Maturity	Duration
$90	$82.5688	0.08257	1	0.08257
90	75.7512	0.07575	2	0.15150
1,090	841.6800	0.84168	3	2.52504
				2.75911

Duration = 2.76 years

25.17

Payment	PV	Relative value	Maturity	Duration
$90	$82.5688	0.08257	1	0.08257
90	75.7512	0.07575	2	0.15150
90	69.4965	0.0695	3	0.2085
1,090	772.1835	0.7722	4	3.0888
				3.5315

Duration = 3.53 years

25.18

Payment	PV	Relative value	Maturity	Duration
$50	$47.6190	0.04762	1	0.04762
50	45.3515	0.04535	2	0.09070
50	43.1919	0.04319	3	0.12957
1,050	863.8376	0.86384	4	3.45536
				3.72325

Duration = 3.72 years

25.19

Year	Payment	PV	Relative value
1	0	0	0
2	0	0	0
3	$20,000	$13,150.32	0.30458
4	$20,000	$11,435.06	0.26485
5	$20,000	$9,943.53	0.23030
6	$20,000	$8,646.55	0.20027
		$43,175.47	1.0000

Duration = $1 \times 0 + 2 \times 0 + 3 \times 0.30458 + 4 \times 0.26485$
$\qquad + 5 \times 0.23030 + 6 \times 0.20027$
$\qquad = 4.33$ years

25.20 a. Dollar amounts are in millions.

$0 \times (\$43 / \$1,255) + 0.33333 (\$615 / \$1,255) + 0.75 \times (\$345 / \$1,255)$
$+ 5 \times (\$55 / \$1,255) + 15 \times (\$197 / \$1,255)$
$= 2.943$ years

b. Dollar amounts are in millions.

$0 \times (\$490 / \$1,110) + 1.5 (\$370 / \$1,110) + 10 \times (\$250 / \$1,110)$
$= 2.752$ years

c. No. Besdall is not immune to interest rate risk since the product of market value times duration is different for assets than for liabilities.

25.21 a. $2.943 \times \$1,255$ million = duration $\times \$1,110$ million
Liability duration = $2.943 (\$1,255) / \$1,110$
$= 3.327$

b. Duration $\times \$1,255$ million = $2.752 \times \$1,110$ million
Asset duration = $2.752 (\$1,110) / \$1,255$
$= 2.434$

25.22 a. Duration of assets
$= 0 \times \$100 / \$1,800 + 1 \times \$500 / \$1,800 + 12 \times \$1,200 / \$1,800$
$= 8.278$ years
Duration of liabilities
$= 0 \times \$300 / \$1,200 + 1.1 \times \$400 / \$1,200 + 18.9 \times \$500 / \$1,200$
$= 8.242$ years

b. No, it is not immunized from interest rate risk.
Duration of asset $\times$ market value of asset
$= 8.278 \times \$1,800$
$= \$14,900.4$
Duration of liability $\times$ market value of liability
$= 8.242 \times \$1,200$
$= \$9,890.0$
To be immunized from interest rate risk, either (1) increase the duration of liabilities without changing the duration of the assets or (2) decrease the duration of assets without changing the duration of liabilities.

25.23 a. Yes, there is an opportunity for the Miller Company and the Edwards company to benefit from a swap. Miller has the comparative advantage in the Fixed-rate market while Edwards has the comparative advantage in the floating rate market.

	Fixed Rate	Floating Rate
Miller Company	10%	LIBOR +0.3%
Edwards Company	15%	LIBOR +2.0%

In the floating rate market, the lender usually has the opportunity to review the floating rates every 6 months. If the creditworthiness of Edwards Company declined, the lender has the option of increasing the spread over LIBOR that is charged.

b. The Strategy:
1. Miller borrows at fixed rate loan of 10%.
2. Edwards borrows at floating rate loan of LIBOR +2.0%
3. Enter into a swap (with a notional principal)

Miller: 3 sets of interest-rate cash flows.
1. It pays 10% per annum to outside lenders.
2. It receives 11.65% per annum from Miller.
3. It pays LIBOR +0.15% to Edwards.

Edwards: 3 sets of interest-rate cash flows.
1. It pays LIBOR +2.0% per annum to outside lenders.
2. It receives LIBOR +0.15% from Miller.
3. It pays 11.65% to Miller.

Miller $\Rightarrow$ Borrowing at LIBOR +0.15% floating rate (cheaper by 0.15% than it would have to pay if it borrows directly from the floating rate market.)

Edwards $\Rightarrow$ Borrowing at 11.65% Fixed (cheaper by 3.35% than it would pay if it borrows directly from the fixed rate market.)

Both sides are better off by 1.50% per annum.

Chapter 26: Corporate Financial Models and Long-term Planning

26.1 Forecast sales:

$S = 0.00001$ GNP $= 0.00001$ ($2,050 billion) $= \$20,500,000$

Compute the other values:

CA $= \$500,000 + 0.25$ ($20,500,000) $= \$5,625,000$

FA $= \$1,000,000 + 0.50$ ($20,500,000) $= \$11,250,000$

CL $= \$100,000 + 0.10$ ($20,500,000) $= \$2,150,000$

NP $= 0.02$ ($20,500,000) $= \$410,000$

Compute the new amount of retained earnings:

$\Delta RE = NP (1 - 0.34) = \$410,000 (0.66) = \$270,600$

RE $= \$3,400,000 + \$270,600 = \$3,670,600$

Compute the new amount of bonds:

Debt-to-Asset Ratio $= (\$1,100,000 + \$2,500,000) / (\$3,000,000 + \$6,000,000) = 0.40$

Bonds $= [(CA + FA) \times 0.40] - CL$

$= (\$5,625,000 + \$11,250,000) (0.40) - \$2,150,000 = \$4,600,000$

Compute the new amount of stock:

Stock $= [(CA + FA) - (CL + Bonds + RE)]$

$= (\$5,625,000 + \$11,250,000) - (\$2,150,000 + 4,600,000 + 3,670,600)$

$= \$6,454,400$

Balance Sheet

Current Assets	5,625,000	Current Liabilities	$2,150,000
Fixed Assets	11,250,000	Bonds	4,600,000
Total Assets	$16,875,000	Common Stock	6,454,400
		Retained Earnings	3,670,600
		Total Liabs & CS	$16,875,000

26.2 $\Delta S = 330 - 330 / (1 + 10\%) = \$30$ million

a. External funds needed

$= (25\% + 150\%) \times 30 - (40\% + 45\%) \times 30 - (12\% \times 330) (1 - 40\%)$

$= \$3.24$ million

b. Current assets $= 25\% \times 330 / (1 + 10\%) = 75$

Fixed assets $= 150\% \times 330 / (1+10\%) = 450$

Total assets $=$ Current assets + Fixed assets $= 75 + 450 = \$525$ million

Short term debt $= 40\% \times 330 / (1+10\%) = 120$

Long term debt $= 45\% \times 330 / (1 + 10\%) = 135$

Common stock $= 50$

Retained earnings $= 220$

Total liabilities $= \$525$ million

c. Pro Forma Balance Sheet
Current assets = 25% x 330 = 82.5
Fixed assets = 150% x 330 = 495
    Total assets = $577.5 million
Short term debt = 40% x 330 = 132
Long term debt = 45% x 330 = 148.5
Common stock = 50
Retained earnings = 243.76
    Total liabilities = 574.26
    External fund needed = 577.5-574.26 = $3.24 million

26.3 a. Compute the sustainable growth using the formula from the text.
$$\frac{\Delta S}{S} = \frac{P(1-d)(1+L)}{T - P(1-d)(1+L)} = \frac{0.05(.5)(2)}{1 - 0.05(0.5)(2)} = 0.0526 = 5.26\%$$

b. Yes, it is possible for the actual growth to differ from the sustainable growth. If any of the actual parameters (P, T, L or d) differ from those used to compute the sustainable growth rate, the actual growth rate will deviate from the sustainable growth rate.

c. Stieben Company can increase its growth rate by doing any of the following.
i. Sell new stock
ii. Increase its debt-to-equity ratio by either selling more debt or repurchasing stock
iii. Increase its net profit margin
iv. Decrease its total assets to sales ratio
v. Reduce its dividend payout

26.4 a. Since you are making a projection for one year in the future it is reasonable to assume that fixed costs do not change. Thus, if sales grow 20%, then net income will grow 20%. Net income is $2,000,000(1.2) = $2,400,000.
Determine total uses of funds.
ΔNWC = 0.20 ($16,000,000 - $10,000,000) = $1,200,000
ΔINV = 0.20 ($16,000,000) + Dep = $3,200,000 + Dep
Dividend = 0.70 ($2,400,000) = $1,680,000
Total uses = ΔNWC + ΔINV + Dep + Dividend = $6,080,000 + Dep
Operating sources = Net income + Dep = $2,400,000 + Dep
New External Funds = Total uses - Operating sources
    = ($6,080,000 + Dep) - (2,400,000 + Dep) = $3,680,000

To maintain its debt-to-equity ratio, Optimal Scam must issue $2,880,000 of new stock and $800,000 of new long-term debt.

b.

Pro Forma Balance Sheet
Optimal Scam Company

Current assets		$19,200,000
Fixed assets		19,200,000
	Total assets	$38,400,000
Current liabilities		$12,000,000
Long-term debt		4,800,000
	Total liabilities	$16,800,000
Common stock		$16,880,000
Accumulated retained earnings		4,720,000
	Total equity	$21,600,000
	Total liabilities and equity	$38,400,000

c. $$\text{Sustainable growth} = \frac{\Delta S}{S} = \frac{P(1-d)(1+L)}{T - P(1-d)(1+L)}$$

$$= \frac{0.0625(.3)(1.7778)}{1 - 0.0625(0.3)(1.7778)} = 0.0345 = 3.45\%$$

d. Optimal Scam is far below its growth rate objective. Cutting the dividend to zero will not be enough. It could only attain a 12.5% growth rate by eliminating the dividend. Optimal Scam must increase its asset utilization and/or its profit margin substantially to be able to achieve its objective growth rate. Optimal could also increase its debt load; this action will increase ROE.

26.5

a.

$$\text{Sustainable growth} = \frac{\Delta S}{S} = \frac{P(1-d)(1+L)}{T - P(1-d)(1+L)}$$

$$= \frac{0.10(.50)(2)}{1.5 - 0.10(0.50)(2)} = 0.0714 = 7.14\%$$

b. MBI Company can achieve its zero growth objective by reducing its profit margin to zero or increasing its dividend payout ratio to one. Reduction of the profit margin to zero, however, will hurt stockholders. Thus, a 100% payout ratio would probably be MBI's best choice.

26.6 Undertaking positive NPV projects is how companies increase shareholders' value. Financial planning allows the company to determine the interrelationships among the different aspects of managerial finance that will ultimately allow management to correctly utilize the NPV approach.

26.7 The new MBA is correct though perhaps naively so. The two formulas are essentially the same.

$$\frac{\Delta S}{S} = ROE(1-d) = \frac{\text{Net Income}}{\text{Net Worth}}(1-d)$$

$$= \frac{\text{Net Income}(1-d)}{TA - \Delta RE - B}$$

Divide by sales, S,

$$= \frac{(NI/S)(1-d)}{TA/S - \Delta RE/S - B/S}$$

$$= \frac{(NI/S)(1-d)}{TA/S - (NI/S)(1-d) - (B/TA)(TA/S)}$$

Since $NI/S = P$, $TA/S = T$,

$$= \frac{P(1-d)}{T - P(1-d) - LT/(1+L)}$$

$$= \frac{P(1-d)}{T/(1+L) - P(1-d)}$$

$$= \frac{P(1-d)(1+L)}{T - P(1-d)(1+L)}$$

26.8

    a.

$$\text{Sustainable growth rate} = \frac{ROE(1-d)}{1 - ROE(1-d)}$$

$$= \frac{16\%(1-60\%)}{1 - 16\%(1-60\%)} = 6.84\%$$

    b. $\dfrac{P(1-60\%)(1+50\%)}{175\% - P(1-60\%)(1+50\%)} = 6.84\%$

        $P = 18.67\%$

26.9 The two shortcomings of financial-planning models we should beware of are:
     i. financial-planning models don't indicate which financial policies are the best.
    ii. financial-planning models are too simple that they don't fully reflect real-world complications.

                                                        Answers to End-of-Chapter Problems

Chapter 27: Short-Term Finance and Planning

27.1 Assets = Liabilities + Equity
Current assets + Fixed assets = Current liabilities + Long-term debt + Equity
Net working capital + Fixed assets = Long-term debt + Equity
Cash + Other current assets - Current liabilities = Long-term debt + Equity - Fixed assets
Cash = Long-term debt + Equity - Net working capital (excluding cash) - Fixed assets

27.2 a. Decrease
b. Decrease
c. No change
d. Increase
e. No change
f. No change
g. Increase
h. No change
i. Increase
j. Decrease
k. Increase
l. No change
m. No change
n. No change
o. Decrease
p. Decrease
q. No change
r. Decrease

27.3

Sources and Uses of Cash
Country Kettles, Inc.
19X6

Sources of cash:	
Cash from operations	
Net income	$68,600
Depreciation	5,225
Decrease in net working capital	
Increase in accounts payable	5,500
New stock	3,000
	$82,325
Uses of cash:	
Increase in fixed assets	$12,725
Dividends	30,800
Increase in net working capital	
Investment in inventory	3,750
Increase in accounts receivable	9,750
Decrease in accrued expenses	3.300
Decrease in long-term debt	15,000
	$75,325
Change in cash balance	$7,000

27.4

Sources and Uses of Cash
S/B Corporation
19X6

Sources of cash:

Cash from operations

Net income	$83,000
Depreciation	50,000

Decrease in net working capital

Decrease in inventory	114,000
Increase in accounts payable	23,000
Increase in loans payable	376,000
	$646,000

Uses of cash:

Increase in fixed assets	$139,000
Dividends	100,000

Increase in net working capital

Increase in accounts receivable	251,000
Decrease in taxes payable	132,000
Decrease in accrued expenses	11,000
	$633,000
Change in cash balance	$13,000

27.5

$$\text{Inventory turnover ratio} = \frac{\text{Costs of Good Sold}}{\text{Average Inventory}} = \frac{200}{(40+60)/2} = 4$$

$$\text{Receivable turnover ratio} = \frac{\text{Credit Sales}}{\text{Average Receivables}} = \frac{240}{(30+50)/2} = 6$$

$$\text{Accounts payable turnover ratio} = \frac{200}{(10+30)/2} = 10$$

a. $\text{Operating cycle} = \dfrac{365}{4} + \dfrac{365}{6} = 152.1(\text{Days})$

b. $\text{Cash cycle} = 152.1 - \dfrac{365}{10} = 115.6(\text{Days})$

27.6 a.   The operating cycle begins when inventory stock arrives at a firm and ends when cash is collected from receivables. The operating cycle is also the sum of the cash cycle and the accounts payable period.

    b.   The cash cycle begins when cash is paid for materials and ends when cash is collected from receivables. The cash cycle is the time between cash disbursement and cash collection.

    c.   The accounts payable period is the length of time the firm is able to delay payment on the purchase of manufacturing resources.

27.7

	Cash cycle	Operating cycle
a.	Decrease	No change
b.	No change	Decrease
c.	Increase	No change
d.	Decrease	Decrease
e.	Increase	Increase
f.	Decrease	Decrease

27.8 a. A flexible short-term financing policy maintains a high ratio of current assets to sales. The policy includes limited use of short-term debt and heavy reliance on long-term debt.

b. A restrictive short-term financing policy entails a low ratio of current assets to sales. This policy relies upon the use of short-term liabilities.

c. If carrying costs are low and/or shortage costs are high, a flexible short-term financing policy is optimal.

d. If carrying costs are high and/or shortage costs are low, a restrictive short-term financing policy is optimal.

27.9 Shortage costs are those costs incurred by a firm when its investment in current assets is low. These costs are of two types.

i. Trading or order costs. Order costs are the costs of placing an order for more cash or more inventory.

ii. Costs related to safety reserves. These costs include lost sales, lost customer goodwill and disruption of production schedules.

27.10 a. The current assets of Cleveland Compressor are financed largely by retained earnings. From 19X1 to 19X2, total current assets grew by $7,212. Only $2,126 of this increase was financed by the growth of current liabilities. Pnew York Pneumatic's current assets are largely financed by current liabilities. Bank loans are the most important of these current liabilities. They grew $3,077 to finance an increase in current assets of $8,333.

b. Cleveland Compressor holds the larger investment in current assets. It has current assets of $92,616 while Pnew York Pneumatic has $78,434 in current assets. The main reason for the difference is the larger sales of Cleveland Compressor.

c. Cleveland Compressor is more likely to incur shortage costs because the ratio of current assets to sales is 0.57. That ratio for Pnew York Pneumatic is 0.86. Similarly, Pnew York Pneumatic is incurring more carrying costs for the same reason, a higher ratio of current assets to sales.

27.11 A long-term growth trend in sales will require some permanent investment in current assets. Thus, in the real world, net working capital is not zero. Also, the variation across time for assets means that net working capital is unlikely to be zero at any point in time.

27.12a. To solve this problem you must assume that all sales are on credit and the remaining 30% of credit sales (100% - 30% - 40%) are never collected. They are bad debts that are written off the books.

Let S be the sales in December. 30% of S will be collected in December and 40% of S will be collected in January. You are told that the balance of account receivable at the end of December is $36,000. $30,000 of this amount is uncollected December sales. That amount must be the difference between S and 0.3 S. Therefore,

$$S - 0.3S = \$30,000$$
$$0.7S = \$30,000$$
$$S = \$42,857$$

December collections = 0.3 ($42,857) = $12,857
January collections = 0.4 ($42,857) = $17,143

b.

	December	January	February	March
Credit sales	$42,875	$90,000	$100,000	$120,000
Collections of current month	12,875	27,000	30,000	36,000
Collections of previous month		17,143	36,000	40,000

January: $27,000 + $17,143 = $44,143
February: $30,000 + $36,000 = $66,000
March: $36,000 + $40,000 = $76,000

27.13

	1	2	3	4
Sales (basic trend)	100	120	144	172.8
Seasonal adjustments	0	-10	-5	15
Sales projections	100	110	139	187.8
Collection within month	30	33	41.7	56.34
Collection next month		50	55	69.5
Cash Collection from Sales		83	96.7	125.84

27.14

Credit sales and Collections
Pine Mulch Company
Second Quarter, 19X5

	March	April	May	June
Credit sales	$180,000	$160,000	$140,000	$192,000
Collections of current month		80,000	70,000	96,000
Collections of previous month		72,000	64,000	56,000
Total Collections		$152,000	$134,000	$152,000

Cash Budget
Pine Mulch Company
Second Quarter, 19X5

	April	May	June
Beginning cash balance	$200,000	$226,000	$282,000
Cash receipts:			
Collections	152,000	134,000	152,000
Total cash available	$352,000	$360,000	$434,000
Cash disbursements:			
Pay credit purchases	$65,000	$68,000	$64,000
Wages, taxes, expenses	8,000	7,000	8,400
Interest	3,000	3,000	3,000
Equipment purchases	50,000	0	4,000
Total cash disbursed	$126,000	$78,000	$79,400
Ending cash balance	$226,000	$282,000	$354,600

27.15 The considerations in determining the most appropriate amount of short-term borrowing are:

i. Cash reserves. Flexible financing strategy can reduce financial distress possibility, but it may reduce the return on equity.

ii. Maturity hedging. Financing long-term assets with short-term borrowing is inherently risky as short-term interest rate is more volatile.

iii. Term structure. On average, long-term borrowing is more costly than short-term borrowing.

27.16 Short-term external financing options include:

i. unsecured loans that can be either committed or uncommitted lines of credit.

ii. secured loans that include blanket inventory lien, trust receipt, field-warehouse financing etc.

iii. other sources like banker's acceptances, commercial paper, ..., etc.

Chapter 28: Cash Management

28.1 Firms need to hold cash to:
  a. Satisfy the transaction needs. For example, cash is collected from sales and new financing and disbursed as wages, salaries, trade debts, taxes and dividends.
  b. Maintain compensating balances. A minimum required compensating balance at banks providing credit service to the firm may impose a lower limit on the level of cash a firm holds.

28.2 a. Decrease. Examine the Baumol model. As the interest rate (k) increases, the optimal cash balance must also rise.
  b. Increase. Examine the Baumol model. As brokerage costs (F, the per transaction costs) rise, the optimal balance increases.
  c. Decrease. Clearly, if the bank lowers its compensating balance requirement, a firm will not be required to hold as much of its assets as cash.
  d. Decrease. If the cost of borrowing falls, a firm need not hold as much of its assets as cash because the cost of running short, i.e. the cost to borrow to fill cash needs, is lower.
  e. Increase. As a firm's credit rating falls, its cost to borrow increases. Thus, the firm cannot as easily afford to run short of cash and its cash balance must be higher.
  f. Decrease. Introduction of direct banking fees would increase the fixed costs associated with holding cash. As fixed costs rise, the optimal balance must also rise.

28.3 The average weekly cash balance is $20,750 [($24,000 + $34,000 + $10,000 + $15,000)/ 4]
  With monthly compounding, the return that the firm can earn on its average balance is
  $20,750 [[(1 + 0.12/12)^{12} - 1] = $2,631.62
  Your answer may differ if you made different assumptions about the interest payments.

28.4 a. The total amount of cash that will be disbursed during the year is:
  $345,000 * 12 = $4,140,000
  Using the optimal cash balance formula,
  $$C* = \sqrt{\frac{2FT}{K}} = \sqrt{\frac{2(\$500)(4,140,000)}{0.07}} = \$243,193$$
  $243,193 should be kept as cash. The balance, $556,807 (=$800,000-$243,193), should be invested in marketable securities.
  b. The number of times marketable securities will be sold during the next twelve months is $4,140,000 / $243,193 = 17 times

28.5

$$C* = \sqrt{\frac{2FT}{K}}$$

$$T = \frac{KC*^2}{2F} = \frac{7.5\% \times (20mil)^2}{2 \times 5,000} = \frac{7.5\% \times 20^2}{0.01} = \$3,000(mil)$$

$$Average\ weekly\ disbursement = \frac{3,000}{52} = \$57.69mil$$

28.6 Use the Miller-Orr formula.

The target cash balance = $Z^* = \sqrt[3]{\dfrac{3F\sigma^2}{4K}} + L$

The upper limit = $H^* = 3Z^* - 2L$

The daily opportunity cost = $K = \sqrt[365]{1.08} - 1 = 0.000211$

$$Z^* = \sqrt[3]{\dfrac{3(\$600)(\$1,440,00)}{4(0.000211)}} + \$20,000 = \$34,536$$

$H^* = \$63,608$

The average cash balance:

$$C^* = \dfrac{4Z^* - L}{3} = \dfrac{4(\$34,536) - \$20,000}{3} = \$39,381$$

28.7 a.

$$Z_g^* = \dfrac{H_g + 2L_g}{3} = \dfrac{200,000 + 2 \times 100,000}{3} = \$133,333$$

$$Z_s^* = \dfrac{H_s + 2L_s}{3} = \dfrac{300,000 + 2 \times 150,000}{3} = \$200,000$$

b. Gold Star:

$$s_g^2 = \left(Z_g^* - L_g\right)^3 4K_g / 3F_g = \dfrac{(133,333 - 100,000)^3 \times 4 \times 0.000261}{3 \times 2,000} \approx 6,444,251$$

$$K_g = \sqrt[365]{1.10} - 1 = 0.000261$$

Silver Star:

$$s_g^2 = \left(Z_g^* - L_g\right)^3 4K_g / 3F_g = \dfrac{(200,000 - 150,000)^3 \times 4 \times 0.000236}{3 \times 2,000} \approx 15,733,333$$

$$K_g = \sqrt[365]{1.09} - 1 = 0.000236$$

So, Silver Star Co. has a more volatile daily cash flow.

28.8 Garden Groves float = 150 ($15,000) = $2,250,000
Increase in collected cash balance if a 3 day lockbox is installed = 3($2,250,000)
= $6,750,000
Annual earnings from this amount = $6,750,000 x 0.075 = $506,250

The system should be installed if its cost is below this amount.
Variable cost $ 0.5 x 150 x 365 = $27,375
Fixed cost   = 80,000
Total cost   =$107,375
The lockbox system should be installed. The net earnings from the use of the system are
$398,875 (= $506,250 - $107,375)

28.9 To make the system profitable, the net earnings of installing the lockbox system must be non-negative. The lower limit for acceptability is zero profits.

Let N be the number of customers per day.
   Earnings = ($4,500) (N) (2) (0.06) = $540 x N
Costs:
   Variable cost: N (365) ($0.25) = $91.25 x N
   Fixed cost: $15,000
Equate Earnings to total costs:
   N = 33.43
Salisbury Stakes needs at least 34 customers per day for the lockbox system to be profitable.

28.10 Disbursement float = $12,000 x 5 = $60,000
   Collection float = -$15,000 x 3 = -$45,000
   Net float = $60,000 - $45,000 = $15,000
   If funds are collected in four days rather than three, disbursement float will not change. Collection float will change to -$60,000. This change makes the net float equal to zero.

28.11 a.   Reduction in outstanding cash balances = $100,000 x 3 days = $300,000
      b.   Return on savings = $300,000 (0.12) = $360,000
      c.   Maximum monthly charge = $36,000 / 12 = $3,000
           Note: The calculation in part b assumes annual compounding. The answer in part c does not account for the time value of money. With monthly compounding of the interest earned, the return on savings at the end of the year is
                $300,000 [(1.01)^{12} - 1] = $38,047.51
           The present value of this amount is $38,047.51 / (1.01)^{12} = $33,765.23
           Compute the monthly payment as an annuity with a discount rate of 1% per period for twelve periods. That annuity factor is 11.2551. Thus, the payment is
                $33,765.23 = (Payment) (11.2551)
                   Payment = $3,000
           Notice, as long as the treatment of the cash flows is the same, the payment is the same.

28.12 The cash savings are the earnings from the interest bearing account. Assuming daily compounding, the three-day return to the delayed payment is
   ($200,000)[(1.0004)^{3}-1] = $240.096
   The interest rate for two weeks is 0.5615% (=(1.0004)^{14}-1).
   Therefore, the present value of this annuity is

$$(\$240.096)\left[\frac{1-\dfrac{1}{(1.005615)^{26}}}{0.005615}\right] = \$5,793.12$$

   The Walter Company will save $5,793.12 per year.

28.13 If the Miller Company divides the eastern region, collections will be accelerated by one day freeing up $4 million per day. Compensating balances will be increased by $100,000 [=2($300,000)-$500,000]. The net effect is to have $3,900,000 to invest. If T-bills pay 7%

per year, the annual net savings from the division of the eastern region is $3,900,000 x 0.07 = $273,000.

28.14 Lockbox: interest saved = 7,500 x 250 x 1.5 x0.0003 = $843.75
Annual saving (Annual charge) = 843.75 x 365 - 30,000 - 0.3 x 250 x 365
$$= \$250,593.75$$
Annual saving (Concentration Banking)   = 7,500 x 250 x1 x 0.0003 x 365
$$= 562.5 \text{ x } 365 = \$205,312.5$$
So the lockbox system is recommended.

28.15 The important characteristics of short-term marketable securities are:
  i.   maturity
  ii.   default risk
  iii.   marketability
  iv.   taxability

Chapter 29: Credit Management

29.1 North County Publishing Company should adopt the new credit policy if its PV, PV (New) is greater than the PV of the current policy, PV (Old).

$$PV(Old) = \frac{\$10,000,000/365}{1+0.1(2/12)} = \$26,948.12$$

Let T = the average number of days until payment for those customers who do not take the discount.

$$0.5 \ (10 \ \text{days}) + 0.5 \ (T) = 30 \ \text{days}$$
$$T = 50 \ \text{days}$$

$$PV(New) = \frac{0.5(\$10,000,000/365)(0.98)}{1+0.1(10/365)} + \frac{0.5(\$10,000,000/365)}{1+0.1(50/365)} = \$26,901.49$$

Because PV(Old) > PV(New), North County Publishing should not adopt the new policy. Notice that the decision is actually independent of the level of credit sales.

$$PV(Old) = \frac{1}{1+0.1(2/12)} = 0.9836$$

$$PV(New) = \frac{0.5(0.98)}{1+0.1(10/365)} + \frac{0.5}{1+0.1(50/365)} = 0.9819$$

29.2 If the credit terms are net 45 and accounts are 45 days past due on average, the average collection period is 90 days. Accounts receivable are

$$\frac{90 \ \text{days}}{365 \ \text{days}}(\$5,000,000) = \$1,232,876.71$$

29.3 The Tropeland Company should adopt the new credit policy if its PV, PV(New), is greater than the PV of the current policy, PV(Old).

$$PV \ (Old) = \frac{\$30,000,000}{1+0.12(2/12)} = \$29,411,764.71$$

Let T = the average number of days until payment for those customers who do not take the discount.

$$0.5(10 \ \text{days}) + 0.5 \ (T) = 30 \ \text{days}$$
$$T = 50 \ \text{days}$$

$$PV(New) = \frac{0.5(\$30,000,000)(0.96)}{1+0.12(10/365)} + \frac{0.5(\$30,000,000)}{1+0.12(50/365)} = \$29,110,225.07$$

Because PV(Old) > PV(New), Tropeland should not adopt the new policy. Notice that the decision is actually independent of the level of credit sales.

$$PV(Old) = \frac{1}{1+0.12(2/12)} = 0.98039$$

$$PV(New) = \frac{0.5(0.96)}{1+0.12(10/365)} + \frac{0.5}{1+0.12(50/365)} = 0.97034$$

29.4   a.   A firm should offer credit if the NPV of offering credit is greater than the NPV of the firm's current, no-credit policy.

NPV(Current policy) = ($35 - $25)(2,000) = $20,000

$$NPV(\text{Credit policy}) = \frac{(0.85)(\$40)(3,000)}{1.03} - (\$32)(3,000) = \$3,029.13$$

Berkshire should not offer credit to its customers.

     b.   Let h be the probability of payment. Berkshire will be indifferent if the NPV of the current policy equals the NPV of the credit policy.

$$\$20,000 = \frac{(h)(\$40)(3,000)}{1.03} - (\$32)(3,000)$$

$$h = 0.9957 = 99.57\%$$

Berkshire should offer its customers a credit plan if the probability that they will pay is greater than 99.57%.

29.5   Offering a credit policy is attractive if the NPV of the credit policy is greater than the NPV of the current, no-credit policy. Let P be the price that would make Theodore Bruin Company indifferent.

$$(\$48 - \$43)750 = \frac{(0.92)(P)(1,000)}{1.027} - (\$45)(1,000)$$

$$P = \$54.42$$

The new price per unit must be greater than $54.42. Thus, the price must increase at least $6.42 (=$54.42-$48).

29.6   Profit under current policy = (900-600) x 5,000 = $1,500,000

$$\text{Profit under credit sales} = -650 \times 9,000 + \frac{900 \times h \times 9,000}{1.015}$$

When the two profits equal, the firm would be indifferent.
Solve for h; h = 92.10%

29.7   If the cost of subscribing to the credit agency is less than the savings from collection of the bad debts, Silver Spokes Bicycle Shop should subscribe.

        Cost of the subscription = $500 + $4(300) = $1,700
        Savings from not selling to bad credit risks = ($240)(300)(0.05) = $3,600

Silver Spokes should subscribe to the collection agency. The shop's net savings are $1,900 (= $3,600 - $1,700).

29.8   In principle, the optimal credit policy occurs at the minimum total-credit-cost point. Total credit cost is the sum of carrying costs (the costs associated with granting credit and making an investment in receivables), and the opportunity costs (the lost sales from refusing to offer credit). In perfect financial market, there's no optimal credit policy. In imperfect financial markets, taxes, bankruptcy costs and agency costs are factors that can influence the optimal credit policy.

29.9 The information commonly used to assess credit-worthiness include:
  i.   financial statements
  ii. credit reports on customers' payment history with other firms
  iii. banks
  iv. the customers' payment history with the firm.

29.10 The average collection period = 0.4(15) + 0.6(40) = 30 days
  Average daily sales = 85,000 x $55 / 365 = $12,808.22
  Accounts receivable = 30 x $12,808.22 = $384.247
  The new credit terms will increase the number of customers who take the discount. As a result, the average collection period will decrease. The drop in the collection period will cause the investment in account receivable to decrease.

29.11 If $600,000 is the average monthly sales, the average investment in account receivable is

$$\frac{\$600,000 \times 90}{30} = \$1,800,000$$

29.12 Per unit revenue $= -1,500 \times (1 - 4\%) + \dfrac{1,500 \times 98\%}{1 + 10\% \times 30 / 365} = \$18$

  Gross profit $= 100,000 \times 18 - 400,000 = \$1,400,000$

Chapter 30: Mergers and Acquisitions

30.1 The new corporation issues $300,000 in new debt. The merger creates $100,000 of goodwill because the merger is a purchase.

Balance Sheet
Lager Brewing
(in $ thousands)

Current assets	$480	Current liabilities	$200
Other assets	140	Long-term debt	400
Net fixed assets	580	Equity	700
Goodwill	100		
Total assets	$1,300	Total liabilities	$1,300

30.2 If the balance sheet for Philadelphia Pretzel shows assets at book value instead of market value, the goodwill will be only $60,000 (=$300,000 - $240,000). Thus, the net fixed assets are $620,000 (=$1,300,000 - $480,000 - $140,000 - $60,000).

Balance Sheet
Lager Brewing
(in $ thousands)

Current assets	$480	Current liabilities	$200
Other assets	140	Long-term debt	400
Net fixed assets	620	Equity	700
Goodwill	60		
Total assets	$1,300	Total liabilities	$1,300

30.3

Balance Sheet
Lager Brewing
(in $ thousands)

Current assets	$480	Current liabilities	$280
Other assets	140	Long-term debt	100
Net fixed assets	580	Equity	820
Total assets	$1,200	Total liabilities	$1,200

30.4 a. False. Although the reasoning seems correct, the Stillman-Eckbo data do not support the monopoly power theory.

b. True. When managers act in their own interest, acquisitions are an important control device for shareholders. It appears that some acquisitions and takeovers are the consequence of underlying conflicts between managers and shareholders.

c. False. Even if markets are efficient, the presence of synergy will make the value of the combined firm different from the sum of the values of the separate firms. Incremental cash flows provide the positive NPV of the transaction.

d. False. In an efficient market, traders will value takeovers based on "Fundamental factors" regardless of the time horizon. Recall that the evidence as a whole suggests efficiency in the markets. Mergers should be no different.

e. False. The tax effect of an acquisition depends on whether the merger is taxable or non-taxable. In a taxable merger, there are two opposing factors to consider, the capital gains effect and the write-up effect. The net effect is the sum of these two effects.

f.   True. Because of the coinsurance effect, wealth might be transferred from the stockholders to the bondholders. Acquisition analysis usually disregards this effect and considers only the total value.

30.5

(in $ millions)	Net Cash Flow Per Year (Perpetual)	Discount Rate (%)	Value
Small Fry	8	16%	50
Whale	20	10%	200
Benefits from Acquisition:	5	11.76%	42.5
Revenue Enhancement	2.5	20%	12.5
Cost Reduction	2	10%	20
Tax Shelters	0.5	5%	10
Whale-Fry	$33	11.28%	$292.5

Per share price = ($292.5-100)/5 = $38.5

30.6 a.   The weather conditions are independent. Thus, the joint probabilities are the products of the individual probabilities.

Possible states	Joint probability
Rain Rain	0.1 x 0.1=0.01
Rain Warm	0.1 x 0.4=0.04
Rain Hot	0.1 x 0.5=0.05
Warm Rain	0.4 x 0.1=0.04
Warm Warm	0.4 x 0.4=0.16
Warm Hot	0.4 x 0.5=0.20
Hot Rain	0.5 x 0.1=0.05
Hot Warm	0.5 x 0.4=0.20
Hot Hot	0.5 x 0.5=0.25

Since the state Rain Warm has the same outcome (revenue) as Warm Rain, their probabilities can be added. The same is true of Rain Hot, Hot Rain and Warm Hot, Hot Warm. Thus the joint probabilities are

Possible states	Joint probability
Rain Rain	0.01
Rain Warm	0.08
Rain Hot	0.10
Warm Warm	0.16
Warm Hot	0.40
Hot Hot	0.25

The joint values are the sums of the values of the two companies for the particular state.

Possible states	Joint value
Rain Rain	$200,000
Rain Warm	300,000
Warm Warm	400,000
Rain Hot	500,000
Warm Hot	600,000
Hot Hot	800,000

b. Recall, if a firm cannot service its debt, the bondholders receive the value of the assets. Thus, the value of the debt is the value of the company if the face value of the debt is greater than the value of the company. If the value of the company is greater than the value of the debt, the value of the debt is its face value. Here the value of the common stock is always the residual value of the firm over the value of the debt.

Joint Prob.	Joint Value	Debt Value	Stock Value
0.01	$200,000	$200,000	$0
0.08	300,000	300,000	0
0.16	400,000	400,000	0
0.10	500,000	400,000	100,000
0.40	600,000	400,000	200,000
0.25	800,000	400,000	400,000

c. To show that the value of the combined firm is the sum of the individual values, you must show that the expected joint value is equal to the sum of the separate expected values.

Expected joint value
$= 0.01(\$200,000) + 0.08(\$300,000) + 0.16(\$400,000) + 0.10(\$500,000) +$
$\quad 0.40(\$600,000) + 0.25(\$800,000)$
$= \$580,000$

Since the firms are identical, the sum of the expected values is twice the expected value of either.
Expected individual value $= 0.1(\$100,000) + 0.4(\$200,000) + 0.5(\$400,000) = \$290,000$
Expected combined value $= 2(\$290,000) = \$580,000$

d. The bondholders are better off if the value of the debt after the merger is greater than the value of the debt before the merger.

Value of the debt before the merger:
The value of debt for either company
$= 0.1(\$100,000) + 0.4(\$200,000) + 0.5(\$200,000) = \$190,000$
Total value of debt before the merger $= 2(\$190,000) = \$380,000$

Value of debt after the merger
$$= 0.01(\$200,000) + 0.08(\$300,000) + 0.16(\$400,000) + 0.10(\$400,000) + 0.40(\$400,000) + 0.25(\$400,000)$$
$$= \$390,000$$

The bondholders are $10,000 better off after the merger.

30.7   The decision hinges upon the risk of surviving. The final decision should hinge on the wealth transfer from bondholders to stockholders when risky projects are undertaken. High-risk projects will reduce the expected value of the bondholders' claims on the firm. The telecommunications business is riskier than the utilities business. If the total value of the firm does not change, the increase in risk should favor the stockholder. Hence, management should approve this transaction. Note, if the total value of the firm drops because of the transaction and the wealth effect is lower than the reduction in total value, management should reject the project.

30.8   If the market is "smart," the P/E ratio will not be constant.
   a. Value = $2,500 + $1,000 = $3,500
   b. EPS = Post-merger earnings / Total number of shares
       =($100 + $100)/200 =$1
   c. Price per share = Value/Total number of shares
       =$3,500/200 =$17.50
   d. If the market is "fooled," the P/E ratio will be constant at $25.
       Value = P/E * Total number of shares
           = 25 * 200 = $5,000
       EPS = Post-merger earnings / Total number of shares
       =$5,000/200 = $25.00

30.9 a.   After the merger, Arcadia Financial will have 130,000 [=10,000 + (50,000)(6/10)] shares outstanding. The earnings of the combined firm will be $325,000. The earnings per share of the combined firm will be $2.50 (=$325,000/130,000). The acquisition will increase the EPS for the stockholders from $2.25 to $2.50.

   b.   There will be no effect on the original Arcadia stockholders. No synergies exist in this merger since Arcadia is buying Coldran at its market price. Examining the relative values of the two firms sees the latter point.
       Share price of Arcadia = (16 * $225,000) / 100,000=$36
       Share price of Coldran = (10.8 * $100,000) / 50,000=$21.60
       The relative value of these prices is $21.6/$36 = 0.6. Since Coldran's shareholders receive 0.6 shares of Arcadia for every share of Coldran, no synergies exist.

30.10 a.   The synergy will be the discounted incremental cash flows. Since the cash flows are perpetual, this amount is
$$\frac{\$600,000}{0.08} = \$7,500,000$$

b. The value of Flash-in-the-Pan to Fly-by-Night is the synergy plus the current market value of Flash-in-the-Pan.

$$V = \$7,500,000 + \$20,000,000$$
$$= \$27,500,000$$

c. Cash alternative = $15,000,000

Stock alternative = 0.25($27,500,000 + $35,000,000)
$$= \$15,625,000$$

d. NPV of cash alternative = V - Cost
$$= \$27,500,000 - \$15,000,000$$
$$= \$12,500,000$$

NPV of stock alternative = V - Cost
$$= \$27,500,000 - \$15,625,000$$
$$= \$11,875,000$$

e. Use the cash alternative, its NPV is greater.

30.11 a. The value of Portland Industries before the merger is $9,000,000 (=750,000x12). This value is also the discounted value of the expected future dividends.

$$\$9,000,000 = \frac{\$1.80 \times 250,000)1.05}{(r - 0.05)}$$

r = 0.1025 = 10.25%

r is the risk-adjusted discount rate for Portland's expected future dividends. the value of Portland Industries after the merger is

$$V = \frac{(\$1.80 \times 250000)1.07}{(0.1025 - 0.07)}$$

$$= \$14,815,385$$

This is the value of Portland Industries to Freeport.

b. NPV = Gain - Cost
$$= \$14,815,385 - (\$40 \times 250,000)$$
$$= \$4,815,385$$

c. If Freeport offers stock, the value of Portland Industries to Freeport is the same, but the cost differs.

Cost = (Fraction of combined firm owned by Portland's stockholders)
x(Value of the combined firm)

Value of the combined firm = (Value of Freeport before merger)
+ (Value of Portland to Freeport)
$$= \$15 \times 1,000,000 + \$14,815,385$$
$$= \$29,815,385$$

$$\text{Fraction of ownership} = \frac{600,000}{1,000,000 + 600,000} = 0.375$$

Cost = 0.375 x $29,815,385
$$= \$11,180,769$$

NPV = $14,815,385 - $11,180,769
$$= \$3,634,616$$

d. The acquisition should be attempted with a cash offer since it provides a higher NPV.

e. The value of Portland Industries after the merger is

$$V = \frac{(\$1.80 \times 250{,}000)1.06}{(0.1025 - 0.06)} = \$11{,}223{,}529$$

This is the value of Portland Industries to Freeport.

$$NPV = Gain\text{-}Cost$$
$$= \$11{,}223{,}529 - (\$40 \times 250{,}000)$$
$$= \$1{,}223{,}529$$

If Freeport offers stock, the value of Portland Industries to Freeport is the same, but the cost differs.

Cost = (Fraction of combined firm owned by Portland's stockholders)
x(Value of the combined firm)

Value of the combined firm = (Value of Freeport before merger)
+ (Value of Portland to Freeport)
= $15x1,000,000 + $11,223,529
= $26,223,529

$$\text{Fraction of ownership} = \frac{600{,}000}{1{,}000{,}000 + 600{,}000} = 0.375$$

Cost = 0.375 * $26,223,529=$9,833,823
NPV = $11,223,529 - $9,833,823=$1,389,706
The acquisition should be attempted with a stock offer since it provides a higher NPV.

30.12 a. Number of shares after acquisition
=30 + 15 = 45 mil
Stock price of Harrods after acquisition = 1,000/45=22.22 pounds
b. Value of Selfridge stockholders after merger:
$\alpha * 1{,}000 = 300$
$\alpha = 30\%$

$$30\% = \frac{\text{New Shares Issued}}{\text{New Shares Issued} + \text{Old Shares}}$$

$$= \frac{\text{New Shares Issued}}{\text{New Shares Issued} + 30}$$

New shares issued = 12.86 mil
12.86:20 = 0.643:1
The proper exchange ratio should be 0.643 to make the stock offer's value to Selfridge equivalent to the cash offer.

30.13 To evaluate this proposal, look at the present value of the incremental cash flows.

Cash Flows to Company A
(in $ million)

Year	0	1	2	3	4	5
Acquisition of B	-550					
Dividends from B	150	32	5	20	30	45
Tax-loss carryforwards			25	25		
Terminal value						600
Total	-400	32	30	45	30	645

The additional cash flows from the tax-loss carry forwards and the proposed level of debt should be discounted at the cost of debt because they are determined with very little uncertainty.

The after-tax cash flows are subject to normal business risk and must be discounted at a normal rate.

Beta coefficient for the bond $= 0.25 = [(8\%-6\%)/8\%]$.

Beta coefficient for the company $= 1 = [(0.25)^2 + (1.25)(0.75)]$

Discount rate for normal operations:

$r = 6\% + 8\% (1) = 14\%$

Discount rate for dividends:

The new beta coefficient for the company, 1, must be the weighted average of the debt beta and the stock beta.

$1 = 0.5(0.25) + 0.5(\beta_s)$

$\beta_s = 1.75$

$r = 6\% + 8\%(1.75) = 20\%$

$$NPV = -\$400 + \frac{\$32}{1.2} + \frac{\$5}{(1.2)^2} + \frac{\$20}{(1.2)^3} + \frac{\$30}{(1.2)^4} + \frac{\$45}{(1.2)^5} + \frac{\$25}{(1.08)^2} + \frac{\$25}{(1.08)^3} + \frac{\$900}{(1.14)^5} - \frac{\$300}{(1.08)^5}$$

$= -\$400 + \$26.67 + \$3.47 + \$11.57 + \$14.47 + \$18.08 + \$21.43 + \$19.85 + \$467.43 - \$204.17$

$= -\$21.2$

Because the NPV of the acquisition is negative, Company A should not acquire Company B.

30.14 The commonly used defensive tactics by target-firm managers include:
  i.   corporate charter amendments like super-majority amendment or staggering the election of board members.
  ii. repurchase standstill agreements.
  iii. exclusionary self-tenders.
  iv. going private and leveraged buyouts.
  v.   other devices like golden parachutes, scorched earth strategy, poison pill, ..., etc.

Mini Case: U.S.Steel's case.

You have 3 choices: tender, or do not tender or sell in the market. If you do sell your shares in the market, at some point, somebody else would need to make a decision in "tender" or "not tender" as well.

It is important to recognize that the firm has about 60 million shares outstanding (since 30 million shares will give US Steel 50.1% of Marathon shares). Let's consider the possible selling prices, which you will receive for each of the following scenarios:

	US Steel Tender offer	
	Succeeds	Fails
Tender	A pro-rated Price between $125 and $85	Market price
Do not Tender	$85	Market price

If US Steel's tender offer fails, you are equally well off since your share value is determined by the market price.

If you choose not to tender, and 30 million shares were tendered US Steel succeeds to gain 50.1% control, you will only receive $85 a share. If you do tender, the price you will receive will be no worse than $85 a share and can be as high as $125 a share. Depending on the number of shares tendered, you will receive one of the following prices.

1. If only 50.1% tendered, you will get $125 per share.
2. If the shares tendered exceed 50.1% but less than 100%, you will get more than $105 a share.
3. If all 60 million shares were tendered, you will get $105 per share. (which is
$\frac{30}{60}(\$125) + \frac{30}{60}(\$85))$

It is clear that, in the above 3 cases, when you are not sure about whether US Steel will succeed or not, you will be better off to tender your shares than not tender. This is because at best, you will only receive $85 per share if you choose not to tender.

Chapter 31: Financial Distress

31.1 Financial distress is often linked to insolvency. Stock-based insolvency occurs when a firm has a negative net worth. Flow-based insolvency occurs when operating cash flow is insufficient to meet current obligations.

31.2 Financial distress frequently can serve as firm's "early warning" sign for trouble. Thus, it can be beneficial since it may bring about new organizational forms and new operating strategies.

31.3 Under the absolute priority rule (APR), you should propose the follows.

Claims	Distribution of liquidating value	
Trade credit	1,000	1,000
Secured notes	1,000	1,000
Senior debenture	3,000	3,000
Junior debenture	1,000	---
Equity	---	---
	6,000	5,000

31.4 There are many possible reorganization plans. One that might work here is

Assets		Claims	
Going concern value	15,000	Senior debenture	10,000
		Junior debenture	4,000
		Equity	1,000

The holders of multiple bonds would receive senior debentures in equal amounts.
The holders of senior debentures would receive junior debentures (subordinated of your equity) worth $500.

The holders of the junior debentures would receive equity worth $500, 50% of the new firm.

31.5 a. APR: Absolute priority rule, which is the priority rule of the distribution of the proceeds of the liquidation. It begins with the first claim to the last in the order of administrative expenses, unsecured claims after a filing of involuntary bankruptcy petition, wages, employee benefit plan, consumer claims, taxes, secured and unsecured loans, preferred stocks and common stocks.
   b. DIP: Debtor in possession. Bankruptcy allows firms to issue new debt that is senior to all previously incurred debt. This new debt is called DIP debt.

31.6 There are four possible reasons why firms may choose legal bankruptcy over private workout.
   i. It may be less expensive (although legal bankruptcy is usually more expensive.
   ii. Equity investors can use legal bankruptcy to "hold out".
   iii. A complicated capital structure makes private workouts more difficult.
   iv. Conflicts of interest between creditors, equity investors and management can make private workouts impossible.

Chapter 32: International Corporate Finance

32.1 a. In direct terms, $1.6317 / Pound
In European terms, DM1.8110 / $

b. The Japanese yen is selling at a premium to the U.S. dollar in the forward markets. Today, at the spot rate, U.S.$ 1 buys ¥143, while at the 90-day future rate, U.S.$ 1 buys only ¥142.01. Clearly, Yen are getting more expensive in dollar terms.

c. It will be important to Japanese companies that will receive or make payments in dollars. It will also be important to other international companies outside Japan that must make or receive payments in yen. For these companies, future cash flows depend on the exchange rate.

d. The 3 month forward exchange rate is $0.6743 / SF. The amount of Swiss francs received will be SF148,301.94. $= \left[\dfrac{\$100,000}{\$0.6743 / SF} \right]$. We should sell dollars.

e.

$$S_{E/DM} = S_{Pound/\$} \times S_{\$/DM}$$

$$= (Pound0.6129 / \$)(\$0.5522 / DM) = Pound0.3384 / DM$$

$$S_{Yen/SF} = S_{Yen/\$} \times S_{\$/SF}$$

$$= (Yen143.00/\$)(\$0.6691/SF) = Yen95.6813/SF$$

f. Both banks reduce their exposure to foreign exchange risk. If a bank finds another bank with a complimentary mismatch of cash flows in terms of foreign currencies, it should arrange a swap since both banks' cash flows would be more closely matched.

32.2 a. $1.8 \times 2 \neq 4$
b. $100 / 2 = 50$
c. $100 / 7.8 \neq 14$
There are arbitrage opportunities in a and c, but not in b.

32.3 a. False. On the contrary, according to Relative Purchasing Power Parity, an expectation of higher inflation in Japan should cause the yen to depreciate against the dollar.

b. False. Assuming that the forward market is efficient, any expectation of higher inflation in France should be reflected in discounted French francs in the forward market. Therefore, no protection from risk would be available by using forward contracts.

c. True. The fact that other participants in the market do not have information regarding the differences in the relative inflation rates in the two countries will make our knowledge of this fact a special factor that will make speculation in the forward market successful.

32.4 Approximate spot rate at year-end
$$= 2.5 \times (1 + (10\% - 5\%))$$
$$= \text{BD } 2.625 / \text{WD}$$

32.5 a.   Forward rate = $6 \times (1 + 8\% / 4) / (1 + 5\%/4) = \text{FF}6.04 / \$$

     b.   Enter the buy-side position of a 3 month FF forward contract worth
$1,000,000 \times 6.04 = \text{FF}6.04$ million

32.6 a.   <u>Investment in the U.K.:</u>
The treasurer can obtain 2.5 million Pounds [= \$5 million / (\$2 / Pound)]. After
investing in the U.K. for three months at 9% he will have 2,556,250 pounds [= 2.5
million pounds $\times (1 + 0.09 / 4)$]
The forward sale of pounds will provide \$5,150,843.75 (= 2,556,250 Pounds $\times$
\$2.015 / Pound).

<u>Investment in the U.S.:</u>
After investing in the U.S. for three months at 12%, the treasurer will have
\$5,150,000 [= \$5,000,000 $\times (1 + 0.12 / 4)$].

     b.   Forward rate $= \dfrac{1 + i_{US}}{1 + i_{UK}} \times S(0) = \dfrac{1.13}{1.08} \times \$1.50 / \text{Pound} = \$1.57 / \text{Pound}$

     c.   It all depends on whether the forward market expects the same appreciation over the
period and whether the expectation is accurate. Assuming that the expectation is
correct and that other traders do have the same information, there will be value to
hedging the currency exposure.

32.7 a.   Investment in the foreign subsidiary will be appropriate if this investment provides
direct diversification that shareholders could not attain by investing on their own.
The case of a country that represents a political risk would be where the home
subsidiary investment would be preferred. Indonesia can serve as a great example of
political risk. If it cannot be diversified away, investing in this type of foreign
country will increase the systematic risk. As a result, it will raise the cost of the
capital.

     b.   Using the interest rate and purchasing power parity, the expected exchange rate is
$$E[S_{\$/DM}(1)] = \frac{1 + i_{US}}{1 + i_{WG}} \times \$ / DM(0) = \frac{1.113}{1.06} \times \$0.5 / DM = \$0.525 / DM$$
Similarly,
$$E[S_{\$/DM}(2)] = (\frac{1.113}{1.06})^2 \times \$0.5 / DM = \$0.5513 / DM$$
$$E[S_{\$/DM}(3)] = (\frac{1.113}{1.06})^3 \times \$0.5 / DM = \$0.5788 / DM$$

$$NPV = (-DM10,000,000 \times \$0.5/DM) + \frac{DM4,000,000 \times \$0.525/DM}{1.15} +$$

$$\frac{DM3,000,000 \times \$0.5513/DM}{1.15^2} + \frac{(DM3,000,000 + DM2,100,000) \times \$0.5788/DM}{1.15^3}$$

$$= -\$5,000,000 + \$1,826,087 + \$1,250,586 + \$1,940,909$$

$$= \$17,582$$

c. Yes, the firm should undertake the foreign investment. If, after taking into consideration all risks, a project in a foreign country has a positive NPV, the firm should undertake it. The net present value principle holds for foreign operations.

d. Yes, because it has exchange rate risk. If the foreign currency depreciates, the U.S. parent will experience an exchange rate loss when the foreign cash flow is remitted to the U.S. This problem could be overcome by selling forward contracts. Another way of overcoming this problem would be to borrow in the country where the project is located.

32.8 a. Euroyen is yen deposited in a bank outside Japan.

b. False. If the financial markets are perfectly competitive, the difference between the Eurodollar rate and the U.S. rate will be due to differences in risk and government regulation.

c. The difference between a Eurobond and a foreign bond is that the foreign bond is denominated in the currency of the country of origin of the issuing company. Eurobonds are more popular than foreign bonds because of registration differences. Eurobonds are unregistered securities.

d. A foreign bond. In this particular case, a Yankee bond.